Healing the nation

Published in our centenary year
2004
MANCHESTER UNIVERSITY PRESS

Cultural History of Modern War

Healing the Nation

Soldiers and the culture of caregiving in Britain during the Great War

JEFFREY S. REZNICK

Manchester University Press
Manchester and New York
distributed exclusively in the USA by Palgrave

Published by Manchester University Press
Oxford Road, Manchester M13 9NR, UK
and Room 400, 175 Fifth Avenue, New York, NY 10010, USA
www.manchesteruniversitypress.co.uk

Distributed in the United States exclusively by
Palgrave Macmillan, 175 Fifth Avenue,
New York, NY 10010, USA

Distributed in Canada exclusively by
UBC Press, University of British Columbia, 2029 West Mall,
Vancouver, BC, Canada V6T 1Z2

British Library Cataloguing-in-Publication Data is available

Library of Congress Cataloging-in-Publication Data is available

ISBN 978 0 7190 6975 8 paperback

First published by Manchester University Press in hardback 2004

This paperback edition first published 2011

Printed by Lightning Source

Contents

List of illustrations

Acknowledgements

The experience of thinking about this project during the past dozen-plus years proved immensely rewarding, and I am grateful for immeasurable support I received from family, friends, colleagues and the many individuals I met along the way.

Stewart Weaver introduced me to the Great War as I was completing my undergraduate education at the University of Rochester. This book has its roots in his lectures and our many conversations. It also has origins in the mentorship I received at Rochester from Tom DiPiero and Tom Hahn. I thank them for their unwavering support of this project and for helping me to see history hand-in-hand with literature and to appreciate that it is the journey, not the arrival, that matters.

In the History Department at Emory University, where the original version of this book took shape as a doctoral dissertation, Margot Finn offered helpful comments every step of the way. Every graduate student should be so fortunate to receive such guidance in research and writing. Walter Adamson and Kathy Amdur gave generously of their time to read and comment on my work, and I thank them for their insights.

I appreciate the institutional support I received during the course of completing this project. A graduate fellowship from Emory University made possible fifteen months of research in Britain. An Emory Dean's Teaching Fellowship, followed by the opportunity to serve as assistant editor of the *Journal of British Studies*, enabled me to complete the first full draft of the original work. Completion of final archival research and the penultimate version of the typescript would not have been possible without the opportunity to serve as executive director and senior research fellow at the Orthotic and Prosthetic Assistance Fund (OPAF). I thank the OPAF board of directors and Julie Besaha, OPAF Director of Operations, for their support.

In Britain, archivists, librarians and specialists provided me with much advice, assistance and encouragement. I wish to express particular thanks to Geoffrey

Palmer for his hospitality and for sharing with me his extensive knowledge of the Young Men's Christian Association (YMCA). I also thank Shirley Dixon at the Wellcome Library for the History and Understanding of Medicine, Jonathan Morgan and Caroline Townend at the Order of St John, John Smith at the headquarters of the Church Army, Peter H. Starling at the Royal Army Medical Corps Museum and Stephen Walton at the Imperial War Museum. At Emory, Marie Hansen and the staff of the Interlibrary Loan Department in Woodruff Library made available to me a great deal of material that was essential to completing my work. I thank them for their generous assistance.

I presented portions of this project to numerous audiences, and I am especially grateful for thoughts I received at meetings sponsored by the Atlanta Medical History Society; Emory University History of Medicine Group; Delaware Valley British Studies Seminar, Villanova University; Department of Foreign Languages, University of Barcelona; Minda de Gunzburg Center for European Studies, Harvard University; Institute of the History of Medicine at The Johns Hopkins University; North American, Northeast, Mid-Atlantic and Southern Conferences on British Studies; Rehabilitation Research and Development Center, Atlanta Veterans Administration Medical Center; Seminar on Modern Social History, Institute of Historical Research, University of London; Society for Literature and Science; Society for the History of Authorship, Reading, and Publishing; Society for the Study of Narrative Literature and Western Front Association, East Coast Chapter.

My work immediately after graduate school afforded great opportunities to discover new perspectives on my subject and on my training as an historian. I appreciate the support I received from Howard Rollins, who brought me on as assistant director of Emory's Institute for Comparative and International Studies, Randall Packard, who gave me the opportunity to become a research fellow at the Center for the Study of Health, Culture and Society at Rollins School of Public Health, and Walter Adamson, who enabled me to design and teach a senior seminar on 'healers and patients' as an adjunct instructor in Emory's Department of History.

Many friends and colleagues listened patiently and offered helpful thoughts and encouragement during the hard work of researching and writing. Thanks especially to Charlotte Barraclough, Timothy Bowman, Miriam Chirico, Deborah Cohen, Graham Cooke, Paul Courtright, Stuart Crenshaw, Ana Sofia Ganho, Michele Garfinkel, Vishal Gulati, Nicoletta Gullace, Susan Grayzel, Lesley Hall, Stephen Kern, Seth Koven, Lara Kriegel, Jonathan Lewis, Jeffrey Lesser, Alexandra Lord, Aran Mackinnon, Peter Mandler, Maryn McKenna, Paul Menair, James Mokhiber, Gordon Newby, Matthew Payne, Kim Pelis, Sidney Perkowitz, Jonathan Prude, Rakesh Ranjan, Mair Salts, Alta Schwartz, Robert Silliman, Ellen Strain, Colin Talley, Julie Taddeo, Douglas Unfug, Chris Warren, Dana White, Jack Sammons, Angela Woollacott and Kira Zender . Thanks also to David Gerber for his encouragement and for his helpful comments on an earlier version of Chapter 6, which appears in his edited volume *Disabled Veterans in History* (2000).

The love of my family was a constant through every phase of this project. To my parents, Bernard and Ellen Reznick, and to my sister and brother-in-law, Dana and Paul Ginsburg: thank you for everything. Allison Kletter gave me inspiration during the final year of this project. For her support and her love I am especially grateful.

My editors at Manchester University Press, Alison Welsby and Jonathan Bevan, offered generous assistance in preparing the material for publication. Kathy Amdur, Michael Flannery, Brendan Kane, Jay Winter and my anonymous referees read the penultimate typescript and provided excellent suggestions for its improvement. My father also read the script and offered his insights, which I appreciated enormously. His love of history has been an inspiration since our first outings together to the libraries, museums and art galleries of Rochester, Buffalo and Toronto. For introducing me to history, and for his support of my efforts along the way, I dedicate this book to him.

Permission to quote from documents in their collections or from copyrighted materials is acknowledged with thanks from the following individuals and institutions: British Red Cross Archives and Library, Margaret Armstrong, Rhys Griffith of the London Metropolitan Archives, Colm McLaughlin and the Trustees of the National Library of Scotland, Roger Middlebrook, John Norman, R.J. Palmer of Lambeth Palace Library, Anthony Richards of the Imperial War Museum, Freda Rodgers, Roy Sutcliffe, Mari Takayanagi and the Clerk of the Records of the House of Lords Record Office and Pat Utechin.

To the end of preparing the images reproduced in this book I received the assistance of Pauline Allwright, David Bell and Michael Moody of the Department of Art, Imperial War Museum; Andrew Bamji and the staff of the Gilles Archives, Queen Mary's Hospital, Sidcup, Kent; Richard Henchley of the Periodical Publishers' Association; Clive Coward of the Wellcome Trust Medical Photographic Library; Christopher Jakes and James Yardley of the Cambridgeshire Collection, Cambridge Central Library; Philip Johanson of the Church Army; Jane Kimber of Hammersmith and Fulham Archives and Local History Centre; Alastair Massie of the National Army Museum; Philippa Bassett and Sue Ralph of the YMCA Archives at the University of Birmingham; Christopher Shea of the Ministry of Defence Intellectual Property Rights Group; Gordon Taylor of the Salvation Army International Heritage Centre, London and I.C. Wallace of Bamforth and Co. Every effort has been made to trace the copyright holders of texts and images reproduced here. Should holders step forward after publication, due acknowledgement will gladly be made.

In exploring specific features of the wartime culture of caregiving on the western front and the British home front, this book makes no claim to be an exhaustive study. The subjects that receive attention here deserve further analysis across different regions of the country and in the context of rest, recovery and rehabilitation arrangements for soldiers of Dominion nations. Fortunately, several scholars are undertaking local and thematic studies that hopefully will enable comparative studies to emerge and new features to be identified. I hope that the projects of Hazel Basford, Robin Barlow, Samantha Bird, Michael Bull,

Robert Brown, Stephen Gower, Christine Hill and others will combine with my own to yield a comprehensive study of similarities and differences that obtained in the culture of caregiving as it developed across wartime Britain and as it figured after the conflict in efforts to come to terms with loss.[1]

I hope, too, that my readers will forgive errors that appear in my text. For these I alone am responsible.

J.S.R.

Note

1 Hazel Basford, 'Kent VAD During the First World War', M.A. thesis, University of Kent at Canterbury; Robin Barlow, 'Carmarthenshire in the Great War', Ph.D. dissertation, University of Wales; Samantha Bird, 'War and Peace in the Metropolitan Borough of Stepney, *c.* 1910–1955', Ph.D. dissertation, North London University; Michael Bull, 'Rochdale and Wigan during the Period of the Great War', Ph.D. dissertation, Salford University; Robert Brown, 'The Great War and the Great Flu Pandemic of 1918', Ph.D. dissertation, Syracuse University; Stephen Gower, 'Wolverhampton during the Great War', Ph.D. dissertation, Birmingham University, and Christine Hill, 'The Healthcare of Troops on the Western Front, 1914–18', Ph.D. dissertation, University of Central Lancashire.

1

Soldiers and the culture of caregiving in Britain during the Great War

The First World War continues to fascinate scholars and general audiences alike, and efforts to understand its events and aftermath are as strong as ever. Inspired by and contributing to this vast body of work, this book reveals aspects of life on the western front and the British home front that have not received the attention they deserve. Its focus is the culture of caregiving: the product of medical knowledge and procedure, social relationships, *matériel*, institutions and physical environments that informed experiences of rest, recovery and rehabilitation in sites administered by military and voluntary-aid authorities.[1] Through this framework, we explore how soldiers, their caregivers and the public made sense of the war in the context of healing sites used to sustain manpower for battle as well as mass support for the war effort. Concerned chiefly with conditions for British soldiers of non-officer 'other ranks', or men, while examining those for officers for comparison, this book illuminates experiences common to the vast majority of men who served King and Country on the western front.

Our story takes place between the front lines of battle and the home front, along the 'lines of communication' as military authorities called this route, 'from battlefield to Blighty' as many soldiers described it. This system was designed chiefly to ensure manpower through the return of soldiers as rapidly as possible to active duty or, if they were unfit for further service, through discharge to civilian life.[2] Informed by precedent and by the exigencies of war, these lines constituted a network of distinct and often overlapping sites. They included regimental aid posts, advanced dressing stations, casualty clearing stations and general and stationary hospitals. They also included distinct modes of transport such as motor ambulances, ambulance trains and hospital ships and barges, several of which provided specialized treatments for illness and injury.

One of the greatest hopes among British soldiers, or 'Tommies', serving overseas, especially after the first year of the war, was to receive a 'Blighty wound' that meant they would be returned home.[3] Those men who had their wish fulfilled began a journey through the lines determined chiefly by the chaos of war and by the nature of injury. This book examines the development of and soldiers' experiences within four components of this route: voluntary-aid rest huts, which complemented formal caregiving environs, general military hospitals and their associated convalescent facilities and hospitals set aside uniquely for the rehabilitation of disabled men. Extant written, printed and visual materials reveal a detailed picture of these sites and soldiers' experiences in and around them. Sources also suggest that these sites afford greater opportunities for social and cultural analysis than either their stationary-mobile counterparts, whose mark in the historical record is not as prominent, or medicine as practised in the trenches.[4] Organizing evidence loosely around places and periods of wartime caregiving – essentially around space and time, two of the most fundamental categories of human experience – the narrative of this book reflects the progression of men themselves along the lines of communication, from huts behind the lines to hospitals and convalescent facilities to specialized institutions of caregiving for those who lost limbs in the war.[5]

The war machine

The work of preparing and repairing men for battle was at once a component of the military-civilian system of resources mobilized to engage the enemy and defend the nation. As Daniel Pick contends, the idea of such a system, a 'war machine', has roots in mid-nineteenth-century Prussian military might, subsequent German unification and *fin-de-siècle* 'rationalisation' of industry, space and time.[6] In modern cultural representation that emerges from these trends, Pick argues, the idea of war as a machine takes on 'two decisively significant and contradictory permutations'.[7] The first permutation portrays war 'as increasingly under the sway of the logic of technology, science and planning' and thus beyond 'the conscious will of the commander'. This conceptualization persists through the twentieth century 'often anchored in the "moral" of the Somme'. Pick concludes: 'War would be a natural science, albeit of great complexity.'[8] The second permutation is essentially the opposite of the first. In this case 'the reassuring (Clausewitzean) image of human control, science, politics, instrumentality, racial improvement through war, is overthrown in a more nightmarish image of crisis. War is no longer the stable object of representation, but the threat of a more drastic foreclosure of meaning. War is internal and external; the catastrophic destroyer of its own author'.[9] One of Pick's chief aims in revealing these lineages is to show that the First World War 'as archetype of the modern war (and world) demands further analysis'.[10] We should not view this event as immediately 'modern' from which emerged our image of the war machine. Within the 'war to end all wars', Pick argues, 'resonates in contradictory fashion the first permutation of the idea of the war machine, as product of rationalisation and the second, as anarchy and madness'.

This book adopts Pick's interpretation of the war machine to reveal how experiences that played out in the wartime culture of caregiving, as in the trenches and at home, involved rational and familiar processes combining with stark realizations of the futility of rationalization and unfamiliar – indeed, unprecedented – circumstances. Here we learn that military authorities developed their caregiving initiatives based on pre-war plans and well-known forms of architectural design and institutional administration. Voluntary-aid authorities developed their work based on enduring forms of religion, domesticity and ideals of manhood. For military authorities, the resulting culture was essential to sustaining manpower needs and morale among soldiers and civilians alike. For voluntary-aid workers, it was integral to preserving manhood at war for the nation. That many weary, sick and wounded men often welcomed this culture warmly should not be surprising since it offered conditions more peaceful than life in the trenches. However, this culture represented to many men a continuation of the war machine at play in their lives, an extension of the combined rationalization–anarchy–madness they had experienced at the front. As one soldier explained while recovering in Lancashire's Military Convalescent Hospital toward the end of the war, 'We are after all but cog wheels in a vast machine, a machine designed to and built up to grind the Hun elements to such an ultimate degree of fineness that man will once more be able to resume his normal life on this planet.' Acknowledging his proper place within the order of a system designed to yield a peaceful conclusion, he continued: 'It may be that we are, indeed, very small cog wheels, nevertheless, small cog wheels as well as big ones are found in any engine and no matter how far removed the small cog wheels be from the heart of the engine, the efficiency of the engine is as dependent on the small cog wheels as it is on the bigger, stronger and fitter cog wheels close to its very heart ...'[11] The conditions were no different at Keighley War Hospital, where every patient, whether to be discharged or to remain in the institution for eventual return to battle, was a 'wheel in a complicated machine [and] all must work together otherwise disorder and chaos would inevitably result'.[12] Across the Channel, at Le Havre base camp, a Royal Army Medical Corps (RAMC) officer described each man leaving for the front as a 'living machine' that needed to be kept clean from venereal disease and no less fit and in good working order so as to function properly within the larger war machine itself.[13] Near the seaside town of Trouville, site of numerous British and allied convalescent depots, Miss Irene Rathbone, a YMCA volunteer, looked to the beauty of the male body to find meaning in light of its destruction by the mechanisms of war. She observed 'over the expanse of salty grass, in among the pools and up to the edge of the water ... soldiers bathing'. The scene was 'a beautiful sight, hundreds of white bodies stark naked, running in the sunlight all far away enough to make a picture'. She concluded: 'This is what men were made for, not to kill each other with hideous machinery but to dance and bathe and leap in the sunlight and the sea – naked, unmarred and beautiful.'[14]

Framing these and other perceptions of wartime caregiving in terms of the war machine shows that 'healing the nation' in wartime Britain involved much more than treatment of shell shock, a subject that has received substantial attention in recent years.[15] It involved voluntary-aid workers establishing and conceptualizing rest huts as 'homes away from home'. It entailed institutional authorities seeing their hospitals as havens while recovering soldiers criticized this view and articulated a comradeship of healing within and beyond the hospital environment. Healing the nation involved public praise of convalescent soldiers. It involved systems of work therapy that trained disabled men to make and repair their own limbs and to produce limbs for other disabled men. And healing the nation meant healing writ large, society coming to terms with unprecedented loss through the culture of caregiving we examine here. Our subject, therefore, helps to illuminate experiential bridges and gulfs at a time when classes mixed in ways that they had not done previously in a country so rigidly defined by class.[16] Environments of rest, recovery and rehabilitation contributed to the sharp distinctions that developed during the war between the experience of these conditions by soldiers themselves and the rhetoric of these experiences expounded by government leaders, elite opinion makers and managers of Britain's mobilized society. At the same time, despite soldiers feeling distant from the public, the culture of caregiving became the focus of intense public pride, a means by which those who remained at home to experience the war in their own way could articulate support of the conflict and its heroes. Examining these experiential bridges and gulfs along with the complicity of the wartime culture of caregiving in the failure to produce Lloyd George's promised 'home fit for heroes' helps to reveal that the men who survived to become the vast majority of Britain's 'generation of 1914' constituted a group bound as much by their comradeship of healing as by their comradeship of the trenches.

Our story begins behind the trenches, along the lines of communication, where Church Army, Salvation Army and YMCA workers drew upon pre-war ideals of male paternal authority and experiences of saving the urban poor and destitute in efforts to establish distinctive rest huts for war-weary soldiers. While competing on traditional religious grounds to ameliorate the war-weary soul, these agencies embraced a new economic competitiveness driven by the war, one that especially coloured their relationship with the military establishment. Although the military was forced to rely on the help of voluntary aid owing to the large scale of the war effort, it consistently defended its traditional right to regulate the provision of comforts to resting soldiers and claim profits that were reinvested into services provided. The existence of economic competition and official concerns about efficiency and economy in the voluntary-aid effort reveals that the provision of comforts to soldiers, and no less the publicity of such efforts at home, was as much a contested form of business constrained by the public sphere of the wartime economy as a form of caregiving concerned with traditional bourgeois ideas of domesticity and codes of moral behaviour. In identifying both the persistence of pre-war ideological tensions into the war period and the exacerbation of these tensions by the exigencies of war, we learn that hut culture helped voluntary-aid and military authorities define the resting soldier according to a masculine code of conduct that fitted with both pre-war and wartime societies. These sites framed expectations of voluntary-aid leaders and military authorities that the war-weary soldier would remain strong, morally courageous and sexually pure. Huts also became means by which the public could express support of Tommy's service to King and Country. And the vast majority of soldiers appreciated hut culture for fostering an *esprit de corps*, offering the company of women and providing opportunities to become consumers of comforts such as decent meals, non-alcoholic refreshments and proper entertainment.

From the homes away from home that helped in large measure to define the voluntary-aid contribution to the war effort, we turn to the development of two general military hospitals on the home front, institutions set aside almost completely for the care of other ranks. Interpreting the development of the First Eastern General Hospital at Cambridge and London's King George Hospital in terms of the broader history of institutions and institutional design in Britain we learn that these sites testified to the endurance into the war years of the central features of nineteenth-century institutional architecture as well as to traditional elite perceptions of institutional design. However, as with contemporary rest huts, wartime issues of efficiency, economy, discipline and morale loomed large in the culture of both hospitals. Here were essential components of the war machine, sites assumed by authorities to be havens of healing and means by which the public could learn about the supposedly positive healing experience of soldiers. Hospital culture, like hut culture, became a means by which those who remained at home could articulate appreciation of those who were 'doing their bit' overseas.

Such positive views of recovering soldiers stand in stark contrast to how men themselves represented their experiences in the hospital environment. Military-hospital magazines, official publications in which men published prose, poetry and illustrations about their combat and healing experiences, testify to this conclusion. Through this material, which has been largely overlooked by scholars, we learn that soldiers saw routines in hospital as they understood the institution itself, as an extension of the war machine that allowed rationalization–anarchy–madness to continue to play out in their lives and complicate their masculine identity. Like the soldier's experience of rest in rest huts, therefore, his experience of recovery in hospitals helped to solidify a comradeship of healing that combined with comradeship of the trenches to underscore a collective sense among men that they remained a class apart from those who expressed appreciation of war service overseas but had little if any idea of what this service entailed.

From the subject of hospitalization our focus shifts to convalescence and to the distinctive blue uniform that military authorities required recovering other ranks to wear in hospital and in public, after which they popularly became known as 'convalescent blues'. These ill-fitting, bright-coloured and pocketless outfits had substantial precedents in pre-war institutional culture as they functioned during the war to promote a comradeship of healing among men. Here was a mark of discipline, a mark of the war machine itself, upon the body of the convalescent soldier. This mark failed to confer a deserved dignity of public appearance and a sense of masculine independence. But some blue-clad soldiers did find positive value in this mark when civilians, especially young women, praised convalescent blues for their heroism. The hospital-blue outfit, therefore, like the environment and daily routines of the general hospital itself, further complicated the masculinity of soldiers and underscored their sense of being a class apart from the rest of society.

The final chapter of this book examines the wartime culture of caregiving as it played out in the context of physical rehabilitation at one of Britain's sixteen regional orthopaedic facilities set aside uniquely for the care of men who lost limbs in battle. At Shepherd's Bush Military Orthopaedic Hospital in London assumed historical distinctions between work and non-work time overlapped in the context of wartime healing, as they did in other arenas of confinement previous to the war, to provide a context of work therapy in which diverse interests struggled to control the soldier's body. The efforts of military-medical authorities at Shepherd's Bush to 'reclaim' disabled soldiers involved a diverse range of well established approaches to treating both physical and mental illness and injury. Examining wartime rehabilitation from this perspective illuminates the fact that military-medical elites conceived disabled men as 'cripples' who required treatments based on established societal forms of physical rehabilitation. Through their distinctive work-therapy programme, which made Shepherd's Bush a centre of teaching and industry as well as healing, authorities further identified disabled soldiers as 'schoolboys' who needed to be taught a new trade. Here authorities harnessed the skill and energy of disabled soldiers to make and repair artificial limbs and other essential after-care equipment. Authorities intended this distinctive work not only to help recovery rates among patients but also to help maintain efficiency in the economies of Shepherd's Bush and its provincial satellite hospitals. The disabled soldier therefore became an integral part of the hospital economy as well as the larger war machine, helping to promote efficiency and economy in the medical service and encouraging public support for the war effort. In contrast, disabled servicemen themselves ultimately saw such work in terms of creating false hopes, underscoring their sense of being members of a class apart and helping to turn a 'home fit for heroes' into a wasteland in which government and industry drove those who 'did their bit' to poverty and unemployment.

That the wartime culture of caregiving, along with the experience of the trenches, helped to shape the camaraderie of Britain's generation of 1914 there is little doubt. But what remains unclear is the role of this culture in post-war memorialization by individuals in their recollections and by communities in their monuments. In what ways have individuals and communities evoked this culture as means to remember – and to forget – the war? The conclusion of this book poses this question alongside others to help chart further study of healing the nation during and after the war to end all wars.

Historiography

While a handful of scholars have written specifically on medicine in the Great War, no one has yet offered a study that illuminates the different views and representations of as well as experiences within the culture of caregiving described. This book takes on this challenge, drawing on and moving in new directions the distinctive branch of literature that explores life in Britain during the period *c.* 1914–18. In many interpretations this historiography begins with Paul Fussell's understanding of the war machine and the impact of its systematized slaughter on survivors of the conflict. For Fussell, the First World War was nothing less than a 'collision' between traditional modes of thinking and gross realities of modern industrial life. A 'hideous embarrassment to the prevailing meliorist myth which had dominated the public consciousness for century', the conflict gave birth to an unprecedented way of thinking about the world while marking the death of a generation of youth. Out of this cauldron, Fussell contends, emerged 'modern consciousness', an ironic frame of mind that produced a 'yawning gap' between pre-war and wartime societies in addition to an experiential separation between those who had suffered the war first-hand and those who remained at home.[17] This book takes issue with such conclusions, arguing that the apparent 'gaps' between societies and experiences were not as deep as Fussell claims.

In adopting this view, this book also engages interpretations of the war that emerged during the two decades following the appearance of Fussell's landmark study. Drawing on Fussell's arguments, Eric Leed, Robert Wohl and Samuel Hynes, among others, claim that the conflict marked a watershed in the development of modernism, decisively severing connections with a discredited traditional heritage. For Leed, the psychological trauma wrought by the Great War was 'a nodal point in the history of industrial civilization' which constituted a collision of material realities and traditional mentalities. This trauma, Leed argues further, was so profound for soldiers, on the one hand, and so incomprehensible to noncombatants, on the other, that it helped to engender two opposing views of the world. Soldiers' common endurance of mental shock, in addition to their sense of comradeship produced by trench life, set them apart from the rest of society, which remained physically distant from the war.[18] Wohl also argues that an experiential gap set the so-called generation of 1914 apart from the rest of society. 'What bound the generation of 1914 together,' Wohl concludes, was not just their experiences during the war, as many of them later came to believe, but the fact that they grew up and formulated their first ideas in the world from which the war issued, a world framed by two dates, 1900 and 1914. This world was the 'vital horizon' within which they began conscious historical life'.[19] Hynes takes a similar interpretation in his study of the 'Myth of the War Experience' which explains how 'imaginative versions of the war' that grew out of both the conflict itself and post-war memory illustrate 'a sense of radical discontinuity of present from past'. This 'Myth', Hynes concludes, helped to engender the idea among contemporaries, as well as among historians, that the war to end all wars represented nothing less than severance from the past.[20]

Since the 1980s this school of thought has been increasingly challenged by interpretations that have suggested that despite its unprecedented slaughter the Great War was not necessarily a watershed event after all. Modris Eksteins, for example, sees the period *c.* 1914–18 as a capstone to the development of a modern era that had emerged before the horrors of the western front became evident.[21] Historians concerned with the relationship between the Great War and the inter-war and post-war periods have linked the destruction of the Great War with that of the Second World War. George Mosse argues that because the Great War marked the first occurrence of mass death, it provided an unprecedented hallmark for the twentieth century.[22] Jay Winter demonstrates how bereavement prompted a revival of traditional modes of aesthetic expression, revitalizing classical, romantic and religious themes of the past. The resurgence of these modes of expression was a means to reconnect a grieving generation with its familiar past.[23]

These most recent interpretations constitute the immediate historiographical foundations of this book. The war as it was played out at the front did bring dramatic change.[24] The war machine did shape new attitudes toward efficiency, economy, morale and state intervention. But this book emphasizes social and cultural continuity within this environment of change, upholding recent scholars' arguments that the period *c.* 1914–18 was not universally a time of dramatic transformation but rather a time during which contemporaries made sense of events through traditional points of reference. This book, therefore, places the admitted horrors of warfare in the broader context of rest, recovery and rehabilitation, to identify new patterns of cultural continuity that informed how contemporaries made sense of the change playing out around them. The analytical framework employed here also enables us to see how such drawing on the past helped to foster camaraderie among men and structure both bridges and gulfs between these men and those who stayed at home.

In addressing these issues, this book establishes a dialogue with scholars of gender who question assumed gaps between men's and women's wartime experiences to insist that debates about experience in wartime should include the full array of experiences as well as their relationships to each other. Angela Woollacott and Laura Lee Downs demonstrate that women factory workers saw themselves as being on the front lines of battle as they took up work in munitions and metalworking industries making the weapons of war. Susan Kingsley Kent argues that such work prompted soldiers to see women as emasculating them and benefiting from their absence on the home front.[25] But even as the entrance of women into the wartime workplace subverted traditional gender roles, Woollacott and Downs observe, it also served to deepen misogyny by highlighting the privileged wartime status of most women as noncombatants and present or future mothers.[26] Similarly, Nicoletta Gullace, Susan Grayzel and Janet Watson argue that despite the war's clear challenges to traditional gender roles, these roles survived through maintenance of and re-emphasis on soldiering and mothering as the core of gender and national identities.[27] Situated within these historiographical contours this book demonstrates that wartime sites of healing, like trenches and munitions factories, help to reveal the instability of the divides between pre-war and wartime societies, between home front and war front, and between men and women. More to the subject of gender relationships, the analysis presented here offers insights into the crisis of masculinity that occurred during the First World War.[28]

As it played out on the front lines, the war shattered and disabled mens' bodies in numbers and ways unseen. It also shocked their minds, often taking one or more of their senses. As the conflict played out at home, it destabilized male authority and spheres of activity. Wreaking such havoc, the war ultimately eroded the ways men traditionally thought of themselves as men.[29] Joanna Bourke and Seth Koven reveal nuances in this process by highlighting the significance of pre-war medical and welfare programmes for wartime and post-war identity.[30] Focusing on the curative programme at Chailey Heritage Hospital in Sussex, Koven has shown how crippled boys, who were traditionally objects of rescue in orthopaedic healing programmes, became agents of healing during the Great War. By pairing a disabled soldier with a crippled boy, medical authorities at Chailey intended to help the soldier remember his duty in the face of adversity, urging him to remain a brave 'soldier', fighting to regain his role as a citizen, a breadwinner and a productive member of civilian society.[31] Bourke's study of disabled men takes up key themes in Koven's work in order to extend our understanding of wartime masculinity. She identifies the endurance of traditional masculine discourse in the attempts of both the public and the government to reconcile the damage wrought on the bodies of dismembered soldiers. These men, Bourke argues, were not viewed as passive, weak or emasculated, but rather as whole men who could reclaim their roles as breadwinners and productive citizens. Moreover, Bourke demonstrates that crippled soldiers themselves drew on traditional forms of masculine expression, like male bonding, as means of coping with their injuries and reconstituting their lives after the war. Bourke concludes that the conflict was less a successful onslaught on the male body than an event which reinforced pre-war gender conventions by which men understood themselves and their shared sense of kinship with other men.[32] This book extends Bourke's conclusions, arguing that expressions of and attempts to preserve manliness within the wartime culture of caregiving had outcomes that ranged from reinforcement to destabilization of manliness as defined by the male-breadwinner ideal and by emphasis on independence, moral courage, sexual purity, athleticism and stoicism.

The important task of situating this book in the historiography of the Great War would not be complete without attention to scholarship that focuses on propaganda, visual culture and the history of medicine. Studies of Britain's wartime propaganda machine, such as those by Gary Messinger, Bernard Waites and others, emphasize not only how the character of this machine changed over time commensurate with state direction, popular feeling, the tide of battle and the return home of casualties but also how it contributed to defining relationships between soldiers and those who remained at home.[33] This book adds to this literature a view of wartime sites of healing, especially of rest huts and hospitals, as foci of efforts to construct heroic images of soldiers and their service and to sustain morale among soldiers and civilians alike. Much of the material I use to develop these and other arguments is highly visual, so work on visual culture by Ludmilla Jordanova and Peter Burke has been enormously helpful and influential.[34] In helping me to read hospital-magazine and related images with a critical eye, these studies have also provided guidance in connecting this project with the development and utilization of wartime medicine, and no less environments of wartime caregiving, in the contexts of the prelude to war, the conflict itself and the post-war world. Historians working in this area have rightly urged their colleagues to consider the 'civilianisation of medicine in war and its militarisation during peacetime'.[35] As Roger Cooter argues, 'the theatres of war and medicine must be studied as part and parcel of the societies and cultures in which they were set and ... they must be seen as economically and ideologically constitutive with those societies'. In taking this approach, Cooter explains further, 'the study of war and medicine ceases to be epiphenomenal to the rest of history and to the rest of the social history of medicine in particular'.[36] This book adopts Cooter's view as it highlights the significance of pre-war medical and welfare programmes for the wartime culture of caregiving and traces the influence of this culture itself on the fostering of camaraderie among weary, sick and wounded men.

Notes

1 As historians seem to have overlooked the value of the term 'culture of caregiving' for capturing the richness of the healing experience, whether during peace or war, anthropologists, ethicists, policymakers and sociologists, among others, have employed the term to convey a range of ideas and arguments. See, for example, Heidi Keller, Ype H. Poortinga and Axel Schölmerich (eds), *Between Culture and Biology: Perspectives on Ontogenetic Development* (Cambridge: Cambridge University Press, 2002), in which contributors evoke the 'material culture of caregiving' in the context of evolutionary cultural anthropology and efforts to learn more about the evolutionary nature of culture and social reproduction. For use of the term in the context of family health, health professionals and health policy see Carol Levine and Thomas H. Murray (eds), *The Cultures of Caregiving: Conflict and Common Ground among Families, Health Professionals and Policy Makers* (Baltimore MD: Johns Hopkins University Press, 2004). Hillel Goelman uses the term in the context of early childhood development. See, among his other works, 'The language of caregiving and caretaking in child care settings' in the online proceedings of the 18 October 2002 symposium *Enhancing Caregiving Language Facilitation in Child Care Settings* held at the Hanen Centre, Toronto, Ontario, *www.cllrnet.ca/index.php?fa=caregiver.workshop.*

2 An overview of this system appears in the two-part article 'The Royal Army Medical Corps and its work', *British Medical Journal* (18 August 1917), 217–224, and (25 August 1917), 254–260.

3 On the etymology of 'Tommy', which was 'a standard term for the representative British private soldier', see Angela Woollacott, *On Her Their Lives Depend: Munitions Workers in the Great War* (Berkeley CA: University of California Press, 1994), 6.

4 This book complements work on wartime resuscitation wards, military ambulances, hospital ships and ambulance trains. See Kim Pelis, 'Taking credit: The Canadian Army Medical Corps and the British conversion to blood transfusion in WWI', *Journal of the History of Medicine* 56:3 (2001): 238–277; John S. Haller, Jr, *Farmcarts to Fords: A History of the Military Ambulance, 1790–1925* (Carbondale IL: Southern Illinois University Press, 1992); John H. Plumridge, *Hospital Ships and Ambulance Trains* (London: Seeley, Service and Co., 1975) and David Noonan, 'Ships of Mercy: The Hospital Ship in the First World War', BSc. dissertation, Wellcome Institute for the History of Medicine, 1999.

5 This approach is inspired partly by methodology employed by Stephen Kern, *The Culture of Time and Space, 1880–1918* (Cambridge MA: Harvard University Press, 1983), and by the field of historical geography which demonstrates how geographical perspectives can reveal histories of power, control and identity in changing physical environments. On this field see especially Robin A. Butlin, *Historical Geography: Through the Gates of Space and Time* (London: Edward Arnold, 1993).

6 Daniel Pick, *War Machine: The Rationalisation of Slaughter in the Modern Age* (New Haven CT: Yale University Press, 1993).

7 Ibid., 165.

8 Ibid., 165.

9 Ibid., 166.

10 Ibid., 189.

11 H.O.M.B., 'On cog wheels', *Return: Journal of the King's Lancashire Military Convalescent Hospital* (September 1918): 4.

12 *Recollections of the War Hospital Keighley and its Auxiliaries, 1916–1919* (London: Wadsworth and Co., *c.* 1919), 32–33.

13 F.F. McCabe, *A Living Machine* (London: Grant Richards, 1921).

14 Imperial War Museum, Department of Documents (hereafter IWM, DOD), Papers of Miss Irene Rathbone, 557 90/30/1, diary entry, 23 August 1918.

15 See Wendy Holden, *Shell Shock* (London: Channel 4 Books, 1998); Peter Leese, *Shell Shock: Traumatic Neurosis and British Soldiers of the First World War* (New York: Palgrave Macmillan, 2002); Elaine Showalter, *The Female Malady* (New York: Pantheon Books, 1985) and Chris Feudtner, '"Minds the dead have ravished": Shell shock, history, and the ecology of disease-systems', *History of Science* 31:4 (1993): 377–420.

16 It is important to recognize, of course, as others have noted in discussions of the British army following Kitchener's call to arms and conscription, that there is no easy correlation between rank and social status and how these categories together played out in the general experiences of the men who served King

and Country, no less their specific experiences within the wartime 'culture of caregiving'. See Richard Holmes, *The Western Front: Ordinary Soldiers and the Defining Battles of World War I* (New York: TV Books, 1999), 11–12.

17 Paul Fussell, *The Great War and Modern Memory* (New York: Oxford University Press, 1975), 8.

18 Eric J. Leed, *No Man's Land: Combat and Identity in World War One* (Cambridge: Cambridge University Press, 1979), 193.

19 Robert Wohl, *The Generation of 1914* (Cambridge MA: Harvard University Press, 1979), 210.

20 Samuel Hynes, *A War Imagined: The Great War and English Culture* (New York: Collier Books, 1990). For a view of modernism in the broader culture of the Great War see Allyson Booth, *Postcards from the Trenches: Negotiating the Space between Modernism and the First World War* (New York: Oxford University Press, 1996).

21 Modris Eksteins, *Rites of Spring: The Great War and the Birth of the Modern Age* (Boston MA: Houghton, Mifflin, 1989).

22 George Mosse, *Fallen Soldiers: Reshaping the Memory of the Two World Wars* (New York: Oxford University Press, 1990).

23 Jay M. Winter, *Sites of Memory, Sites of Mourning: The Great War in European Cultural History* (Cambridge: Cambridge University Press, 1995). See also Ted Bogacz, '"Tyranny of words": Language, poetry, and anti-modernism in England in the First World War', *Journal of Modern History*, 58:3 (1986): 643–668; Rosa Bracco, *Merchants of Hope: Middlebrow Writers of the First World War* (Providence RI: Berg, 1993) and Allen Frantzen, *Bloody Good: Chivalry, Sacrifice and the Great War* (Chicago: University of Chicago Press, 2003).

24 On life at the front see, among many other works, Tony Ashworth, *Trench Warfare, 1914–1918: The Live and Let Live System* (New York: Macmillan, 1980); John Ellis, *Eye-deep in Hell: Trench Warfare in World War I* (Baltimore MD: Johns Hopkins University Press, 1976) and Denis Winter, *Death's Men: Soldiers of the Great War* (New York: Penguin Books, 1978).

25 Susan Kingsley Kent, *Making Peace: The Reconstruction of Gender in Interwar Britain* (Princeton NJ: Princeton University Press, 1993). On the sense of estrangement felt by men see also Sandra M. Gilbert and Susan Gubar, 'Soldier's heart: literary men, literary women, and the Great War', in Sandra M. Gilbert and Susan Gubar, *No Man's Land: The Place of the Woman Writer in the Twentieth Century* II (New Haven CT: Yale University Press, 1989).

26 Laura Lee Downs, *Manufacturing Inequality: Gender Division in the French and British Metalworking Industries, 1914–1939* (Ithaca NY: Cornell University Press, 1995); Woollacott, *On Her Their Lives Depend.* See also Miriam Cooke and Angela Woollacott (eds), *Gendering War Talk* (Princeton NJ: Princeton University Press, 1993); Margaret Higonnet (ed.), *Behind the Lines: Gender and the Two World Wars* (New Haven CT: Yale University Press, 1987) and *Lines of Fire: Women Writers of World War I* (New York: Plume, 1999) and Sharon Ouditt, *Fighting Forces, Writing Women: Identity and Ideology in the*

First World War (New York: Routledge, 1994).

27 Nicoletta Gullace, *The Blood of Our Sons* (New York: Palgrave Macmillan, 2002); Susan R. Grayzel, *Women's Identities at War: Gender, Motherhood, and Politics in Britain and France during the First World War* (Chapel Hill NC: University of North Carolina Press, 1999) and Janet S.K. Watson, *Fighting Different Wars: Experience, Memory, and the First World War in Britain* (Cambridge: Cambridge University Press, 2004). See also Susan R. Grayzel, *Women and the First World War* (New York: Longman, 2002); Nicoletta Gullace, 'White feathers and wounded men: Female patriotism and the memory of the Great War', *Journal of British Studies* 37:2 (1997): 178–206, as well as Susan Pedersen, *Family, Dependence, and the Origins of the Welfare State: Britain and France, 1914–1945* (Cambridge: Cambridge University Press, 1993).

28 Literature on masculinity is vast and continues to grow at a fast pace. See especially Adrian Caesar, *Taking it Like a Man: Suffering, Sexuality, and the War Poets* (Manchester: Manchester University Press, 1993); Graham Dawson, *Soldier Heroes: British Adventure, Empire, and the Imagining of Masculinity* (New York: Routledge, 1994); Stefan Dudnik, Karen Hagemann and John Tosh (eds), *Masculinities in Politics and War* (Manchester: Manchester University Press, 2003); Joshua S. Goldstein, *War and Gender: How Gender Shapes the War System and Vice Versa* (Cambridge: Cambridge University Press, 2001); George L. Mosse, *Nationalism and Sexuality: Respectability and Abnormal Sexuality in Modern Europe* (New York: Howard Fertif, 1985), *Fallen Soldiers*, and *The Image of Man: The Creation of Modern Masculinity* (New York: Oxford University Press, 1996); Michael Roper and John Tosh (eds), *Manful Assertions: Masculinities in Britain since 1800* (New York: Routledge, 1991); Jonathan Rutherford, *Forever England: Reflections on Race, Masculinity, and Empire* (London: Lawrence and Wishart, 1997); Claire M. Tylee, *The Great War and Women's Consciousness: Images of Militarism and Womanhood in Women's Writings, 1914–64* (Iowa City IA: University of Iowa Press, 1990) and Stephen M. Whitehead and Frank J. Barrett (eds), *The Masculinities Reader* (Malden MA: Polity Press, 2001).

29 Deborah Cohen, *The War Come Home: Disabled Veterans in Britain and Germany, 1914–1919* (London: University of California Press, 2001), and Sophie Delaporte, *Gueules cassées: Les blessés de la face de la Grande Guerre* (Paris: Noesis, 2001). On the subject of disability and wartime/post-war identity see also Roxanne Panchasi, 'Reconstructions: Prosthetics and the rehabilitation of the male body in World War I France', *Differences* 7:3 (1995): 109–140 and the work of Ena Elsey, 'The Rehabilitation and Employment of Disabled Ex-servicemen after Two World Wars', Ph.D. dissertation, University of Teesside, 1995 and Andrew P. Latcham, 'Journey's End: Ex-servicemen and the State during and after the Great War', D.Phil. dissertation, Oxford University, 1997.

30 Similar arguments have been made in the vast literature on shell shock. Again, see Holden, *Shell Shock*; Leese, *Shell Shock*; Showalter, *The Female Malady* and Feudtner, '"Minds the dead have ravished"'.

31 Seth Koven, 'Remembering and dismemberment: Crippled children, wounded soldiers, and the Great War in Great Britain', *American Historical Review*, 99:4 (October 1994): 1167–1202. Koven's study complicates existing histories of disabled soldiers in both Western Europe and the United States, including Antoine Prost, *In the Wake of War:* Les Anciens Combattants *and French Society*, trans. Helen McPhail (Providence RI: Berg, 1992) and Robert Whalen, *Bitter Wounds: German Victims of the Great War, 1914–1939* (Ithaca NY: Cornell University Press, 1984).

32 Joanna Bourke, *Dismembering the Male: Men's Bodies, Britain, and the Great War* (Chicago: University of Chicago Press, 1995), 190.

33 Gary S. Messinger, *Propaganda and the State in the First World War* (Manchester: Manchester University Press, 1992) and Bernard Waites, 'The government of the home front and the "moral economy" of the working class' in Peter H. Liddle (ed.), *Home Fires and Foreign Fields* (Washington DC: Brassey's Defense Publishers, 1985), 175–193. See also Cooke and Woollacott (eds), *Gendering War Talk*; Cate Haste, *Keep the Home Fires Burning: Propaganda in the First World War* (London: Allen Lane, 1977); Ouditt, *Fighting Forces*, 71–88, and Jay M. Winter, 'Propaganda and the mobilization of consent' in Hew Strachan (ed.), *World War I: A History* (Oxford: Oxford University Press, 1999), 216–226.

34 See especially Peter Burke, *Eyewitnessing: The Uses of Images as Historical Evidence* (London: Reaktion Books, 2001) and the critical review article by Ludmilla Jordanova, 'Medicine and visual culture', *Social History of Medicine* 3:1 (1990): 89–99.

35 Roger Cooter, Mark Harrison and Steve Sturdy (eds), *War, Medicine, and Modernity* (Stroud: Sutton Books, 1998), 6.

36 Roger Cooter, 'Medicine and the goodness of war', *Canadian Bulletin of Medical History* 12 (1990): 147–159, at 149. See also Cooter, *Surgery and Society in Peace and War: Orthopaedics and the Origin of Modern Medicine, 1880–1940* (London: Macmillan, 1993) and 'War and modern medicine' in W.F. Bynum and Roy Porter (eds), *Companion Encyclopedia of the History of Medicine* (New York: Routledge, 1993), 1536–1573 and Mark Harrison, 'Medicine and the management of modern warfare', *History of Science*, 34:4 (1996): 379–410 and 'The medicalization of war – the militarization of medicine', *Social History of Medicine* 9:2 (1996): 267–276.

2

Homes away from home: rest huts and war-weary soldiers

On 28 November 1916, the *Times* published a dramatic description of the voluntary-aid effort for Britain's war-weary soldiers, focusing on the establishment of rest huts by the Church Army. 'Enter a crowded hut,' the author, P.K. Lang, wrote,

> and think for yourself that each man in it, not many hours before, has been elbowing death, dodging death, defying death and you will shiver at the pull of the fell magnet that has made men fight to the death through the ages. The soldier thinks nothing of this. Nor is there any pose in him. In the hut he wants to forget it all. He does forget it all. He rests. Without the hut he might rest his body somehow, but there would be no blessed respite, no forgetting. In the hut he forgets everything in his games, or in a magazine story …[1]

Few studies of the Great War consider such contemporary observations of the rest hut. Those that do typically focus only briefly on how authorities used these sites and their associated social activities to help keep the morale of soldiers high and their malingering to a minimum.[2] While accurate, such straightforward interpretation of rest huts belies the role of these sites in the wartime culture of caregiving, in public efforts to articulate support for Tommy, and in fostering camaraderie among men.

Lang's romanticized view of the rest hut was characteristic of the perspectives of the popular press and voluntary-aid leaders. Here was a space that did more than supplement the work of the traditional regimental canteen. The rest hut, no matter which voluntary-aid agency established it, sought to bring a 'touch of home' to the lives of men fighting overseas for King and Country. In huts close to the front lines, during lulls in fighting or when on leave from duty, soldiers could escape from trench life by enjoying a cup of tea and a biscuit, reading a newspaper, listening to a gramophone record, joining in a sing-along, playing a game or participating in a religious service. In huts located behind the lines and at home, men could enjoy these same comforts in the company of middle-class women. These volunteers had one key purpose: to replicate whenever and wherever possible the meaning and social experience of the middle-class 'home away from home', a space alternative both to the trenches and to local recreations.[3] The hut therefore aimed to 'bring "Blighty" to the soldier', structuring a bridge between the familiar – indeed, familial – and the unfamiliar and chaotic experiences of the war.

Three of Britain's most prominent wartime voluntary-aid organizations – the Church Army, Salvation Army and YMCA – drew upon Victorian and Edwardian religious views and competing experiences of 'saving' the urban poor and destitute in their efforts to ameliorate the wartime weariness of servicemen. Exacerbated by the exigencies of war, such persistent religious ideological and socio-economic antagonisms among these organizations helped to underscore expectations among authorities that resting soldiers would retain their roles both as defenders of King and Country and as consumers of goods that could help them fulfil their wartime service. The provision of huts to soldiers therefore was as much a contested form of business constrained by the public sphere of the wartime economy as a form of caregiving connected with traditional bourgeois ideas of domesticity and codes of moral behaviour.

During the last quarter of the nineteenth century, the widespread reform efforts of the Church Army, Salvation Army and YMCA reflected the faith that contemporaries had in the voluntary effort being the most desirable motor of social improvement. But while these organizations shared the vision of spiritual regeneration as the true end of philanthropy, conflict arose among them owing to their different programmes of social reform, which dictated the conversion of the poor to different forms of Christianity.[4]

Established in 1844 by the businessman, evangelist and temperance advocate George Williams, the YMCA pursued an interdenominational yet Anglican-based brand of evangelicalism, stressing the value of self-help and the 'celebration of the active and manly'. Most important, the YMCA drew its leadership from the respectable middle classes, who held to the conviction that only educated men could properly interpret and spread the word of God.[5]

William Booth, a minister in the Methodist New Connexion sect, founded the Salvation Army in 1865. The Army distinguished itself from the YMCA not only by drawing its leaders and its rank and file largely from the working classes but also by mobilizing working-class men and women as preachers to help their fellows better themselves and establish a right relationship with God. Furthermore, unlike the YMCA, the Salvation Army steeped its programme of displaying and defining working-class masculinity in terms of ecstatic preaching and military rhetoric, including uniforms, marching bands, parades, flags and a system of ranks to order its leadership. These policies offended YMCA leaders and other middle-class individuals, who saw them as direct criticisms of the dominant and relatively staid ideas about evangelicalism.[6]

The Church Army, like the YMCA but unlike the Salvation Army, was loyal to the Anglican Church.[7] Founded in the early 1880s, its programme of social reform included use of militaristic rhetoric and related trappings. The Church Army also sought to train working-class men and women to be lay evangelists.[8]

Despite their ideological differences, the leaders of these associations understood the value of domestic rhetoric in structuring social reform programmes. To varying degrees they employed dominant notions of domesticity that served as 'defence against material conditions and recalcitrant human beings', indeed as 'a focal point' of morality, propriety and cleanliness that gave concrete shape to the principle that individuals, especially men, had the potential to become, with God's help, captains of their own fate.[9]

YMCA leaders used rest, recreation and holiday homes to deliver to the needy religious and secular education programmes and recreations like gymnastics, cricket, cycling, rowing and swimming. These activities, YMCA officials held, sought to promote 'the permanent welfare of all young men, spiritually, intellectually, socially and physically'.[10] During the 1890s, under the guise of the Soldiers' Christian Association, YMCA leaders continued their programme by establishing home-like huts, tents and marquees in British military garrisons around the world. In these venues they sought 'to keep the Troops happily employed during the hours of leisure; to relieve the monotony of Game … ; [and] to provide counter-attractions to all places of evil resort'.[11] At Mrs Todd Osborne's 'Soldiers' Home' in Cairo, for example, soldiers could enjoy 'an open door, a loving welcome and consecrated efforts to lead them towards right and God' away from the 'streets … teeming with pitfalls and snares, [and] heartless wretches of both sexes watching to drag [soldiers] into sin and ruin'.[12]

Like the YMCA, the Salvation Army used a wide variety of 'Rescue Homes' and 'Rescue Missions' in its pre-war efforts to halt social decay among working-class men and women.[13] Similarly, the Church Army found value in configuring its reform efforts in terms of domestic ideology. Its sites for poor mothers and children were 'Fresh Air Homes' and 'Holiday Homes'.[14] Those for 'lost women' were 'Rescue Homes'.[15] 'Labour Homes' and 'Lodging Homes' were established for 'broken men, whom the lure of false hopes ... tempted to make the plunge into the maelstrom of the Metropolis which knows no mercy'.[16]

By the turn of the century, owing chiefly to the experience of the Boer War, fears about the economy and concerns about 'national efficiency', government leaders concluded that society required greater state intervention alongside voluntary aid in order to promote British strength abroad and social and economic improvement at home.[17] Evident in the areas of education, criminal policy and medicine and public health,[18] this trend was also a hallmark of the extensive military reforms of R.B. Haldane, Secretary of War from 1905 to 1912. In response to administrative and operational inefficiencies displayed since the Boer War, Haldane aimed to improve co-ordination and cohesion between civilian and military authorities by establishing a better general staff to plan and conduct operations. Haldane also created an expeditionary force which could be dispatched quickly to meet a threat from Germany and he formed a Territorial Army out of existing volunteers, which was to be used for home defence.[19] All of these reforms helped to shape the military machine with which Britain entered the Great War.

Significantly, Haldane's promotion of military efficiency and economy had left the forces with a shortage of regimental and battalion canteens, the traditional means by which military authorities provided basic comforts to soldiers. Run by private civilian contractors, these venues were sanctioned by the military to turn a small profit as long as the contractor agreed to donate the majority of his receipts to the associated military camp.[20] Thus, as Haldane's reforms promoted greater state intervention in military planning, they prompted authorities to recognize the established value of voluntary aid in military circles. Because the Church Army, Salvation Army and YMCA had claimed to improve the lives of soldiers without profiteering, commanding officers were willing to admit these organizations into military camps in larger numbers than ever before.[21]

From the perspective of military officials, canteens run by all agencies were vital to operations at home and overseas. By providing decent meals, non-alcoholic refreshments and proper entertainment, they helped to

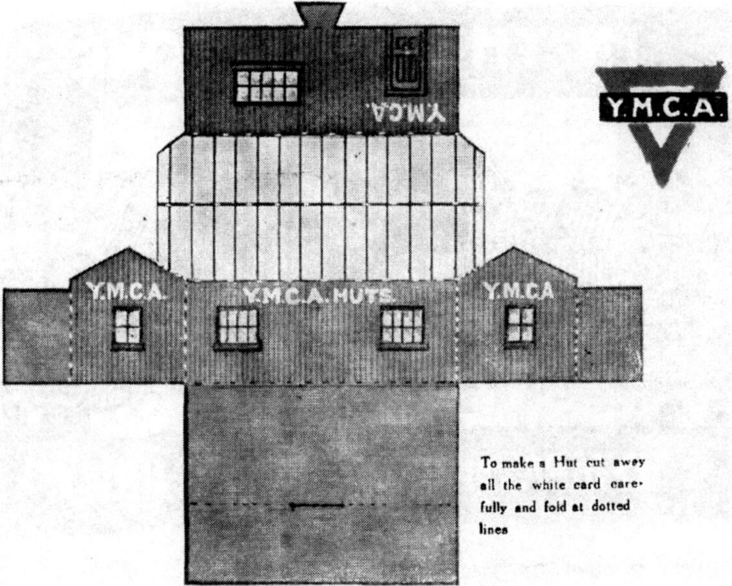

Figure 1 YMCA publicity postcard, *c.* 1916

keep men fit, prepared for battle and out of trouble while on leave. On the western front rest huts countered the perception, shared by many soldiers, that 'the object of a visit to a French city is one of two: boozing or … visit[ing] the red lamp'.[22] In home camps, as YMCA officials confirmed for military authorities, rest huts helped young men fight their battles against 'drink, vice and gambling', elements that were 'more to be feared than the shot and shell of the enemy'.[23]

At the outset of the Great War, Britain's voluntary-aid organizations based their hut work squarely on the rhetoric of middle-class domestic ideology. Testifying to this continuity were distinct mottoes chosen by agency leaders to assist in securing financial support and attracting named-sponsorships for soldiers' huts. These mottoes pervaded publicity campaigns directed toward soldier-patrons and potential civilian supporters. On frontline pointers, posters and marquees, the YMCA distinguished its huts as 'Little Bits of Heaven'.[24] At home YMCA publicity campaigns described huts at 'Homes Away From Home'.[25] They also offered the vast majority of individuals who could not afford to sponsor a hut outright the opportunity to purchase one – albeit a miniature made

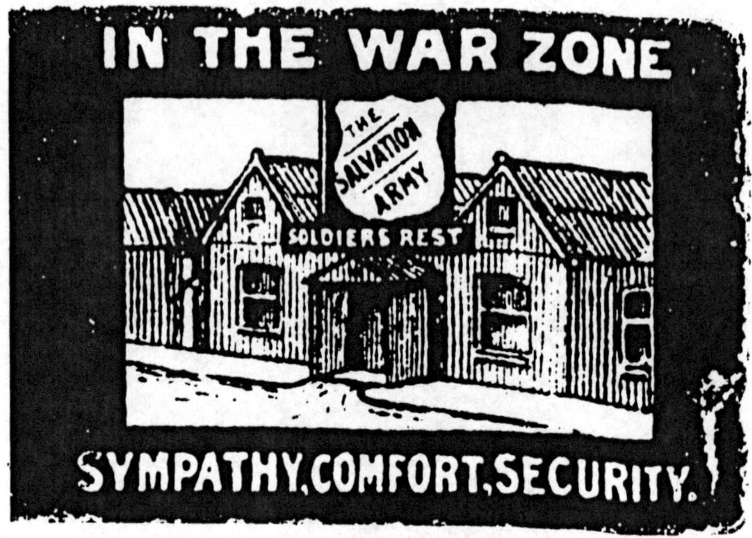

Figure 2 Salvation Army 'Flag Day' lapel pin, *c.* 1914–18

of paper – ostensibly for display in their own home or in public to show their support both for the YMCA and for Tommy[26] (see Figure 1). The Church Army offered a similar opportunity to potential supporters of its hut campaign, selling various-sized 'collecting boxes' in the shape of a hut.[27] Such venues were 'Huts of Silence' containing essential comforts for weary soldiers.[28] These sites also gave men shelter from the mud of the trenches, a condition that meant nothing less than 'misery and suffering' for those who were 'sick and shattered'.[29] Similarly, while front line and home front advertisements by the Salvation Army identified its huts as 'Soldiers' and Sailors' Rests' run by 'motherly women' volunteers,[30] the organization sold hut-themed lapel pins on 'Flag Days' to raise public contributions. One of these pins described the soldier's hut as a 'Home from Home' that supplied 'Sympathy, Comfort, Security' (see Figure 2).

The fact that voluntary-aid authorities intended their venues to be home-like not only in name but also in appearance and atmosphere demonstrates further how domestic peacetime priorities informed wartime programmes. The YMCA especially went to great lengths to make its huts bulwarks of home-like comfort and behaviour. The Association's *Red Triangle Handbook* instructed hut administrators and staff in the idea that 'the ideal of the YMCA Hut is 'A Home from Home' for the soldier. Cheerful and welcoming homeliness, and everything that helps that, must be its climate. Cleanliness, order, brightness, the supply of many small wants, opportunity to read, write and prayer, entertainment, friendship must be sought and given.'[31] Moreover, the *Handbook* prescribed, 'an attractive hut' was a 'homelike and comfortable hut', one 'more like a club and … less like a barrack-room'.[32] Domestic detail was central to this vision of the rest hut. Its main hall was supposed to include 'a dado finished off with a light picture-frame mould'. The colour of the hut interior deserved 'careful consideration', as did its decoration, which was to include 'windows, curtains, table cloths and pictures'. As for the canteen section of the hut, the *Handbook* pointed out, 'care should be taken to avoid a shoppy appearance … A lining of wallpaper behind the shelving and an absence of gaudy advertisements is to be commended … [and] the counter and tables used for refreshments [covered] with an inlaid linoleum [and] tables stained a rich walnut and polished daily with beeswax'. Domestic rather then military ideals, the *Handbook* recommended, should govern the style and arrangement of the furniture of the hut, which should not involve the 'use of [regimented] forms', but rather the placement of tables and chairs 'along the walls at the sides of the hut'. This 'adds greatly to the comfort of the hut', creating a place 'where men can "unlimber"'.[33]

Thus physical appearance was vital, but what truly made the YMCA hut a 'home', according to the *Handbook*, was the 'good work' of the Association's women workers. 'Treat the hut as a home and your men will value it accordingly,' the *Handbook* encouraged them.[34] Echoing this sentiment, an observer of the YMCA wrote in 1918:

> What a difference it makes to the atmosphere of a canteen of the YMCA, when she serves behind the counter, taking a sisterly (if young) or motherly interest (if of maturer years) in the men and never once have I found it abused and the roughest of men are most chivalrous and an oath is never heard inside, however prevalent they may be outside.[35]

Such configurations of the female hut worker as a 'sister' and/or 'mother', as opposed to a 'wife', are significant. They not only reflect the persistent aim of voluntary aid to make the man the head of the home but also underscore the wartime goal of these organizations to reinforce the manliness of the resting Tommy.

During the war, the Salvation Army also instructed its workers in the importance of establishing a 'home-like' atmosphere in the soldiers' hut.

Such a place, the army's 1919 *Year Book* explained in an article entitled 'The home touch of the hut', was the 'comfort corner, far removed from officialdom – although it may be next door to the drill ground!' Here, workers served 'good cups of freshly-made tea and … bread and butter, cake or scone, perhaps a little home-stewed fruit and custard, or a piece of pie baked by a woman's skill'. Here, too, were 'music [and] the recreation and writing room, where paper, ink and pens are supplied gratis to make the home letter an easy task'. However, the article pointed out, what made the hut and its attractions 'irresistible' was the '*home touch!*' The Salvation Army, in 'its methods, its uniform, its practicability, its tender sympathy and [its] helpfulness all the world over, [offered] the touch of *home* … in the Hut: the remembrance of the Open-Air corner or the street march at home'.[36]

As with the YMCA, however, the feature which Salvation Army officials truly believed made many of its huts venues of domestic comfort was the help of devoted women volunteers, who 'toil incessantly to provide the mother-and-sister sense which calls for satisfaction in the heart of every "boy" when far from home'.[37] F.A. McKenzie's account of Salvation Army war work, which described how those 'boys' who 'most need mothering are mothered',[38] underscored this view. Salvation Army women volunteers helped to 'supply … that much missed element on war service – the touch of home'. These women, 'pure-souled [and] devoted', made the activities of the hut itself 'prove a powerful counter-attraction to those coming within its influence'.[39] They had '"Ma's" character and that in the good, homely Hertfordshire way she can be the disciplinarian as well as the comforter'.[40]

Like their counterparts in the YMCA and Salvation Army, Church Army officials also intended the atmosphere of their huts to evoke familiar features of home at the front. The Church Army hut, as one of the organization's publicity leaflets explained, sat amidst 'raging disorder in earth and sky'. As 'rain falls in cold, slanting sheets at intervals, making the ground a worse quagmire than any ploughed field', the hut provided 'luxury, rest and ease compared with the trenches of the morrow'. Here was 'peace, perfect peace', with 'the artillery booming around on three sides and bombs from the sky … The great majority of men sleep through a German fusilade [*sic*] undisturbed, dreaming of home and loved ones – always home and loved ones'.[41]

War-weary men shared this positive view of rest huts because these sites helped them to be men. As market places, they offered opportunities to express a degree of economic independence, to continue to play the role of breadwinner. Here soldiers could manage whatever amount of money they possessed, keeping it when comforts were free of charge or spending it as they chose when desired comforts were available. John Middlebrook suggested such appreciation in a letter to his mother and father, writing that 'in the YMCAs the goods are duty free and so are cheaper but a lookout is kept to see Tommy doesn't sell them to the Frenchies'.[42] Jock McLeod suggested in a letter to his sweetheart that huts gave men an opportunity to express an opinion about the wartime economy: 'I *do* know [the YMCA] charge[s] more for stuff than anybody else out there, ask any Tommy who's been!' McLeod concluded that 'The Salvation Army is the best, the boys are always "grousing" about the Y.M.C.A. prices'.[43]

As homes away from home, huts also gave men opportunities to express camaraderie through common enjoyment of hot drinks, hearty meals and the company of women. T.H. Newsome drew physical strength from the comforts provided by the Salvation Army's huts. The hot drinks, no less the comfort, security and general sustenance, gave him the strength he needed in order to get through the war. 'If I ever get through this war safely,' Newsome wrote in his diary, 'I shall certainly never forget the Salvation Army.'[44] Similarly, H.W. Harwood expressed appreciation of the YMCA huts for the sense of independence and freedom they offered all soldiers. 'Taken all round, there is no place to which soldiers flock more readily after duties than to the various recreation huts.'[45] Private Gerald Warry recalled shortly after the war that while military authorities did not allow the troops into the town of Etaples, they did provide the men with 'many institutions such as Y.M.C.A.'s and Church Army Huts where we could go in an evening and have quite a decent meal'. Warry especially appreciated this comfort since 'the food in the camp was very poor and [there was] very little of it'. Alongside good food, what Warry appreciated most about YMCA and Church Army huts was that 'they were nearly all run by ladies'. Private C.J. Woosnam shared such sentiments about a YMCA hut near Rouen. 'We were marched off to a large YMCA Hut, already half full of convalescents and sat down to an excellent tea, followed by a concert, in which Lena Ashwell appeared. One of the most pleasant surprises I have had for a long time.'[46] Perhaps the most positive testimony to the value that the soldier attached to the rest hut was in the context of Christmas. On Christmas eve 1916, Frederick William Sutcliffe wrote in his diary that he 'went to YMCA carol singing. The rooms were very nicely decorated and several Christmas trees which reminded me of home very much.'[47] Two days later, following a Christmas celebration in the dining hall, complete with a concert, cigarettes and oranges, cold ham and beef, pickles, bread and cheese and a 'very good tea', Sutcliffe 'got a good feed' again at the nearby YMCA hut. Harold Wilson recalled that 'the YMCA do splendid work, their huts are everywhere. I am writing this in one.' Wilson suggested further that despite 'all letters [being] censored by the Captain', he valued 'the peace and quiet provided by the Y'.[48]

Some soldiers also appreciated huts for being the spiritual comfort they could offer. [49] As John Middlebrook wrote to his mother and father, 'This morning we again had Church parade and as on last Sunday, so also today, we nonconformists went to the YMCA. We had a splendid service and finished up with the communion service. I shall regard it infinitely more as a privilege in days to come to be able to attend public worship than I did before.'

Rest huts therefore played a prominent role in fostering camaraderie among men. Meeting expectations of their administrators, military authorities, an appreciative public and men themselves, these sites became immensely popular and one of the most prominent features of the wartime voluntary-aid effort.

Although the Church Army, Salvation Army and YMCA shared a common domestic rhetoric in establishing huts for soldiers, they approached this work in different ways These approaches reflected their traditionally divergent and often opposing reform programmes. Following its long-standing effort to celebrate the active and manly, the YMCA emphasized the importance of first serving the needs of the soldier's weary body through recreational activities, like popular music, games and athletics. This attention, Association leaders held, was the best way to reach the two other essential components of the soldier's being, his mind and his soul. While Salvation Army and Church Army officials certainly recognized the value of this approach, they believed the rest hut should chiefly serve the needs of the soldier's inner self. Driven by their common dedication to a militaristic brand of evangelicalism, these organizations concentrated their efforts on proselytizing through conventional sermons, hymns and religious services.

YMCA leaders believed that 'to bring men under Christian moral influences' and 'to counteract the temptations inseparable from life in the great city',[50] they needed to provide for the 'whole man'. This endeavour, they held, should begin by attending to his body, the proper welfare of which would lead to a healthy mind and a healthy soul.[51] Association officials therefore believed that wholesome recreation, like musical programmes, educational classes, lectures and indoor and outdoor athletics and competitive games, were the most effective ways to build healthy bodies and to encourage good thoughts and behaviour among soldiers. Such activities comforted souls, bringing them closer to God. The Association's *Handbook* therefore advised hut workers that:

> To interest a man in your work you must interest yourself in him and the fact must be borne in mind that a large part of a Citizen Army consists of men keen on athletics. Apart from the physical and educational value of athletics, hardly anything gives the Association Leader a greater opportunity of getting into personal touch with the men and influencing them for the highest ideals, always provided this is kept to the forefront.[52]

Fitting with the Association's established goals, the *Handbook* claimed, this programme 'largely made possible [the Association's] spiritual appeal' among 'the nation's manhood'.[53]

Contemporary accounts of YMCA wartime work demonstrate further the dedication that Association hut workers had to configuring wartime rest primarily according to the physical needs of soldiers. The YMCA hut, as Arthur Copping explained, was 'an emporium' for the soldier. 'It was ... a restaurant, furnished with many chairs and tables, where a lad or a party of chums could rest while partaking of refreshments. The wooden pavilion was also a club; for other chairs and tables were associated with reading matter, writing materials and quietude.' Moreover, it was 'a scene of cinema entertainments, concerts and even dramatic performances, a raised platform in many cases carrying proscenium associated with wings, scenery and footlights.' Finally, the hut was 'a church, part of the premises being probably partitioned off as a 'Quiet Room' for meditation and prayer, while the YMCA workers, even if laymen (and the great majority were ministers), would be representatives of religion, available as counselors [*sic*] and living happy, laborious lives of brotherly service'.[54] These activities provided the soldier with 'some of the strength and helpful leisure of a home from home'. Moreover, they shaped the 'climate' of the hut, helping to distinguish it from 'mere canteens' and other places of rest'.[55] The Association's wide range of 'pledge cards', which were intended to encourage the soldier to give up drink, gambling and prostitution, served to reinforce authorities' efforts to make the hut a proper, home-like place of rest.

Like their YMCA counterparts, Salvation Army and Church Army workers understood the value of catering to the physical and intellectual needs of the soldier. Salvation Army officials acknowledged that soldiers' comforts had to involve free reading and writing materials and cheap, good food. As F.A. McKenzie explained, 'the young soldier hasn't much to spend on extras and it is our business to see that we can give him a better meal than he can buy anywhere else for the same money'.[56] At the same time, however, McKenzie argued that 'while you must first give the soldier practical help – serve, feed him when he is hungry and give him warmth when he is cold, if you end there your work is less than half done'. Suggesting that the efforts of some voluntary-aid associations were misdirected, McKenzie concluded that 'a work of help that comforted their bodies and left their souls untouched would not be enough'.[57] Implying similar criticism while declaring the agency's own wartime success in providing for the soldier, the Salvation Army's *Year Book* suggested that recreation was important 'but it is The [Salvation] Army's religion, most of all, that attracts. In the thought of the future danger, a strong desire exists to know more of God, whose Spirit does, when sought, pervade the very atmosphere of The Army Hut.'[58]

Similarly, Church Army hut workers tended to cater to the weary soldier chiefly through sermons and services. As one worker suggested in a letter describing the character of his effort, the job of the YMCA huts was to feed and entertain the men while the real challenge was to pay attention to the 'spiritual side of the work' which was 'so often crowded out in the rush of Canteens'. While the hut catered to the soldiers' physical needs, this worker claimed, he could 'better devote my time to other things'. By this, he meant that providing for the spiritual needs of the men was most important.[59]

Such divergent approaches to comforting the soldier sharpened pre-war ideological antagonisms and differences among all three voluntary-aid agencies, but especially between the Church Army and the YMCA. Supporters of the Church Army, drawn chiefly from the Church of England, resented the YMCA's high degree of visibility and financial success in its war effort. They also expressed dismay at the physical means by which the Association had achieved its success. These approaches corrupted what the Church Army held to be the chief purpose of the rest hut, namely to provide comfort for the soul. As one supporter wrote in the *Christian*, 'While [we are] most thankful for such an effort to win our soldiers to Christ, we [remain] deeply concerned [about] much of the normal activity of the YMCA amongst the troops, which seem to express a departure from the Evangelical and spiritual ideals for which the Association has so long and so honourably stood.' Among the Association's supposedly pernicious actions were 'the flagrant secularizing of the Lord's Day, the merely secondary place afforded to any thing like definitely spiritual objective in the many centres where the provision of social pleasures is made the first aim and the introduction of certain forms of amusement of a positively doubtful character'. These failings, this critic explained further, 'have all caused great uneasiness to large numbers of people who have been life-long friends and supporters of the YMCA'. In many of their centres:

> We have known Christian soldiers who felt themselves unable to take any part in YMCA activities ..., for to have done so would have been a going back to the things which they forswore at their conversion! And we have known of others – young believers, brought to Christ through other agencies at work among the troops, or by the faithful personal witness of their comrades – actually turning from the music-hall entertainments in the YMCA Huts as part of their first witness to the Saviour!

Undoubtedly, this individual acknowledged, some of these developments were 'the more or less inevitable outcome of an organisation hastily extemporised to meet the challenge of unprecedented circumstance'. Nevertheless, they represented a departure from 'traditional methods of evangelical work'. In an effort to confirm and justify his criticism of the YMCA, the author cited a statement by Arthur Yapp, president of the Association, which defended his organization's wartime work among soldiers. 'We have not in the least departed from the very rigid lines laid down for us by our Evangelical founders,' Yapp claimed. 'What I feel we are doing is ... naturalising religion; ... making it human; a matter of everyday life.' Thus, Yapp concluded, 'we do not hesitate to sandwich a religious address between two comic songs, if need be'. Contradicting his initial claim, Yapp concluded, 'You see this War is changing all our ideas of values.' In fact, Yapp's critic argued, 'while the Association's 'avowal of the spirit of compromise has at least the merit of frankness', it simply was an extension of the long-standing, wrongheaded programme of the Association. The 'so-called Evangelicalism [of the YMCA has forgotten] its own distinctive message and commission. [T]he teaching of Christ can only be made human by elimination of the Divine.' Yapp's critic continued:

> As for the sandwiching of a religious address between two comic songs, we can only say that such an idea betokens a strange ignorance of the necessity of securing as far as possible an atmosphere in which the Holy Spirit can work, if the Message is to be effective to the salvation of souls. We know the kind of religious address which is at home between two comic songs; and we neither envy the man who can deliver it, nor those to whom it is made.

This supporter of the Church Army sealed his condemnation of the YMCA by asking two questions: 'Whither? [Can the YMCA] be saved, to become a more powerful instrument for the extension of the Kingdom of God than it has ever yet been?' Alternatively, he observed, 'can [the Association] become the friend and victim of the World?'[60]

Contemporary memoirs written by Church Army and Church of England hut workers provide further testimony to the real ideological antagonism between the Church Army and the YMCA. As one Church of England chaplain recalled, in some camps behind the lines, Church Army and YMCA leaders clashed on the format of evening services for soldiers, including their duration, location and how many and what kinds of musical interludes to incorporate between prayer readings. Such disagreement, he explained, resulted in a certain degree of religious 'friction' between organizations on the western front.[61]

Significantly, concerns among Church Army authorities about the secularization of evangelical work also existed on the home front during the war. Church officials and Church of England army chaplains expressed concern that a 'YMCA Church may be set up', despite the fact that 'the YMCA themselves recognized the danger of a washy undenominationalism'. 'Do you think we can trust the HQ of the YMCA?' the Reverend H.W. Blackburne asked a group of chaplains and the Archbishop of Canterbury in January 1919. The archbishop responded that 'at present [the answer was] yes. The Committee are satisfied themselves. But personnel changes. There was obviously a danger'.[62]

While ideological antagonism persisted among voluntary-aid associations, this antagonism had an economic dimension in monetary competition, one that was fuelled significantly by concerns about wartime 'profiteering'. As we have seen, since the War Office needed to provide services to soldiers at little expense to its structure it gave this opportunity to the voluntary sector. However, when authorities saw competition emerge with its own canteens, they became adversarial toward aid associations. Authorities feared such pecuniary competition and therefore instituted strict regulations. The development of rest huts as practical places of business within these trends served to underscore the identity of the soldier as a consumer of commodities.

Many voluntary-aid leaders and the rank-and-file hut workers understood their work for soldiers in strict business terms. In the case of the YMCA, the Reverend George Henderson, a volunteer Association hut worker, recounted in his wartime memoir that some of the greatest problems that plagued the Association were those that related to its character as a business. Often, he wrote, 'the high-pressured labour of selling [lemonade, tea and other refreshments] was greatly increased by the hindrance of financial exchange, taking English silver and giving back the change in French money, or of changing the 5-franc notes in which the men received their pay. Often, too, we had to change English Postal Orders, giving the proper French equivalent.' Further emphasizing the 'business side' of his work, Henderson explained the necessity of maintaining long hours of 'counter work' and keeping 'the shelves ... constantly filled up with goods from the store-room'. Henderson reiterated the economic aspects of this voluntary activity, including 'counting and carefully tabulating the drawings for the day' and 'preparing financial statements'. 'In short', Henderson concluded, 'the Hut Leader had to run a shop doing a large business'.[63] Similarly, despite the claims of one Salvation Army leader that his 'Officers are friends and not patronizers of the Tommies [and] they are not in France to "sell" to the soldier, but to help him',[64] another worker saw the Army as exemplifying 'Good Business Capacity'.[65]

Like their YMCA and Salvation Army counterparts, Church Army officials interpreted their rest hut initiatives in competitive business terms. In an April 1918 letter to the Archbishop of Canterbury, the president of the Church Army, H. Pike Pease, conveyed his concern not only about the widespread popularity of the YMCA among soldiers but also about the consistent success of the Association's public appeals for funds. 'We are privately advised', Pease explained, 'that our friendly rivals, the YMCA intend to make a great advertisement of their losses [in the war] in the course of a few days and unless we move quickly and it is made clear to Church people that we have some claim in [*sic*] their support, the bulk of their subscriptions is likely to find its way into their coffers'.[66] Such business concerns among Church Army officials also existed abroad, as passages in the August 1917 diary of the Reverend H.D.F. Pollock suggest. Pollock, a superintendent of the Church Army Hut at Pernes, observed that when he arrived at Pernes, a YMCA hut already stood in the vicinity. Pollock thus had serious reservations about the value of his own hut. 'I can see that Mr Anderson [of the] YMCA is sore about the CA putting up a hut here and it is quite natural. At present there is not enough to keep him and the orderly busy. I don't understand why the CA fixed on this place for a hut.'[67] This apparent rivalry coexisted with friendly interaction, as Church Army and YMCA officials did spend leisure time together. Nonetheless, Pollock remained critical of the administration of the Church Army and resentful of the financial successes of the YMCA.

In September 1917 he wrote in his diary that 'The whole Church Army system seems to be in need of organisation – a long way behind the YMCA – one thing is certainly needed i.e. to deliver goods round to the Huts.'[68]

As the war dragged into 1915 and concern about 'profiteering' became more widespread, this businesslike conceptualization of soldiers' huts began to worry some government and military officials.[69] Increasingly, it seemed, this supposedly non-profit 'home-like' venue was becoming a for-profit business that had the potential to threaten the economic welfare of the military camps in which they were established. Officials levelled this accusation against all voluntary-aid huts based on evidence that singled out the YMCA for allegedly siphoning business from traditional regimental canteens. Ultimately, ignoring the long-established, sanctioned profiteering of the private contractors who ran these venues, chiefly because they had long ago agreed to turn over the bulk of their receipts to military authorities,[70] the War Office condemned the 'incursion of … expansive voluntary-aid efforts' on the grounds that 'Regimental Funds suffer directly from business done outside the Military Canteen'.[71] As a penalty, it sought to impose strict regulation on all Association huts, both at home and on the front.

This War Office regulation consisted of three parts. It dictated that the YMCA should stop selling temperance refreshments and purchase goods only through the private contractors who ran regimental canteens. The regulation also stated that private canteen contractors should enter YMCA facilities and be responsible for the business side of the organization's work, including paying expenses and taking profits. Finally, the regulation dictated that the YMCA should pay a percentage of its gross takings to the army. The army intended this final rule to prevent further loss of income to regimental funds. This tax was 2½ per cent more than that which had been levied by the War Office since the beginning of the war on general business contractors, whom the army hired to organize, establish and administer regimental canteens.[72]

Official correspondence between the War Office and Executive Committee of the YMCA, the body which represented all voluntary-aid agencies, details the grounds on which the Association protested against army regulation generally and the hut tax in particular. Above all, the Association claimed that its war work was completely unlike that of the general contractor.

> The root of the demand for the 10 per cent lies in the assumption that contractors and voluntary bodies … are on one and the same footing … It

> is absurd that anyone should for one moment contend that a religious organisation like the YMCA should in any way be treated like a contractor ... It should be naturally understood by everyone that the YMCA is solely and entirely for the good of the soldier and whenever with the consent of the General Officer Commanding or the Commanding Office ... If refreshments are sold ... it is for the comfort of the men.

Moreover, YMCA officials argued that

> The voluntary bodies concerned see an essential difference between themselves and the contractors [in that the latter is] a highly organised business [which] relies on a steady custom in permanent camps, [while the YMCA is] a voluntary and philanthropic body which is doing emergency work for the most part in temporary camps under the shifting conditions of a great War.[73]

Thus the YMCA relied on its established religious character to avoid taxation, even as its competitors made a point of undercutting that self-definition by attacking the YMCA as unduly secular.

Drawing upon this distinction, Association leaders argued that 'to allow the paid agents of the contractors to come into the YMCA and supervise the trading would in our judgement, alter the whole character of our work'. Moreover, the Association argued, it should be exempt from regulation generally and taxation in particular because it was simply unable to pay the 10 per cent tax. 'Such a considerable tax', the president of the YMCA explained to the War Office, 'would take from the funds of the [Association] at least £50,000 a year'.[74] These funds, Yapp argued further, were not profit. 'Every penny which [the Association] receives both from trading and from public subscriptions [and] surpluses in one camp [is] transferred [if not used] to other camps in the same district.'[75]

With regard to the cessation of the sale of non-alcoholic refreshments, Association officials argued that this was not simply 'an integral part of the YMCA work' but also in the best interest of the troops – a great convenience to the men and one of the most effective aids to temperance. Finally, in response to the military's insistence that the Association should purchase goods only from contractors, leaders argued that quality and quantity could not be assured at all times. Such conditions would certainly not benefit the soldier.

Ultimately, after nearly two years of negotiations, the YMCA and its counterparts won their battle against the hut tax. Military officials realized that it was impractical, if not impossible, owing to 'the enormous extent of the war', to ask voluntary-aid agencies to keep close track of their finances and to pay a regular tax on items sold in every rest hut. The tax was thus left 'in abeyance' until the end of the war. However, given the need to maintain strict control of the military economy, regulation of voluntary-aid huts was in fact extended to include inspection of all items sold and price controls determined by amounts charged at the regimental canteen.[76]

Evidence collected by the Charity Organisation Society (COS) upheld the claim by the War Office that voluntary-aid agencies seemed to be profiteering.[77] In early 1915, the Salvation Army came under investigation by the COS for allegedly profiting from public appeals made during its 'Self Denial Weeks'.[78] The following year, the COS launched an investigation of the YMCA based on a comprehensive study of the regimental, YMCA and Salvation Army rest huts located at Tidworth military camp. This study concluded that it was 'obvious that the charitable catering associations must deplete the funds of the Regimental Institutes'.[79]

At Tidworth, officials observed that the aggregate net profits of these venues for three months amounted to £6,000. 'If [these profits] had all been earned by the regimental canteen', they concluded, 'the R.I. [Regimental Institute] would have received £480: as a matter of fact it received only £160, [which was] the tax on the R.C. [Regimental Canteen].' This outcome, investigators claimed, was unfair and attributable to the profiteering motives of competing voluntary-aid agencies. 'Charitable associations confine themselves to [the most lucrative] branch [of hut work], namely coffee, beer and groceries, [while they] plead inability to pay the 10% tax.' At the same time, the contractors 'contrive to remunerate themselves' while making 'a welcome contribution to the Regimental Institute funds'. What made this situation worse, investigators suggested, was the fact that the YMCA functioned with 'equally efficient management as the regimental canteen', so much so that they 'ought to be able to show a profit of something like £20,000 a month on their total trade'. Investigators concluded further that 'the confession of business failure on the part of the Association and other agencies seems hardly to constitute a sound claim to increased public support, at a time when we are all being rightly urged to strict economy'.[80]

Such public criticism of the YMCA continued into the final year of the war when the organization continued to charge fees for social service rendered to soldiers fresh from the trenches. Echoing the long-standing sentiments of the COS, the editors of the *World* accused the 'properly managed' YMCA of 'making what is vulgarly known as "pots of money"', even as the organization continued to receive a great deal of public financial aid and a 'large measure of official support' in the form of exemption from the hut tax.[81] Despite issuing public responses that denied any profit motive, the YMCA and its counterpart organizations became victims of their own propaganda. In conceiving their huts simultaneously as venues outside the wartime cash nexus – as homes – yet also as businesses fundamentally unlike those of the traditional regimental canteen – voluntary-aid leaders made their work highly problematic and subject to criticism by the War Office and by the public. These debates and discussions underscored the identity of the resting soldier as a consumer of the comforts he needed to remain fit for battle and to retain his peacetime identity as a breadwinner for home and family.

Serving simultaneously as an idealized domestic space and as a business, rest huts had substantial implications for the identity of soldiers just as contemporary canteens for women munitions workers had implications for their patrons. Like huts, canteens reflected the persistence into wartime of pre-war ideas about rest in work environments. Originating in nineteenth-century Lancashire textile manufacturing towns, factory canteens were the result of employers seeking to break up the monotony of the work routine, to generate sociability among workers and to inculcate thrift, respectability, sobriety and deference. Combined with the holiday, weekend and tea break, factory canteens became major features of modern industrial life during peacetime.[82] This function continued during wartime. Beginning in 1916, these sites were key components of Lloyd George's prohibition campaign, established by many of the same voluntary-aid organisations involved in providing huts to ameliorate the psychological and physical states of weary men at war.[83] Situated in the workplace itself, canteens were intended by authorities to help to make women more efficient producers of the weapons of war.[84] By 1917 these sites had proved their value, as authorities realized their ability to increase 'the efficiency and productivity of the worker and, therefore, of the factories of the country'.[85]

Soldiers' huts and women's canteens had different implications for wartime gender roles. Whereas soldiers' huts were supposed to be homes away from home – alternatives to the 'workplace' of the trenches and to local recreations – munitions canteens for women were intended to be purely utilitarian and extensions of the workplace itself. In huts, authorities expected soldiers to partake of home-like comforts therefore sustaining their peacetime roles as breadwinners for home and family. In factory canteens, as contemporary accounts and illustrations of these venues suggest, authorities expected 'Tommy's sister' to forgo serious leisure activity – taking tea while she worked – so that she could continue to 'do her bit' in the war effort. Rest huts, therefore, underscored codes of masculine conduct, and soldiers appreciated them for doing so. Factory canteens, meanwhile, denied women association with domestic environs and arguably with traditional codes of feminine conduct.

While rest hut ideology emphasized traditional forms of religion and domesticity alongside established ideals of manhood, the actual operation of huts, constrained by concerns about profiteering and about morale among soldiers and civilians alike, illuminates the importance of efficiency, economy and mass support for the war in the contemporary culture of caregiving. Similar parameters structured the contemporaneous development of general military hospitals, highly functional environs intended chiefly for ordinary soldiers. Like rest huts, these institutions testified to the endurance into the war years of nineteenth-century ideals and approaches to caregiving, in particular institutional design and administration. Here, authorities emphasized the appearance of comfort, arguably over comfort itself, to ensure that recovery in home-front 'havens for heroes' not only remained in tune with a society mobilized for total war but also helped to promote public praise of men fighting for King and Country.

Notes

1 P.K. Lang, 'Recreation huts: their value at the western front', *The Times* (28 November 1916), p. 13. This article subsequently appeared in *Church Army Review* (December 1916): 2–4, as a means to bolster support of that agency's wartime welfare efforts.

2 Ilana R. Bet-El, *Conscripts: Lost Legions of the Great War* (Stroud: Sutton Publishing, 1999), 51, 75 and 119; Bourke, *Dismembering the Male*, 90; John Fuller, *Troop Morale and Popular Culture in the British and Dominion Armies, 1914–1918* (Oxford: Clarendon Press, 1991), especially chapter 8, and Winter, *Death's Men*, 141–161. While insightful, work on Talbot House also falls short of engaging the larger issues surrounding the development and role of environments of rest on the western front. See Paul Chapman, *A Haven in Hell: Talbot House, Poperinghe* (Barnsley: Leo Cooper, 2000).

3 F.A. McKenzie, 'Mothering the men', in *Serving the King's Men: How the Salvation Army is Helping the Nation* (London: Hodder and Stoughton, 1918), 11ff.

4 Pat Thane, *Foundations of the Welfare State* (New York: Longman, 1996), 21.

5 On the inculcation of masculine gender roles in these and contemporaneous religious programmes see especially Roper and Tosh (eds), *Manful Assertions*. On the YMCA in particular see Clyde Binfield, *George Williams in Context: A Portrait of the Founder of the YMCA* (Sheffield: Sheffield Academic Press, 1994), 47.

6 On the differences between the Salvation Army and the YMCA see especially Pamela J. Walker, '"I live but not yet I for Christ liveth in me": Men and masculinity in the Salvation Army, 1865–1890', in Roper and Tosh (eds), *Manful Assertions*, 92–112 and Walker, *Pulling the Devil's Kingdom Down: The Salvation Army in Victorian Britain* (Berkeley CA: University of California Press, 2001). See also Gareth Stedman Jones, *Outcast London: A Study in the Relationship between Classes in Victorian Society* (New York: Pantheon, 1971), 281ff and Gertrude Himmelfarb, *Poverty and Compassion: The Moral Imagination of the Late Victorians* (New York: Vintage Books, 1991), 219–234. For a general study of British churches in the First World War see Alison Brown, 'British Churches in the First World War', Ph.D. dissertation, St Andrews University, 1996.

7 See Donald Lynch, *Chariots of the Gospel: The Centenary History of the Church Army* (Worthing: H.E. Walter, 1982), 25.

8 British Library, miscellaneous leaflets *c.* 1914–18, x108/27020, Church Army, *Holidays at Home*, appendix.

9 Leonore Davidoff and Catherine Hall, *Family Fortunes: Men and Women of the English Middle Class, 1780–1850* (Chicago: University of Chicago Press, 1987), 357ff. See also Ellen Ross, *Love and Toil* and 'Hungry children: Housewives and London charity, 1870–1918' in Peter Mandler (ed.), *The Uses of Charity: The Poor on Relief in the Nineteenth-Century Metropolis* (Philadelphia: University of Pennsylvania Press, 1990), 161–196.

10 London Metropolitan Archives (hereafter LMA), Papers of the Charity Organisation Society (hereafter COS), A/FWA/C/D188/1, 'YMCA, *c.* 1900'. The symbol of the YMCA, a red triangle, represented the Association's central aim to provide for the three essential components of man's being: his mind, his body and his spirit.

11 Leeds University Library, Liddle Collection, YMCA Papers, Executive Committee of the National Council of YMCAs, 'YMCA, "National Plan of Campaign" work now being planned, 9 August 1914'.

12 'Soldiers' Christian Association', *The Times* (1 October 1898), p. 7.

13 Norman H. Murdock, *Origins of the Salvation Army* (Knoxville TN: University of Tennessee Press, 1994), 146–171. See also Walker, *Pulling the Devil's Kingdom Down* and Himmelfarb, *Poverty and Compassion*, 219–234.

14 British Library, miscellaneous leaflets *c.* 1914–18, x108/27020, Church Army, *Holidays at Home*, appendix.

15 Himmelfarb, *Poverty and Compassion*, 221.

16 Mary Burns (ed.), *The Pearl Divers: Picture of the Life and Work of Prebendary Carlile and the Church Army* (New York: n.p., 1920). See also Rupert William E. Gascoyne Cecil, *The Church Army: What It is and What It Does* (Oxford: Church Army Press, 1908).

17 Thane, *Foundations of the Welfare State*, 49–93.

18 David Powell, *The Edwardian Crisis: Britain, 1901–1914* (New York: St. Martin's Press 1996), 37. On school reform at the turn of the century see Kevin Joseph Brehony, 'The Froebel Movement and State Schooling, 1880–1914: A Study in

Educational Ideology', Ph.D. dissertation, Open University, 1987. On penal reform see Sean McConville, *English Local Prisons, 1860–1900: Next Only to Death* (New York: Routledge, 1995), and Martin Wiener, *Reconstructing the Criminal: Culture, Law, and Policy in England, 1830–1914* (New York: Cambridge University Press, 1990). On the relationship between 'national efficiency' and public health, particularly the eugenics movement, see Richard A. Soloway, *Demography and Degeneration: Eugenics and the Declining Birth-rate in Twentieth-Century Britain* (Chapel Hill NC: University of North Carolina Press, 1990). See also John M. Eyler, *Sir Arthur Newsholme and State Medicine, 1885–1935* (Cambridge: Cambridge University Press, 1997).

19 Powell, *Edwardian Crisis*, 37. On Haldane and his reforms see also Charles Harris, *Lord Haldane* (Oxford: Oxford University Press, 1928); Frederick Maurice, *Haldane* (Westport CT: Greenwood Press, 1970); Stephen Koss, *Lord Haldane: Scapegoat for Liberalism* (New York: Columbia University Press, 1969), and Hew Strachan, *The Politics of the British Army* (New York: Oxford University Press, 1997).

20 This scheme is detailed in War Office, *Rules for the Management of Garrison and Regimental Institutes*, 1916. For additional background see '"National Plan of Campaign" work now being planned, 9 August 1914' and *Report Presented to the Army Council on the National Scheme for Co-ordination of Voluntary Effort Resulting from the Formation of the Department of the Director-General of Voluntary Organisations, Covering the Period September 1915 to April 1919* (London: HMSO, 1919).

21 Military officials eventually called this scheme the 'co-operative system'. See War Office, *Rules for the Management*. The developments traced here are partially documented in 'YMCA, 1914', LMA, A/FWA/C/D188/1. See also '"National Plan of Campaign" work now being planned, 9 August 1914' and *Report Presented to the Army Committee*. For a general study of profit controls during this period see Anthony J. Arnold, 'Profit Controls and Levies in the First World War' (Ph.D. thesis, University of London, 1995).

22 Leeds University Library, Liddle Collection, Papers of Signaller J. Cockcroft, Cockcroft to an unidentified individual, 14 July 1917.

23 'National Plan of Campaign'. See also YMCA, *The Red Triangle Handbook: Issued for the Personal Information of Workers in the Huts and other Institutes of the Association* (London: Red Triangle Press, 1917), 151ff.

24 This motto appears in the YMCA hut publicity poster lodged in the John Johnson Collection of Printed Ephemera, Bodleian Library.

25 See also 'A touch of home' in Whitehair, *Out There*, 41. These names are also pervasive in official publications of the Association, including *Y.M.: The British Empire YMCA Weekly* (which changed its name in 1917 to *Red Triangle*) and *Red Triangle Bulletin* (*A Weekly Supplement to the Red Triangle*).

26 Evidence suggests that entire public and commercial communities, including 'Christ's College, Cambridge', 'Wigan and District', 'Belfast Scouts', 'Swansea and District' and 'The British Weekly' banded together to sponsor one or

more huts, while members of the royal family, including Princess Victoria and Queen Mary, lent their names and support to these sites. For additional examples see reproductions of a magic-lantern slide depicting locations of YMCA huts on the western front (*c.* 1914–18) held by Mr Geoffrey Palmer.

27 Illustrated leaflet entitled 'Collecting boxes' included in the microfilm collection of Church Army publications held by the library of the Hoover Institution of Stanford University.

28 'One of the Church Army Hut Superintendents on the Western Front', *Over the Top* (London: Church Army Press, 1917), 2.

29 See advertisement for Church Army rest huts, *Church Army Review* (February 1917): 12.

30 McKenzie, 'Mothering the men', 11ff. See also *All the World* (6 June 1917), back page, which depicts a Salvation Army hut near a dock into which soldiers and sailors are streaming. This illustration also appears on the cover of the June 1918 issue of the *War Cry*, another wartime Salvation Army magazine.

31 YMCA, 'Making the hut attractive', *Red Triangle Handbook*, 34–37. Similarly, in its section entitled 'Music: concerts in camp', the *Handbook* emphasized that 'great care should be taken in making [the performance platform] the most attractive [by using, for example] a piece of green baize and a little piece of bunting and hidden lights', 114–115.

32 A photograph of the interior of a YMCA rest hut (*c.* 1914–18), held by Geoffrey Palmer, provides visual evidence of this prescription.

33 YMCA, *Handbook*, 116–117.

34 Ibid., 117.

35 Arthur John Gadd, *Under the Red Triangle* (Gateshead: R. Kelly, 1918), 14.

36 Salvation Army, 'The home touch of the hut', 10.

37 Ibid., 10.

38 Review of McKenzie, *Serving the King's Men*, in *Hospital* (5 October 1918): 22.

39 Salvation Army, 'The Salvation Army and National Service', in *Salvation Army Year Book* (1917), 22.

40 McKenzie, 'Mothering the men', 11.

41 'One of the Church Army Hut Superintendents', *Over the Top*, 2.

42 IWM, DOD, Papers of John B. Middlebrook, 7822 Con Shelf, Middlebrook to his parents, 12 April 1916.

43 IWM, DOD, Papers of Miss M. Semple, 5821 96/50/1 and Con Shelf, Jock McLeod to Semple, 12 May 1916.

44 Leeds University Library, Liddle Collection, Papers of T.H. Newsome, diary entry, undated.

45 H.W. Harwood, 'Y/M's and others', *The Times*, undated, n.p. This article is lodged in Leeds University Library, Liddle Collection, Papers of H.W. Harwood.

46 Leeds University Library, Liddle Collection, Papers of Private C.J. Woosnam, diary entry, 30 May 1916.

47 IWM, DOD, Papers of Frederick William Sutcliffe, diary entry, 24 December 1916.

48 Leeds University Library, Liddle Collection, Papers of Private Harold Wilson, diary entry, 15 November 1915.
49 IWM, DOD, Papers of John B. Middlebrook, Middlebrook to his parents, 19 March 1916.
50 LMA, A/FWA/C/D188/1, unidentified COS official to Mr Bush at COS headquarters, 19 April 1918.
51 Again, the symbol of the YMCA, the red triangle, reflected this three-part goal. As the Association's *Handbook* explained, 'The Triangle stands for the whole man,' 105.
52 YMCA, *Handbook*, 105.
53 Ibid., 105.
54 Arthur E. Copping, *Tommy's Triangle* (New York: Hodder and Stoughton, 1917), 89–90.
55 YMCA, *Handbook*, 20–21. See also Gadd, *Under the Red Triangle*, 128–129.
56 McKenzie, 'Mothering the men', 11.
57 Ibid., 11.
58 Salvation Army, 'The Salvation Army and National Service', in *Salvation Army Year Book* (1919), 10ff.
59 Leeds University Library, Liddle Collection, Reverend H.B. Fawkes to Mrs Disney, 7 March 1918.
60 'YMCA – whither' *Christian* (16 March 1916), pp. 79–80.
61 Bertram Cunningham, *This Also Happened on the Western Front* (London: Hazell, Watson and Viney, 1932), 154.
62 Lambeth Palace Library, Papers of Archbishop of Canterbury Davidson, '"Chaplains" Meeting at Valenciennes (First Army) (Topic: Church Army)', 18 January 1919.
63 George Henderson, *The Experiences of a (YMCA) Hut Leader at the Front* (London: Simpkin, Marshall, Hamilton, Kent and Co., 1918), 44–48.
64 Salvation Army International Heritage Centre, London, England, Salvation Army speech entitled 'On Huts', *c.* 1914–18.
65 McKenzie, 'Mothering the men', 11. These sentiments were echoed by the author of 'On Huts', who pointed out that 'not one penny of profit is taken' from hut sales by the Salvation Army.
66 Lambeth Palace Library, Papers of Archbishop of Canterbury Davidson, H. Pike Pease to Archbishop of Canterbury Davidson, 3 April 1918.
67 IWM, DOD, Papers of Reverend H.D.F. Pollock, 11304 P452, diary entry, 2 August 1917.
68 Ibid., diary entry, 11 September 1917.
69 On 'profiteering' generally see Arthur Marwick, *The Deluge: British Society and the First World War* (New York: Norton, 1965), 123.
70 This phenomenon is an excellent example of the government's real stand on 'profiteering', which, as Gerald DeGroot explains, involved 'turning a blind eye ... as long as supplies remained dependable'. See DeGroot, *Blighty: British Society in the Era of the Great War* (New York: Longman, 1996), 71.

71 YMCA, 'Relations with the military', in *Handbook*, 32–33. For statements on this matter from the perspective of the Salvation Army see McKenzie, *Serving the King's Men*, 34.

72 This rule was Army Order IV of 1915, which, as Sir John Cowans, the Quartermaster General, put it, was drafted chiefly on the basis of 'whether [the Association] was or was not making a profit on its work'. Leeds University Library, Liddle Collection, YMCA Papers, unidentified YMCA official to War Office, 28 July 1918. A YMCA report issued in July 1915 suggests that these terms were to be applied later that year 'to other religious or philanthropic bodies'. See YMCA, 'Report, July 1915', Leeds University Library, Liddle Collection, YMCA Papers. On general War Office concern about profiteering abroad, see Public Record Office (hereafter cited as PRO), WO 95/27, official diary of the Quartermaster General, 23 December 1914. The specific demands of the army are summarized in 'Memorandum by the YMCA on the Demand of the Regimental Institutes' Control Board for 10% of Gross Takings, 28 July 1915' Leeds University Library, Liddle Collection, YMCA Papers.

73 Leeds University Library, Liddle Collection, YMCA Papers, 'Memorandum by the YMCA', 28 July 1915.

74 Ibid., Arthur Yapp to War Office, 13 March 1915.

75 Ibid.

76 Ibid., unidentified YMCA official to War Office, 28 July 1915.

77 On the contentious relationship between the COS and the Salvation Army before the war see Stedman Jones, *Outcast London*, 281ff, and Himmelfarb, *Poverty and Compassion*, 219–234.

78 LMA, A/FWA/C/D123/1, correspondence of COS officials, especially 10, 15 and 22 March 1915.

79 LMA, A/FWA/C/D188/1, E.C.P to COS, 11 March 1916.

80 Ibid.

81 *World* (3 February 1918), p. 7.

82 On nineteenth-century factory canteens see Patrick Joyce, *Work, Society, and Politics: The Culture of the Factory in Later Victorian England* (New Brunswick NJ: Rutgers University Press, 1980), especially chapters 3 and 5.

83 Woollacott, *On Her Their Lives Depend*, 63–65. According to Woollacott, the Central Control Board (Liquor Traffic) was established in 1915 and that same year appointed a canteen committee to oversee the establishment of factory canteens. For reasons of efficiency, and economy, however, the Ministry of Munitions was reluctant to take on the canteen proposals suggested by the committee, so the work was given to voluntary-aid organisations.

84 Ibid., 72.

85 'Canteens at munitions works', *Engineer* (28 September 1917): 269.

3

Havens for heroes: life in two military hospitals

'Looked at from outside', Ward Muir observed of the temporary military hospital in which he worked as an orderly, 'a hut-ward is – to the aesthetic eye – a hideous structure'. Still, he added, 'knowing what it stands for, the science, the tenderness and the fundamental civilisation which it represents, we may descry, behind its stark geometrical outlines, a real nobility and beauty'. Inside, Muir explained, two rows of fifteen beds lined each side of the room, with the Sister's writing table and two coke stoves positioned in the centre aisle. Asbestos-lined walls, located a few feet from the floor, structured a continuous line of windows all down each side of the ward. These windows were of a 'special type', which even when open prevented rain from entering. They also helped to make the ward, like its adjoining verandah, 'not only very well lit, but also airy and odourless … [giving] … the patient … the advantage of indoor comfort plus an out-door atmosphere'. But what was most impressive about the design of this haven for sick and wounded men, Muir concluded, was the way in which it emphasized economy and efficiency. All of its features were 'packed neatly under that one rectangular corrugated roof which looked so ugly and so unpromising from outside'.[1]

Muir's observations offer a window on to the relationship of wartime military hospitals to contemporary systems of efficiency and to the identity of the ordinary soldier in the eyes of military authorities.[2] Historical literature on First World War medical care has given only passing attention to the role of military hospitals in the management of the war and in wartime social relationships.[3] Other studies tend to overlook military hospitals as they seek to reveal connections between these environments and the societies that designed and built them.[4] We extend this body of literature here by examining the 'built environment' of military general hospitals: the physical structure and social meaning of these sites from the perspectives of authorities who constructed and administered them and the popular press that often highlighted them to the public eye.[5] Based in part on an interpretative framework inspired by the field of historical geography, this approach to analysing the leading wartime institutions of caregiving reveals a great deal about priorities in the treatment of soldiers, about elite efforts mobilize mass support for the war and, as the next chapter will reveal, about the camaraderie that emerged among men.

Two case studies, representing the two main types of general hospitals for 'other ranks', constitute our chief focus here. The first study involves the First Eastern General Hospital, Cambridge, a 'temporary' institution, established only for the duration of the war by the War Office in co-operation with local civilian architects. The second study involves a more permanent structure also established by the War Office and professional architects, London's King George Hospital, formerly HM Stationary Office and Office of Works. These studies demonstrate that the chief features of the military hospital, namely the pavilion ward and the associated curative regime of taking fresh air, testified to the endurance into the war years of central features of nineteenth-century institutional architecture and of traditional elite perceptions of institutional design. These studies also reveal how, as in the case of rest huts, official concerns about efficiency and economy figured prominently in the organization, administration and official representations of soldiers' hospitals. Finally, these studies show how issues of propaganda fitted with concerns about the design, layout and presentation of the wartime healing environment by authorities. Praise of hospitals as models of efficiency, economy and comfort shared a common root with propaganda that sought to mask the horrors of wartime life to the end of maintaining mass support for the conflict. As with glorification of munitions factories in the popular press, praise of hospitals like the First Eastern and King George became a means by which those who remained at home could 'do their bit' by expressing appreciation of those who were serving King and Country overseas.[6]

The proposition espoused by Victorian medical authorities, architects and social reformers that the physical environment of an institution could function as an instrument of cure, augmenting the therapies practised within its confines, had its origins in what Felix Driver describes as the late eighteenth-century 'making of healthy space' by the upper classes of society.[7] This broadly Western phenomenon continued into the Victorian era in Britain when it informed middle-class efforts to foster self-discipline among the sick, the poor, the unemployed and the criminal sectors of society. From mid-century, when observers began to realize the limitations of their programme of social reform and thus adopted policies of direct therapeutic intervention,[8] the designs of hospitals, asylums, prisons and workhouses reflected these changing preoccupations.[9]

British hospital architecture had registered upper-class preoccupations with disease and degradation in society since at least the late eighteenth century. But the pavilion design of many mid- to late nineteenth-century British hospitals reflected such concerns among medical and architectural authorities with particular clarity.[10] Consisting of a long, rectangular-shaped room with high ceilings, the pavilion was lined with large windows on opposite sides, against which two rows of beds were positioned at right angles. Access to the ward was at one end only, past the nursing sister's desk and the service rooms. The opposite end of the ward housed the patients' washing facilities.[11] This design had important hygienic value, helping to provide fresh air and sunshine, elements which medical authorities understood to be effective cures for patients. Widely accepted by medical authorities after 1870 as an effective means of treating the sick, the pavilion became a central feature of specialized hospitals for patients suffering from tuberculosis and neurasthenia.[12]

The pavilion had other practical values that complemented its medical virtues. It economized on space and provided efficient supervision of staff and patients by hospital authorities. As Florence Nightingale explained in 1858, when the pavilion was already becoming the standard architectural feature in hospitals across western Europe and in Britain, the idea of this method of organization made 'each ward a cul-de-sac of the main circulation system; thus, each was like a separate minerature [*sic*] hospital, the sister's domain, where intruders would always be noticed'.[13] In this regard pavilion hospitals shared a common purpose with lock hospitals, where authorities sought to instil moral values into working-class female syphilitics by subjecting them to surveillance and to 'lessons in deference, respectability and personal cleanliness'.[14] The designs of nineteenth-century workhouses, asylums and prisons similarly registered authorities' changing conceptions of society generally and the inhabitants of these institutions in particular.[15] During the first half of the century, middle-class social reformers intended the imposing design of the workhouse to promote physical and mental health and the virtues of hard work. Inside, the institution was to be so frightening that it would deter inmates from the self-degradation and pauperization that supposedly ensued from acceptance of poor relief.[16] By mid-century, as the concerns of the middle class shifted from punishing the poor to identifying them as social wreckage in need of better hygienic conditions and therapeutic intervention, the design of the workhouse changed accordingly. Increasingly, authorities created separate workhouse infirmaries and infectious wards based on the pavilion design. They also provided gardens and other large open spaces for the benefit of consumptive patients. This policy was expanded during the Edwardian era, when many workhouse infirmaries included top-floor wards surrounded by open windows and terraces.[17]

The design of the asylum also changed during the course of the nineteenth century as medical authorities developed new ideas about the mentally ill and the insane. Whereas private madhouses and charity asylums of the eighteenth century were designed simply to confine inmates, their nineteenth-century counterparts reflected the gradual shift from punishment to therapeutic treatment. Increasingly, medical authorities called for asylum designs that emphasized more cheerful interiors, large outdoor spaces sufficient for exercise and better separation of inmates according to illness and gender.[18]

Finally, the changing designs of prisons also registered the idea among social elites that the physical environment of these institutions could effectively help to foster a healthier society. Whereas prisons in the early nineteenth century were insanitary places that emphasized the discipline of inmates by hard labour and physical punishment, those in the later nineteenth century saw increased emphasis on inmate hygiene and on punishment by isolation, pacification and observation.[19] The standardization of the prison system after 1870, combined with later Gladstonian penal reform, gave rise to prison arrangements that tended to emphasize greater therapeutic and welfarist priorities.[20]

Of a piece with these related trends in institutional design, the history of British military hospitals in the Great War demonstrates continuity in the face of profound social change. Based on a two-stage plan drawn up in 1907 by War Office authorities in the event of war, the initial mobilization of hospitals in 1914 involved bringing into service, by way of structural and staff modifications, existing voluntary hospitals, workhouses, asylums and a variety of private and public buildings, including large homes, town halls and schools.[21] Authorities saw the basic designs of these structures as central to achieving the main objective of the wartime military hospital, namely 'to get the disabled, physically and mentally, fit to fight again; or, if this is not possible within a reasonable time, to return him to civil life at highest possible value in the labour market, so that he may cost the public purse less'.[22] Authorities especially appreciated the designs of recently constructed asylums and Poor Law infirmaries, which had 'all the resources of hospital institutions', including kitchens and water and electricity supplies, in addition to 'ample and attractive pleasure grounds and gardens, recreation fields, recreation halls and well-equipped stages for concerts and theatricals'.[23] With little modification, authorities argued, these existing facilities could become the efficient and economical establishments that the country needed to have on hand for the care of its soldiers.

However, the initial stage of the War Office mobilization scheme provided only 9,000 hospital beds before August 1914 and roughly 20,000 in October. Consequently, when the War Office faced increased financial duress and estimated that 50,000 hospital beds would be needed for casualties, its authorities activated the second stage of their 1907 plan.[24] This measure provided for the construction from scratch of 'temporary emergency hospitals'.[25] These institutions, like 'converted hospitals', emphasized 'efficiency and economy' through a 'unit principle' of design, involving the use of component parts and mobility so that the facilities could be built cheaply, quickly and on a large scale and could be easily transported where need was greatest.[26] This 'unit principle' also enabled authorities to incorporate into the scheme the traditional pavilion plan.

In October 1914, local architectural firms co-operated with the War Office to erect in Cambridge one of Britain's first and largest 'temporary emergency hospitals', the First Eastern General Hospital.[27] In accordance with established War Office plans, the hospital consisted of two physically distinct and separate parts. Organizers located a nucleus of administrative offices and staff quarters in permanent university buildings and medical and surgical facilities for patients in a few existing lecture and meeting halls. They housed recovering patients in ten 408 ft long 'roughly improvised buildings ... [which were] built quickly and at very small cost', on the cricket pitch of the nearby King's and Clare athletic ground.[28] Constructed of wood frames lined inside with plastic and asbestos sheets and covered outside and on top with corrugated iron, these structures sat on concrete slabs and contained nearly 1,700 beds for sick and wounded servicemen of mainly 'other ranks'.[29]

In the eyes of organizers, administrators and staff, the First Eastern was a model of modern institutional efficiency. Situated entirely on a single level, two central passages connected each ward block to the hospital kitchens and to administrative offices located at the northern end of the institution. As the orderly Ward Muir described the arrangement: 'Corridor branches out of corridor – A Corridor, B Corridor, C Corridor, D Corridor, each with its perspective of doors opening into wards; and shorter corridors leading to store-rooms and the like.'[30] This design provided 'ease of mobility' for all, but especially for hospital staff who could serve meals quickly, administer treatments easily and supervise patients with minimal effort. For the soldier patient, as Muir saw it, he who is:

> on crutches can go anywhere without fear of tripping, the patient in a wheeled chair can propel himself anywhere, the orderlies can push wheeled stretchers or dinner-wagons anywhere … [T]he patient or orderly who has dwelt in a hospital where, though distances are shorter, staircases are involved – or where every trifling coming-and-going of goods or stretchers necessitates the manipulation of a lift – blesses those level, smooth corridors, with their facile access to any ward, to operating theatres, kitchens, stores, X-ray room, massage department, etc. …[31]

Such efficiency through design also characterized the interior of the ward blocks, each of which was significantly larger than the standard thirty-bed ward of a large civilian hospital. Rectangular in shape and flanked on opposite sides by two rows of twenty-five beds and lockers, all the wards of the First Eastern had a wide central aisle through which doctors, nurses and orderlies moved freely from bed to bed. At the end of this aisle was the nursing sister's writing desk, from which she could monitor up to fifty patients in her ward.[32]

Through these arrangements, the First Eastern's wards structured a curative regime comparable to that established in traditional pavilion hospitals. Running east–west on the cricket ground, the ward blocks utilized the natural progression of the sun and wind as key elements in the treatment of patients by open air. The north side of each ward was 'protected by louvres', yet open 'close to the roof to ensure free circulation of air throughout'. The south side opened entirely on to verandahs and small gardens, 'except for a low open railing at the floor level and ordinary sun blinds', which were used to regulate the amount of sunlight streaming into the ward.[33] This arrangement provided 'a stepless exit'[34] for patients into the hospital gardens. Here they could continue their fresh-air treatment either by lounging on the lawn or by 'ample exercise and abundance of simple amusements, including sports and games'.[35] Beyond promoting health, the hospital garden itself had economic and social value, as authorities used such plots to grow vegetables for the institution and medicinal herbs for use in certain treatments. They also saw the garden as a means of 'encouraging economy' in food production and consumption.[36]

While military-medical and architectural authorities generally agreed that the fresh-air regime underpinning the First Eastern's design was sound and valuable, they disagreed on whether the design of the institution was effectively achieving this aim. This disagreement, which was articulated in terms of both the definition and the appearance of comfort in the hospital, reveals the emphasis that authorities ultimately placed on the goal of achieving economy and efficiency in hospital organization, administration and expenditure.

On one side of this debate, some medical officials denounced the supposed quality of the ward construction at the First Eastern, claiming that it provided neither the best-quality open-air treatment nor the best standard of comfort for recovering soldiers. In many wards, one caregiver explained, the absence of gaps in the continuous line of ward windows made it difficult to regulate the ward on hot and cold days.[37] 'Unless some special steps are taken to counteract the downrush of the chilled air on to the heads of the patients on winter nights', this individual concluded, 'we fear it must be most uncomfortable for them'.[38] Additionally, this medical official observed, the ward windows and walls 'opened out like a series of stable doors' and were usually kept open throughout both the summer and the winter. Such an arrangement exacerbated what were already poor conditions for soldiers.[39] Another critic in the medical community revealed that the 'flap and flop' of ward blinds, which caused 'an irregular and intermittent noise at night', made matters even worse. They not only disturbed patients when they were trying to sleep but also proved 'not effective in keeping out the rain'.[40]

Some architectural authorities also criticized aspects of the First Eastern's ward construction. One expert observed that the interior and exterior 'angles' of the hospital were not 'rounded' as in permanent hospitals and some modified facilities, thus reducing the number of aseptic surfaces. 'Dust edges' were also pervasive throughout the entire structure.[41] Another authority pointed out that appliances in ward baths and water closets, as well as in the central kitchens, 'were often supported on rough wooden frames and [their] fittings were not always fixed clean of the walls'. This arrangement 'worsened unhygienic and uncomfortable conditions'.[42] Other architects criticized the beds in the hospital for being 'cheap and old fashioned and too low for proper massage work'.[43]

While these criticisms appeared, some architectural authorities positioned themselves on the opposite side of the debate about the First Eastern's design and its consequences for soldier-patient comfort. These individuals observed that that the goals of efficiency and economy in the wartime hospital were simply 'incompatible with refinement in detail' and the provision of 'comfort' as it was generally understood.[44] Underscoring this position, civil architects involved in the erection of temporary hospitals like the First Eastern went to great lengths to improve ward design by developing features that would 'present a neat appearance'.[45] Other architectural authorities approached heating in hospitals in the same manner. 'When the wards were first built', one observer of the First Eastern wrote in the professional journal *Hospital*, 'no heating whatever was provided'. Authorities thus 'found it necessary to provide a few open fires ... for the appearance of comfort'.[46]

Medical authorities affiliated with the First Eastern also responded to criticism of the First Eastern's construction by emphasizing that the facility should be concerned chiefly with achieving cost-effective and efficient administration and respectable recovery rates. Suggesting that financial duress in wartime necessitated this utilitarian environment, the commanding officer of the First Eastern explained that:

> The cost of [each ward block] remains much the same whether one side of the Ward is left open and blinds provided, or it is closed with windows provided according to fancy ... When all was paid for ... the cost of the entire building to accommodate 1,200 patients ... amounted to £25,000, which works out at £20 per bed. Never before has such excellent and so much accommodation been provided at so small a cost. The main object of a hospital, namely, the provision of conditions, surroundings and facilities for rapid cure of injured and diseased men, was always kept steadily in view, but money was not spent on unnecessary bricks and mortar, which can in no way whatsoever add to the value of the an institution for the restoration to health of the sick and the wounded.[47]

Echoing such praise of the First Eastern's design, Dr Arthur Shipley observed in a speech to the Architectural Association that despite the sun blinds of the wards 'having the disadvantage of flapping at regular intervals', they 'kept out rain when let down vertically'. In such conditions, he argued, 'the patients never complained of suffering from cold, but looked upon the hospital as a paradise after life in the trenches'.[48] Subsequently, Shipley pointed out that in terms of efficiency at the First

Eastern, 'open-air treatment showed a great saving in time: there was in most cases no need for a further stay in a convalescent home and the mortality was astonishingly low among the 6,617 patients who had been admitted up to the date of the latest published returns'.[49] Excusing criticism of the facility's construction, Shipley therefore acknowledged that although 'the raindrops may rattle a shade noisily on the roofs [of the hospital and] the asbestos lining may be devoid of ornamentation, ... the patient still had the advantage of indoor comfort plus an outdoor atmosphere'.[50] Finally, in a *Times* editorial Shipley pointed out that the hospital provided beds for as low as £15 20*s* each, a rate that was not only far below War Office regulations of between £60 and £70 each but also remarkably less than the average cost of between £300 and £400 at large civilian hospitals.[51] What was most essential to remember with regard to the First Eastern, Shipley concluded, was that 'in such a crisis as we are passing through at the present time very cheap and very efficient accommodation can be provided, in a very short time'.[52]

These divergent views of the First Eastern came to a head as the hospital reached its most active point of operation during 1915 and early 1916, a period when casualty rates rose significantly and concerns about patriotism and morale made authorities all the more anxious about the public appearance of their institution. Situated in public view on one of the

Figure 3 Postcard (original in colour), 'First Eastern General Hospital, Cambridge: A Ward Garden', *c.* 1915–18

largest and best-known cricket pitches in Cambridge, the First Eastern was easily seen by local passers-by, who could also visit the facility when rules permitted. This arrangement likely prompted hospital officials to launch publicity campaigns that aimed to promote greater public support for the institution, its staff and its patients. Official postcards of the First Eastern's wards and gardens plainly emphasized the supposedly comfortable environs of an institution well suited to care for Britain's heroes (see Figure 3). Such images upheld a romantic view of the military hospital as a haven of rest containing colourful 'wards [with] neat white cots, flowers, pictures, daintily attired nurses and wounded soldiers dressed up in blue suits with red ties'.[53] Depictions of hospital trains in such popular publications as the *Illustrated London News* conveyed a similar message about the quality treatment of wounded soldiers. On the train 'everything is done to make the 'wards' as bright and cheerful as possible, as in a hospital'.[54]

Modified public buildings commandeered by the government for use as general and auxiliary military hospitals also reflected the primacy of official concerns about the maintenance of economy and efficiency. One of the largest of this group of institutions was London's King George Hospital, which opened in June 1915 adjacent to Waterloo Station. Originally the massive HM Stationery Office and Office of Works Stores, with an 'interminable series of dark trenches, ten feet deep, cut in a thousand directions', this facility was renovated by the government in early 1915 to provide sixty-five wards, containing nearly 1,700 beds for sick and wounded of servicemen of non-officer other ranks.[55] The distinct pavilion arrangement of the hospital's wards, in addition to its prominent and publicly praised 'roof garden', 'roof shelters' and top-floor 'well windows', all of which emphasized open-air treatment, make the King George comparable in many respects to the First Eastern.

As the surgeon Frederick Treves explained in the hospital's publicity brochure, authorities intended the institution's 'day rooms' to function as refuges in the same manner as those found in many civilian hospitals. Here, Treves explained, the recovering soldier could be:

> free from the ward, with its sickly sights, its inauspicious smells, its horrid sounds. Here he is free from the gentle tyranny of the nurse. He can once more express himself in such language as he finds the freest and easiest, since in the wards unrestrained speech is limited to whispers between near bed companions. He can smoke, can write letters, can look over the illustrated papers, play a game of cards and even be beguiled by the hoarse music of the gramophone.[56]

Similarly, authorities intended the 'roof garden' of the hospital to serve the same purpose as those that adorned hospitals for consumptive patients.[57] Here was a place of 'escape' from the monotony of both the ward and the 'common-room atmosphere'.[58] As Treves explained, in the 'roof garden' the recovering soldier could 'let his thoughts wander at will beyond the housetops, undisturbed by the wearisome chatter of the barrack room, by the too familiar joke and by the thousand-times-repeated song'.[59] Also in the garden, where the Union Jack flew prominently as a reminder of King and Country served, the soldier could sit in any one of nearly two dozen 'revolving shelters', designed to 'be so turned as to avoid the rain and the wind or to catch the sun'[60] (see Figure 4). Complementing this distinctive component of the hospital's architecture were the large fourth- and fifth-floor 'Well Windows' located on the institution's south-west face. Simply original fixtures given a new name, these features structured a healthy environment for disabled men who were unable to reach the roof to enjoy the fresh air.[61]

Boat rides on the nearby Thames complemented the architectural features of the King George and fitted with the overall regime of this hospital.[62] Medical authorities deemed these outings, which were sponsored by the British Red Cross and Port of London Authority, as immensely successful 'fresh-air treatments'.[63] By 1918, authorities at over 130 hospitals in the greater London metropolitan region made these outings and associated concerts, tea parties and cigarette give-aways available to over 50,000 convalescent men who were deemed fit enough to travel beyond institutional confines. Once on their way – indeed, once on display – these men became the focus of intense public praise. During one outing 'in the neighbourhood of Temple Pier … the Conservator left the pier, the wounded men being loudly cheered by spectators. The trip was timed to last about four hours and on the way various games were played and tea was provided …'.[64] A subsequent outing involved men being 'photographed from the bridge and saloon deck', after which 'they were given a hearty cheer from the crowds on the Embankment as the yacht steamed away'.[65] And on every journey each man received his own 'pictorial map of the river', which offered soldiers a bird's-eye view of the capital city they helped to defend and in which they could now appreciate the public's appreciation of their service.[66] For Rifleman Maurice Gower, the river-boat experience was an enjoyable despite lack of attention on the part of the organizers to one important detail. 'We started at two and managed to get as far as Kew Bridge', Gower wrote in a letter to his sister, '[T]his is as far as the tide would permit,' since 'the Pilot on board stated

Figure 4 Photograph by Benjamin Disraeli Margerison of the 'roof garden' of the King George Hospital, Waterloo, *c*. 1915–18

that the people who arranged the trips did so without considering tides, he sent them a time-table or wrote to that effect, but they seem to have taken no notice'. Gower wrote further that the pilot 'called them a lot of cold women and was pretty well fed up with the job …' Nonetheless, he concluded, 'the men enjoyed the trip. We had a good tea on board and … [as] I walked back to Victoria from the pier, the station was pretty crowded with troops returning and coming from France, which made me feel extremely contented with my lot …'[67] Gower's sense of fellowship outside the hospital was not atypical, as the following two chapters will demonstrate by examining more closely the routines of hospitalized and convalescent soldiers.

No evidence suggests that official debates about design took place at the King George. However, as with the First Eastern, authorities here were concerned about the appearance of comfort for reasons of economy, efficiency and propaganda. The fact that hospital authorities called the roof of the King George a 'garden' while this space did not in fact contain one is especially revealing. In charge of the development and administration of this space and the 'Well Windows' was the hospital's Administrative Committee, which included the philanthropist Sir Arthur Stanley and the surgeon Frederick Treves, both of whom had been long associated with hospital fund-raising schemes.[68] The committee drew up plans for an elaborate roof 'arrangement of small trees and flowers', an arrangement that the *Times* heralded as a 'New Ideal of Healing' which married 'art and science'. Here soldiers could 'win comfort and cheer' from the view of the city and 'during hot summer days [they] will be able to enjoy the coolness of a relatively high atmosphere without incurring discomfort from the wind'. Moreover, the *Times* medical correspondent assured readers, '[no] fears need be entertained that the roof will be found smoky or dusty. Experiments made on the spot have disposed of that anxiety'.[69] A subsequent article in the *Times* noted further that 'the spotless cleanliness of the hospital and the bright and cheerful atmosphere arrested [the] immediate attention [of the visitor]. Cheerfulness, indeed, was the prevailing note, the patients in their comfortable beds look cheerful and the convalescents in the day rooms more cheerful still.'[70] Such positive reports of life at the King George fit with public interest in expressing appreciation of Tommy. They also enabled wartime efforts of upper-class inidividuals who were concerned to be seen 'doing their bit' by helping the wounded. Ms Anita Cohn of 5 Gloucester Gate, Regent's Park, conveyed these sentiments when she wrote to the *Times* that 'arrangements should be made for admitting the public at a moderate charge to view [the King George] before opening it for patients'. Such an arrangement, Cohn explained, could be used to raise money for endowed beds and to 'get people to take a wider personal interest in this splendid undertaking'.[71]

But hospital records show that the roof scheme described so colourfully by Treves, by the Administrative Committee and by the press was never executed completely. This fact was due chiefly to 'the consideration of the safety of the roof, of expense and also of the curtailment of the space available for exercise'.[72] Disciplinary concerns also played a part in the limitation of the roof plan. As administrative records reveal: 'Great difficulties in [patient] administration and supervision' prevented any extension of the roof scheme into a renovated 'waste ground' opposite the hospital.[73] A Friends' Ambulance Unit volunteer who worked at the hospital observed the entire roof arrangement with some dismay. 'No one quite knew why [the roof was called a garden]. This was just a dismal stretch of concrete bounded by iron railings. The scenery was varied by the presence of a number of wooden shelters and the kitchen ventilating shafts'.[74]

While the appearance of comfort took priority over comfort itself at the First Eastern and the King George, to the end of making these sites conform with wartime efficiency and economy, officers generally did not receive treatment in these and associated institutions. In November 1918 23,242 other ranks and 372 officers were being treated in the entire temporary hutted camp system represented by the First Eastern.[75] Throughout the war, converted public buildings like the King George also housed relatively few officers. According to official statistics from 1917, for example, 43,830 other ranks and 4,806 officers were receiving care in these facilities.[76] Between 1914 and 1918 nearly two-thirds of the total number of officers' beds were in hospitals established in private homes where there was one trained nurse for every four beds.[77] In military hospitals like the First Eastern and King George, there was roughly one trained nurse for every sixteen beds. In Poor Law institutions converted into military hospitals, there was one trained nurse for every forty-four beds.[78]

Because the vast majority of officers' hospitals were in private homes and thus by default associated with homelike comforts, they had more plentiful amenities than barrack-like hospitals for men.[79] Here, therefore, comfort was the norm as well as a priority. While up to fifty soldiers in a single ward at the First Eastern and the King George usually had to share one bathroom, at the Kensington Officers' Home patients had the privilege of two bathrooms on every floor and accommodation in single rooms. Here, one resident medical officer, a matron, three trained nurses and three probationers cared for thirty-five officers.[80] Similar staffing ratios existed at the officers' hospital in London's Arlington Street, a private home whose 'golden drawing room became a ward for ten patients' and 'the ballroom held another twelve'.[81] Red Cross statistics confirm these arrangements, revealing that authorities in charge of officers' hospitals spent twice as much as their counterparts in facilities for other ranks on both '[officer patient] maintenance costs' and 'total average costs [maintenance and administration for patients]'.[82]

Individual accounts of hospital life by officers also testify to plush arrangements. At the Endsleigh Voluntary Aid Detachment (VAD) nursing home for officers, known before the war as the Endsleigh Palace Hotel, Alan Thomas recalled, 'the regime was much less strict that it has been at [Queen Alexandra's Military Hospital] Millbank'. At Endsleigh, Thomas explained, 'I had a private room to myself, daintily furnished and kept well stocked with flowers.'[83] Oscar Orr, a Canadian officer wounded at Ypres, received what he described as 'excellent care' at King Edward VII's Hospital for Officers. 'The butler used to come round the wards before meals and take one's order for dinner. Liquor was available in any form by request. When I was able to be moved, I received through the kindness of

Sister Agnes an invitation to spend some time at Norfolk House, St James's Square. This was living it up indeed. My only complaint was that the wonderful dinner served to the Duke and his guests did not start until about 8:15 p.m.'[84] Orr's experiences were not atypical. Recovering officers were generally allowed greater freedom to smoke where and when they wanted and to leave the hospital for longer periods on recreational 'joy-rides', picnics and walks.[85] Moreover, authorities exempted hospitalized officers from wearing the standard-issue blue uniform, which, as we will see, authorities required all ranks to wear during periods of recovery. Instead, authorities provided officers with 'personal clothing allowances' or permitted them to wear clothing donated by the public and voluntary-aid agencies. 'At Mrs Freddie Guest's in Park Lane', a private home converted into an officers' hospital, 'it was blue silk pyjamas for junior officers on the ground floor and pink silk for senior officers on the floor above'.[86]

The dominance of efficiency and economy in hospitals for men align this feature of wartime caregiving, like hut culture, with contemporary munitions work. In munitions factories, authorities used systems of scientific management in an effort to maximize the efficient production of the weapons of war.[87] Similar systems shaped the blueprints of hospitals like the First Eastern and the King George, which sought to return soldiers as rapidly as possible to duty or to civilian life. But even as hospitals and factories shared this organizational framework, these institutions, like huts for weary soldiers and canteens for working women, had different implications for wartime gender identity. As public assessments of munitions factories identified women workers therein as 'doing their bit', they nearly always emphasized women's energy and productivity over worthiness of receiving rest and comfort for their work.[88] By contrast, hospital authorities expected men returned from the front to be comfortable despite arrangements that offered a contrary experience and one not nearly comparable to that of recovering officers. Such positive elite views structured public images of hospitals as nothing less than havens for heroes who had bravely served King and Country. At the same time, in denying women association with restful environs, public images of factories suggested that the work of Tommy's sister in the factory was indeed valuable but ultimately worth less than the efforts of Tommy himself.

Notes

1 Ward Muir, 'A hut-hospital' in *Observations of an Orderly: Some Glimpses of Life and Work in an English War Hospital* (London: Simpkin, Marshall, Hamilton, Kent and Co., 1917), 47.

2 W.G. Macpherson, *History of the Great War Based on Official Documents: Medical Services, General History* (London: HMSO, 1921) and Brian Abel-Smith, *The Hospitals, 1800–1948: A Study in Social Administration in England and Wales* (London: Heinemann, 1964).

3 Koven, 'Remembering and Dismemberment'; Bourke, *Dismembering the Male*, especially 107–123 and Winter, *Death's Men*.

4 Lindsay Granshaw and Roy Porter (eds), *The Hospital in History* (New York: Routledge, 1989).

5 On the idea of the 'built environment' see especially Michael Ignatieff, *A Just Measure of Pain: The Penitentiary in the Industrial Revolution* (New York: Pantheon, 1978); David J. Rothman, *The Discovery of the Asylum* (Boston MA: Little, Brown, 1971) and Andrew Scull, *Social Order/Mental Disorder: Anglo-American Psychiatry in Historical Perspective* (Berkeley CA: University of California Press, 1989), 213–214.

6 On press coverage of munitions factories see Sharon Ouditt, *Fighting Forces*, 71–85 and Woollacott, *On Her Their Lives Depend*, 6.

7 Felix Driver, *Power and Pauperism: The Workhouse System, 1834–1884* (Cambridge: Cambridge University Press, 1993), 23. On this trend see also David Armstrong, *The Political Anatomy of the Body: Medical Knowledge in Britain in the Twentieth Century* (Cambridge: Cambridge University Press, 1983); Thomas R. Metcalf, *An Imperial Vision: Indian Architecture and Britain's Raj* (Berkeley CA: University of California Press, 1993); P. Rabinow, *French Modern: Norms and Forms of the Built Environment* (Boston MA: MIT Press, 1989) and Richard A. Hayward, 'Changing Hospital Design in the Second Half of the Nineteenth Century' (Ph.D. thesis, University of Keele, 1998).

8 Martin Wiener, *Reconstructing the Criminal: Culture, Law, and Policy in England, 1830–1914* (Cambridge: Cambridge University Press, 1990).

9 This trend also reflected contemporary professionalization, especially during the period 1870 and 1900 when architects and medical authorities were attempting to establish their legitimacy. On the tensions engendered by this trend see Ann Marie Adams, *Architecture in the Family Way: Doctors, Houses, and Women, 1870–1900* (Buffalo NY: McGill-Queen's University Press, 1996).

10 On how contemporary medical understanding guided the design of hospitals and other arenas of rest and recovery see Adrian Forty, 'The modern hospital in England and France: The social and medical uses of architecture' in A.D. King (ed.), *Buildings and Society: Essays on the Social Development of the Built Environment* (New York: Routledge and Kegan Paul, 1980), 61–93 and Dane Kennedy, *The Magic Mountains: Hill Stations and the British Raj* (Berkeley CA: University of California Press, 1996).

11 King, *Buildings and Society*, 76.

12 See F.B. Smith, *The Retreat of Tuberculosis, 1800–1950* (New York: Croom Helm, 1988); M.A. Veeder, 'Diseases of the respiratory system: Why the open-air treatment of consumption succeeds', *Treatment: A Monthly Journal of Practical Medicine and Surgery* (March 1903): 33–34 and J.E. Esslemont, 'Garden cities for consumptives: A plea for a national scheme', *Hospital* (1 November 1913): 115–118, (15 November 1913): 167–170 and (29 November 1913): 221–223. On the value of the hospital environment for neurasthenic women see E.W. Parsey, 'On the treatment of neurasthenia of women by Weir-Mitchell's method', *Treatment* (April 1904): 110–111.

13 Florence Nightingale, *Notes on Hospitals: Being Two Papers Read before the National Association for the Promotion of Social Science, 1858* (London: John W. Parker and Son, 1859), 6–8.

14 See Judith Walkowitz, *Prostitution and Victorian Society: Women, Class, and the State* (New York: Cambridge University Press, 1980), 59–60. See also Donna Andrew, 'Two medical charities in eighteenth-century London: The Lock Hospital and the Lying-in Charity for married women' in Jonathan Barry and Colin Jones (eds) *Medicine and Charity before the Welfare State* (New York: Routledge, 1991), 82–97 and Charles Rosenberg, 'Florence Nightingale on contagion: The hospital as moral universe' in Charles Rosenberg (ed.) *Healing and History* (New York and Folkestone: Dawson, 1979), 116–136.

15 On this trend see F.M.L. Thompson, *The Rise of Respectable Society: A Social History of Victorian Britain* (Cambridge MA: Harvard University Press, 1988) and Deborah E.B. Weiner, *Architecture and Social Reform in Late Victorian London* (Manchester: Manchester University Press, 1994). This trend is also discernible in contemporary public health and educational reforms. On public health see Christopher Hamlin, *Public Health and Social Justice in the Age of Chadwick: Britain, 1800–1854* (Cambridge: Cambridge University Press, 1998). On schools see T. Markus, 'The school as machine' in T. Markus (ed.), *Order in Space and Society: Architectural Form and its Context in the Scottish Enlightenment* (Edinburgh: Edinburgh University Press, 1982), 201–256 and W.A.C. Stewart, *The Educational Innovators* (London: St Martin's Press, 1968).

16 See Thompson, *Rise of Respectable Society*, 348–350.

17 These developments occurred unevenly across Britain. At the turn of the century many small rural workhouses remained places of passive cruelty with bad food and a harsh daily regime. See Jeremy Taylor, *Hospital and Asylum Architecture in England, 1840–1914* (New York: Mansell, 1991), 66–68. Taylor observes, however, that improvements in the design of the workhouse infirmary helped to change this institution into the general hospital. He also points out that this development was one of the chief reasons why many Poor Law institutions were taken over as military hospitals in the Great War. See Taylor, *Hospital and Asylum Architecture*, 73. On this development see Abel-Smith, *The Hospitals*.

18 See Scull, 'Moral architecture: The Victorian lunatic asylum' in Andrew Scull

(ed.), *Museums of Madness: The Social Organisation of Insanity in Nineteenth-Century England* (London: Allen Lane, 1979). See also Scull, *Social Order/ Mental Disorder*.

19 Robin Evans, *The Fabrication of Virtue: English Prison Architecture, 1759–1840* (Cambridge: Cambridge University Press, 1982).

20 See Wiener, *Reconstructing the Criminal*. Victor Bailey has contested this interpretation of prison development by claiming that the English penal system at the turn of the century did not change that substantially. See Bailey, 'English prisons, penal culture, and the abatement of imprisonment, 1895–1922', *Journal of British Studies* 36:3 (1997): 285–324.

21 A. Saxon Snell, 'The War Office model plan and hospitals at Shorncliffe, Leicester, and Norwich: Typical plans illustrating the Chadwick lecture by Mr A. Saxon Snell, FRIBA, on "Emergency Military Hospital Construction"', *Building News* (17 November 1915): 552–554. These plans were part of R.B. Haldane's 1906 reforms of the army, which are discussed in Chapter 1 above.

22 P. Mitchell, *Memoranda on Army General Hospital Administration* (London: Bailliere, Tindall and Cox, 1917).

23 W.G. Macpherson, *History of the Great War*, 79. For general details of the 1907 War Office plan see 'Territorial hospitals: The guiding principles of the scheme', *Hospital* (10 October 1914): 33–34. For an illustration of this plan see Snell, 'The War Office model plan'.

24 Abel-Smith, *The Hospitals*, 273.

25 See *Hospital* (10 October 1914): 23 and 33 and (17 October 1914): 69. In October 1914 the War Office began to issue appeals for additional accommodation, called 'auxiliary military hospitals', via the Joint Committee of the British Red Cross and Order of St John. See Abel-Smith, *The Hospitals*, 253.

26 Snell, 'War Office model plan'.

27 For background on the employment of civil engineers in this type of war work and on the relationship between civil and military engineering in military hospital construction see PRO, WO 32/5104, Chairman of the Institute of Civil Engineers to the War Office, 28 April 1919.

28 A. Saxon Snell, 'Chadwick public lectures: Military Emergency Hospital Construction (lecture to the Royal Sanitary Institute, 6 April 1916)', *Builder* (14 April 1916): 281.

29 An architect's sketch of the First Eastern General Hospital is contained in Joseph Griffiths, *Hospitals: Yesterday, To-day and … Tomorrow* (n.p., [1917–18]).

30 Muir, 'A hut-hospital', 47. For further evidence that the Third London and First Eastern had similar architectural arrangements see Charles F. Skipper, 'A bird's eye perspective view of the 1st Eastern General Hospital, Cambridge' in Joseph Griffiths, *Hospitals: Yesterday, To-day and … Tomorrow* (n.p., [1917–18]).

31 Ibid., 47. Muir added that the ward blocks at the Third London were built along the same lines at the First Eastern and were 'put up at a remarkable pace … [as] an open field vanished in less than a month and [a] 'Bungalo Town' [of fifty huts] appeared' (ibid., 45).

32 See Griffiths, *Hospitals*, n.p.

33 See *Builder* (12 November 1915): 343. This description also points out that 'in cases of a southern gale the beds nearer the southern front can be drawn further back [into the ward]'. For photographic evidence of the designs described here see the 'Ramsey and Muspratt' Collection of Photographs of the First Eastern General Hospital, held by the Cambridgeshire Collection, First Eastern photographs 1–119. This collection constitutes a comprehensive photographic survey of all aspects of daily life at the hospital. For additional photographic evidence see postcards held by the Cambridgeshire Collection, H Eas.K16/4168–9, 'First Eastern General Hospital, Cambridge: Interior of a ward' and 'First Eastern General Hospital, Cambridge: A ward garden'.

34 Contemporary articles in the *Hospital* extolled the practical virtues of the ward-bordered garden in military and civilian hospitals. See, for example, 'Hospital gardens', *Hospital* (10 October 1914): 25–26. At the same time, however, the authors of these articles warned of the infectious potential of this outdoor healing space. See, for example, 'The infectious hospital garden', *Hospital* (2 May 1914): 117.

35 'Hospital provision: Its difficulties and limitations', *Hospital* (23 October 1915): 72.

36 See 'Economy and hospital gardens', *Hospital* (31 July 1915): 380; 'Medicinal herb cultivation in hospital gardens', *Hospital* (22 April 1916): 77; 'A new use for hospital gardens: The cultivation of medicinal herbs', *Hospital* (26 August 1916): 492 and 'Remodelling a hospital garden: A practical example at Hertford', *Hospital* (20 May 1916): 172. Significantly, in the summer of 1916, the Royal Horticultural Society began to publish a series of pamphlets for both civilians and military-medical authorities to 'encourage economy' through food production in the 'home' and in 'hospital gardens'. See 'Economy in hospital gardens', *Hospital* (26 August 1916): 484. Munitions factories also participated in this effort, providing individual garden allotments to workers. See Woollacott, *On Her Their Lives Depend*, 63. On the value of gardens associated with one auxiliary hospital established in a private home in Kent, known as the 'Garden Hospital', see Paul Creswick, G. Stanley Pond and P.H. Ashton, *Kent's Care for the Wounded* (London: Hodder and Stoughton, 1915), 59–62.

37 *Hospital* (9 June 1917): 188. This situation was chiefly due to the fact that glass was a good conductor of heat and cold.

38 Ibid., 188.

39 Ibid., 188. Three years earlier the medical authorities had levelled similar complaints against open-air wards at the Queen's Hospital, where such arrangements 'certainly did not look "comfortable" and seemed open to the objection of getting all the smoke as well as the rain and snow'. See Robert Saundby, MD, 'Open-air hospitals in war-time', *Hospital* (19 September 1914): 673.

40 Shipley pointed to this criticism in his own study of the First Eastern in an effort to refute it. See Shipley, *Open-air Treatment*, 6. A stretcher bearer recalled such criticism in his reminiscences of the First Eastern. The facility, he

wrote, 'consisted of large canvas marquees spaced in parallel and each having one long side open to the healing fresh air (and also wind and rain)'. See Hope Bagenal, *Letters to a Niece,* ed. Rachel Bagenal (Oxford: Oxford Polytechnic, 1983), n.p.

41 Snell, 'Chadwick public lectures', 281.

42 Snell, 'War Office model plan', 552–554.

43 'An open-air hospital: Treatment of wounded at Cambridge', *The Times* (29 June 1915), p. 11.

44 Snell, 'Chadwick public lectures', 281.

45 See 'The Fifth Northern General Hospital, Leicester: The recent additions', *Hospital* (23 October 1915): 81. As the winter of 1915–16 set in, hospital architects developed additional improvements along these lines and put them into place where needed. See 'Weather protection on open-air wards', *Hospital* (1 January 1916): 293.

46 *Hospital* (9 June 1917): 188.

47 Griffiths, *Hospitals*, 29–30.

48 A.E. Shipley, 'The Military Hospital, Cambridge, a paper read at the Architectural Association, November 1915', in *Building News* (10 November 1915): 524. Shipley was Master of Christ's College, Cambridge, and a local fund raiser for and occasional medical consultant to the First Eastern.

49 Shipley, *Open-air Treatment*, 6.

50 Ibid., 6–7.

51 Ibid., 6. See also Shipley, 'Cheap hospital', *The Times* (8 July 1915), p. 9. Shipley wrote this editorial in response to criticism received after the recent praise by *The Times* of the First Eastern in 'Healing in the open: Successful experiment at Cambridge', *The Times* (21 June 1915), p. 5.

52 Shipley, 'Cheap hospital'.

53 'Ward "O": A hospital with peculiarities', *The Times* (7 January 1916), p. 11. See also the 'Ramsey and Muspratt' Collection of Photographs of the First Eastern General Hospital.

54 'A song from home: In a British hospital train', *Illustrated London News* (1 June 1918), cover. This cover-page image depicts nurses in a hospital train attending to bedridden soldiers. Above one of the soldiers is a canary cage. The caption to the image explains this arrangement: 'Even canaries in cages may be seen hung over the cots on occasion to amuse the patients with their song, recalling memories of home.'

55 Frederick Treves, *The King George Hospital: A Short Pamphlet History* (London: Abbey Press, 1915), 6–7. For a similar description of the King George see 'From warehouse to hospital: 3 miles of beds and 9½ acres of linoleum', *The Times* (*c.* 1915), n.p. This article is lodged in a scrapbook kept by a patient at the King George. Wellcome Library for the History and Understanding of Medicine, Contemporary Medical Archives Centre (hereafter WLHUM/CMAC), RAMC 1647. Throughout the war, the King George contained no beds at all for officers. In late 1918 it contained 1882 beds for recovering other

ranks. See IWM, DOD, 75/103/1–2, 'Medical War Records, London District, *c.* 1918'.

56 Treves, *King George*, 12. For evidence of the use of 'day rooms' and 'common rooms' in contemporary civilian hospitals see 'Institutional residents and recreation: The escape from the common-room atmosphere', *Hospital* (13 June 1914): 292. For evidence of use of these rooms in earlier military contexts see *Report of a Committee Appointed by the Secretary of State for War to Inquire into and Report on the Present State and on the Improvement of Libraries, Reading Rooms, and Day Rooms* (London: HMSO, 1861).

57 On the use of these architectural resources for consumptive patients see Taylor, *Hospital and Asylum Architecture*, 72–73 and 'Wooden huts for consumptives', *Hospital* (22 November 1913): 190.

58 Treves, *King George*, 13.

59 Ibid., 13. This description is echoed in 'New ideals of healing. King George Hospital: Roof-garden for wounded soldiers', *The Times* (21 May 1915), p. 11.

60 Ibid., 13. The medical authorities also installed revolving shelters for convalescent soldiers at a British Red Cross auxiliary hospital in Newlands Corner, Surrey. See *Surrey Branch Historical Summary, April 1907–31 December 1953* and Mrs Strachy (Vice-president of Albury and Shere Division of the British Red Cross), *St Loe Strachey: His Life and his Paper* (n.p.: Victor Gollancz Press, 1930).

61 Archives of the Order of St John, Clerkenwell, London First World War collection, 'Minutes of the King George Hospital Committee, 8 June 1917'. This entry also includes a description of a plan to install sun blinds for the windows on the south-west face of the hospital. A British Red Cross report shows further that the authorities initiated a plan to install a lift to the roof so that severely disabled patients could take advantage of its shelters. See 'Summary of Work for the Week Beginning 28th April 1916: The King George Hospital', held in IWM, Department of Printed Books, Red Cross Collection.

62 Hospitals outside London also integrated river-boat trips into their curative schemes. The VAD hospital at Mongewell, Oxfordshire, for example, had a boat launch on its grounds for this purpose. WLHUM, SA/CSP archives, nurse G.M. Weller photograph albums. Wounded soldiers from the Old Court Hospital at Avoncliff boarded a passenger steamer at Kelston Dock on the Kennet and Avon Canal for afternoon trips to Bradford-on-Avon and back. See Niall Allsop, *Images of the Kennet and Avon Canal* (Bristol: Redcliffe, n.a.).

63 The chairmen and/or commanders of over a dozen British and Dominion hospitals in and around London described these outings in such a way. A list of these individuals and their associated institutions appears in Museum of London, Docklands, Port of London Authority, Minutes of Proceedings, 1st April 1915 to 31st March 1916, 15 October 1915.

64 'River trips for wounded. London Port Authority's happy thought', *Times* (*c.* 1914–18), n.p. This article is lodged in a scrapbook kept by a patient at the King George. WLHUM/CMAC, RAMC 1647.

65 Ibid.

66 Museum of London, Docklands, Port of London Authority, Minutes of Proceedings, 1st April 1918 to 31st March 1919, 9 May 1918, p. 53. See also 'Port of London Authority. S.Y. Conservator. A souvenir of an excursion on the river Thames through the port of the Empire: Westminster to Crayford Ness' (London, 1917).

67 IWM, DOD, Papers of Maurice F. Gower, 255 88/25/2, Gower to his sister, 3 September 1918.

68 Stanley was chairman of both the British Red Cross Joint Finance Committee and the *The Times* Fund for the BRCS. Treves had long been involved in publicity campaigns for sick and wounded seamen and the wartime wounded. On Treves see Stephen Trombley, *Sir Frederick Treves: The Extra-ordinary Edwardian* (New York: Routledge, 1989).

69 'New ideals of healing', *The Times* (21 May 1915), p. 11.

70 'A hospital in being. New King George building occupied', *The Times* (1 July 1915), p. 11.

71 'King George's Hospital', letter to *The Times* (24 May 1915), p. 8. No evidence has survived to suggest that Cohn's idea was adopted by the hospital authorities.

72 Archives of the Order of St John, Clerkenwell, London First World War collection, 'Minutes of the King George Hospital Committee, 16 June 1915'. The first of these reasons was likely the result of a Scottish soldier jumping from the roof in 1915. See 'Suicide in hospital. Scottish soldier's jump from the roof', *The Times* (*c.* 1915), n.p. This article is lodged in a scrapbook kept by a patient at the King George. WLHUM/CMAC, RAMC 1647.

73 Archives of the Order of St John, Clerkenwell, London First World War collection, 'Minutes of the King George Hospital Committee, 5 and 12 May 1915'.

74 Meaburn Tatham and James E. Miles (eds), *The Friends' Ambulance Unit, 1914–1919: A Record* (London: Swarthmore Press, 920), 230–232.

75 Macpherson, *History of the Great War*, 77–78. According to Macpherson, in 1917 the First Eastern housed 1,020 other ranks and 153 officers. See ibid., 74.

76 Ibid., 80–82. These statistics include officers and other ranks receiving care in former Poor Law establishments and asylums.

77 Abel-Smith, *The Hospitals*, 272–275 and Macpherson, *History of the Great War*, 74–78 and 80–82.

78 Brian Abel-Smith, *A History of the Nursing Profession* (New York: Springer, 1960), 84–85.

79 Georgina, Lady Dudley supervised hospital arrangements for officers throughout the war. Her contributions in this regard were an extension of the work she undertook during the Boer War. *Reports by the Joint War Committee and the Joint War Finance Committee of the British Red Cross Society and the Order of St John of Jerusalem in England on Voluntary Aid Rendered to the Sick and Wounded at Home and Abroad and to British Prisoners of War, 1914–1919, with*

Appendices (London: HMSO, 1921), 232–235.

80 *Hospital* (16 January 1915): 345.

81 Diana Cooper, *The Rainbow Comes and Goes* (Boston: Houghton Mifflin, 1958), 135. Cooper's mother offered the family home to the Red Cross as a hospital for officers.

82 Abel-Smith, *The Hospitals*, 272–275. See also statistics in *Accounts of Auxiliary Hospitals for the Year Ended 31st December 1918, with Summary of Accounts for the Four Years 1915–1918* (London: British Red Cross Society, 1919).

83 Alan Thomas, *A Life Apart* (London: Victor Gollancz, 1968), 147.

84 Richard Hough, *Sister Agnes: The History of King Edward VII's Hospital for Officers, 1899–1999* (London: John Murray, 1999), 55–56.

85 See *Hospital* (24 April 1915): 82 and (29 May 1915): 185. Despite the disciplinary problems, like drunkenness, that occasionally resulted from such conditions, hospital rules for officer patients remained lenient compared with those for soldier patients. See Abel-Smith, *The Hospitals*, 273–274.

86 Lyn McDonald, *The Roses of No Man's Land* (New York: Penguin Books, 1993), 39. See also Abel-Smith, *The Hospitals*, 275. This may have been the 'luxurious officers' hospital in the region of Park Lane' to which Vera Brittain refers in her search for the wounded colonel who accompanied her brother, Captain Edward Brittain, into battle. See Vera Brittain, *Testament of Youth* (New York: Penguin Books, 1989), 440.

87 Woollacott, *On Her Their Lives Depend*, 72.

88 Ibid., 6 and Ouditt, *Fighting Forces, Writing Women*, 71–80.

4

Hospital magazines: writing about wartime recovery/recovering writing about wartime

> It is my hope that in days to come, in the near future, the men will not only regard death, gashing and gaping wounds, gas-destroyed organs, or even frozen feet…as mere nothings, but that they will be able to joke lightly among themselves in these matters, fortified by the fact that they are giving more gashes, ripping up more bodies and causing more suffering generally than the other side (Brigadier-General F.P. Crozier)…[1]

> Have you lived in Hospital, of course you say 'no'
> Well listen and I will tell you just how all things go …
>
> (Captain J.G.W. Haynes)[2]

Representations of hospital life by recovering soldiers stand in stark contrast to the positive views articulated by institutional authorities. Men made sense of routines in hospital by associating them with the larger war machine and by invoking features of traditional institutional life. Hospital magazines provide abundant testimony to this conclusion. As this official literature helped authorities to sharpen their own vision of the hospital it was intended to – and did – allow recovering soldiers to express their frustration with the institution. Illuminating this dual function of hospital magazines yields further understanding of the military hospital as a site that involved more than total discipline of the soldier's body. Hospital magazines open a window on to the soldier's multifaceted experience of recovery. They also help us gain further insight into soldiers' comradeship of wartime healing, an *esprit de corps* that combined with the comradeship of the trenches to underscore a collective sense of being a class apart from noncombatants in British society.

The classic poets and memoirists of the Great War have received substantial attention,[3] but historians have only recently begun to locate 'amateur' or non-canonical wartime literature in the broader history of print culture and to identify the ways in which this material reflects contemporary social relationships. Stephane Audoin-Rouzeau has shown how French soldiers' production and consumption of trench journals represented an important cultural link between war front and home front that helped men to endure life in the trenches.[4] Similarly, John Fuller has demonstrated how trench literature produced by British forces reflected the endurance of pre-war popular leisure activity into the war years and functioned as a valuable means of building morale on the front lines. Assessing trench journals in terms of the military's concern about discipline, Fuller concludes that this literature functioned as a means of relieving wartime pressures, complaints and frustrations endured by a regiment or battalion.[5] Trench journals were therefore an essential part of the contemporary propaganda machine. Like recruitment posters designed by the Ministry of War and films produced by the Ministry of Information, these publications served to glorify the war and to help boost morale among men.[6]

As Fuller has noted, the creation of trench journals by British and Dominion units was an unprecedented literary achievement in wartime. Never before had so many soldiers of various ranks produced such a volume of literature on a war front and along the military lines of communication. Printed at official army facilities, abandoned French presses and provincial facilities on the British home front, these publications were read chiefly by front-line troops and others on active service. They numbered in the hundreds, but single titles usually included only a handful of issues. And while their censored content reveals the practice of traditional forms of recreation and entertainment on the battlefront, such as musical concerts and football, it also suggests that trench journals themselves functioned as a disciplinary 'safety valve', a means of amusement and venting grievances during periods of rest.[7]

An analysis of hospital magazines reveals a great deal about the production and consumption of this officially sanctioned institutional literature.[8] The first military hospital in Britain to publish its own magazine was the First Eastern General Hospital, Cambridge, beginning on 13 April 1915.[9] By the end of the first year of the war, nearly every general military hospital in the country had initiated a similar literary project. Throughout this period auxiliary hospitals that had sufficient funds and staff also began to publish their own magazines. Like trench journals, therefore, hospital magazines were not produced exclusively during any particular period of the war.[10] And while their front-line counterparts numbered in the hundreds, hospital magazines numbered perhaps only two dozen. However, hospital magazines were much less ephemeral than trench journals: where most trench journals included only a handful of issues, most hospital magazines contained at least a dozen issues. Hospital magazines therefore exerted an impact on soldiers that belies their relatively modest number in the print culture of the Great War.

Just as the commanding officer of a battalion or regiment oversaw the production of his group's trench journal, a hospital's commanding officer supervised the task of editing his institution's magazine. However the editorial work itself often extended beyond officers to the head matron, nursing sisters and ward orderlies. And while the editorial facilities of most magazines were located in the administrative block of associated hospitals, the production process usually took place outside institutions, at local printing presses.[11]

Hospital magazines distinguished themselves from trench journals in terms of distribution and readership. Whereas the distribution of trench journals remained largely limited to the front lines, hospital magazines were sold in the recreation rooms of sponsoring institutions and in those of affiliated hospitals. Editors also often made their publications available to local booksellers and railway news stalls where they could be purchased by the public.[12] Other editors offered postal subscriptions to 'all interested in the Hospital, whether directly connected with it or not'.[13]

As hospital magazine editorials and column by-lines suggest, the chief contributors of literary and artistic material to these publications were also its primary intended audience, the patients and staff of the sponsoring institution. This material, alongside articles about hospital magazines that appeared in the *Hospital*, suggests further that patients and staff in different institutions were avid readers of each other's publications.[14] The fact that some magazines kept track of their 'continental' and 'public' readership demonstrates further that this literature's readership extended beyond the institutional arena both to civilians and to those on active service.[15] As for trench journals, however, the actual readership of a hospital magazine is difficult if not impossible to determine. One individual or possibly dozens could easily have read a single issue.

The format of hospital magazines varied little from first to final issues, averaging between fifteen and twenty-five pages per issue and appearing either bi-weekly or monthly. The consistent physical quality of these publications was impressive for the day, considering limited wartime budgets, manpower and imports of paper and papermaking materials.[16] When paper shortages required editors to choose lower-grade cover sheets for their magazines, for example, colour continued to be used in the printing process. And when the magazine's staff introduced such changes, they usually did so without decreasing the number of pages per issue or increasing the selling price drastically.[17] That editors placed such great value on the appearance and cost of their publications suggests how they saw this material to be of essential importance to their institutions.

The content of hospital magazines depended chiefly on four factors: funds available for production, contributions from staff and patients, recreational activities of the institution and the time that editorial board members, who were also important figures on the hospital's medical staff, were able to contribute to their magazine's creation.[18] Regardless of such differences, this body of literature did share many features, including editorials by the editor, commanding officer or chief matron of the hospital and a wide variety of poems, prose and pen-and-ink sketches authored by soldier patients about life in and around the institution. The magazines also included institutional recreation news and concert announcements, schedules and news about officially sponsored outings, censored humour about staff, patients and ward life and advertisements from local businesses.

Editors justified the existence of hospital magazines in a variety of ways. Intended simultaneously as a history, as a source of mental and physical therapy and as a means of supplying amusement and administrative instruction and camaraderie, this literature effectively served to boost morale among both patients and hospital staff.[19]

Editors drew attention to the historical value of the magazine. It was, as one editor explained, a way of 'reserving for ourselves and for posterity a series of verbal and artistic sidelights on the tone and temper of the day: the obstinate and outwardly irresponsible humour, even frivolity, with which we went about the biggest business which it has ever fallen to the lot of the Empire to tackle'.[20] Like the trench journal, the hospital magazine was the handiwork of individuals who realized that they were witnessing an historic event and, as a result, felt that their experiences should be recorded for future generations.

Editors also justified the creation of hospital magazines by pointing out that these publications fitted into a tradition of proven mental and physical care. Hospital authorities had long emphasized the value of reading in the institution as a useful means of creating a peaceful environment.[21] They had also seen making handicrafts and listening to music to be effective curatives.[22] As in the trenches, where these forms of leisure helped to break up monotonous daily routines and make unfamiliar environs more habitable, in the wartime military hospital they were intended to create a comfortable 'atmosphere of focussed [*sic*] care for [the soldier patients'] well-being'.[23] The process of creating literary and artistic material for institutional magazines, authorities held, was a particularly effective way to keep the hands of recovering ranks busy and their minds occupied. This activity had curative value in itself. As the editor of the *First Eastern General Hospital Gazette* explained in his description of a soldier-patient drawing, entitled 'Suggestions for the curative gymnasium process', this work:

> was done with the left hand (the artist's right arm being wounded). He has taught himself to draw with the left hand since admission to the hospital. The drawing is the artist's idea of how gymnastics can be applied for the cure of injuries to muscles and nerves.[24]

And as another editor explained, the war 'has inspired those with the gift of expression to set down [their experiences] in verse or story'. This creative endeavour, he argued further, gave 'the amateur artist or writer, lying wounded or invalided in a peaceful hospital, ... through the long weeks or months of enforced idleness ..., time for reflection'.[25]

> His is the mind which visualizes and realizes the emotions, the humour and the tragedy which a modern war must bring about. And such an individual has the time to give expression to his thoughts, even though his work in this direction may be crude and lacking the subtleties of professionalism ...[26]

Such expressive work therefore reinforced the official view of the hospital as 'peaceful', a place where the war's tired and broken heroes could deservedly be 'idle' and 'reflective'.[27]

Related to the hospital magazine's function as therapy and as a means of maintaining a restful environment was its purpose to generate income for the delivery of entertainment to patients and staff.[28] The magazine achieved this goal through sales, a portion of the proceeds of which officials combined with voluntary contributions to provide recreations for the entire institution, including concerts and convalescent outings.[29]

Finally, editors saw the magazine as an effective way of maintaining an efficient and harmonious working environment, since it fostered camaraderie among staff and patients. As the editor of the *First Eastern General Hospital Magazine* explained, his publication promoted an 'exchange of ideas and a bond of union', which in turn helped to 'further the interest and increase the pride which we all feel in being on the staff of so important an Institution'.[30] An article on hospital magazines in the *Hospital* underlined this claim, pointing out that whether this literature chronicled the history of the institution, detailed new medical and surgical techniques or simply provided accounts of institutional sporting events, its underlying aim was to uphold the idea that:

> the hospital should be the common bond which unites members of every other organisation. Its affairs should be known to everybody. Its atmosphere should be everywhere appreciated and while these results can only be gained by everyone in some way coming into contact and relation to with the institution, one of the best means of securing intimacy and maintaining interest is by a well-written hospital magazine.[31]

The production of hospital magazines, as this author suggests, helped authorities achieve their essential goals of maintaining good recovery rates and general efficiency in the wartime healing environment.

The fact that editors censored all the material they received for publication, however, reveals the true propagandistic function of hospital magazines.[32] As the editor of the *Gazette of the Third London General Hospital* explained, his magazine helped to encourage the 'community to obey the unwritten rules of commonsense and good form'. It also helped to make the hospital:

> not an 'institution' but a place where there is no atmosphere of institutionalism … [a] complex world of patients, sisters, nurses, officers, orderlies and miscellaneous staff [throughout which] there is a bond of friendly co-operation and mutual comradeship which make for the pleasantest sense of discipline-without-stringency.[33]

Through what this editor called 'happy rule based on a firm belief in the practicability of rulelessness', censorship was intended as a means of encouraging all inhabitants of the hospital to work toward the official goals of efficiency, economy and social harmony. It promoted 'loyalty to the hospital' and this, in turn, fostered in 'every man and woman concerned the spirit of willing service.'[34] More specifically, censorship helped the magazines themselves serve their purpose of siphoning off some of the chief drawbacks of military hospital life, namely 'a superficial restlessness, a craving for excitement, the inevitable reaction from an enforced monotony of bed, the never changing orderly routine [of the institution]' and desires among soldier patients for the 'tinsel and glaring gewgaws of the outside world'.[35]

Military-hospital authorities therefore used their magazines to create a vision of the institution as a relatively relaxed and harmonious environment apart from the horrors of war. But much of the content of these publications, alongside other narratives by soldiers in sources such as personal letters, provides testimony of the repressive nature of the hospital regime. Taken together this evidence conveys the soldiers' resistance to this regime and its routines, to their sense of recovery as being an extension of trench life and to their view of being a unique community of sufferers enduring harsh treatments, aggravating visitors and other daily activities.

Many soldiers appreciated time in bed following their return from the front, Frederick Davison's view of his 'nice, cosy, clean, warm bed' being typical.[36] Others, however, were less positive as they saw the bed to be a source of feelings of discipline and confinement. As the author of 'Beds and bed making' suggested, the soldier patient's bed was 'made at least once every day and 'straightened up' on other occasions, such as [during the] appearance of the Matron, or the Orderly Officer; [or] when the brow of the Charge Sister is clouded; just before the visitors come; just before an inspection; and so on, ad lib, ad nauseum'. The way in which the bed was made, in addition to the frequency of this procedure, involved 'the clothes [being] tucked in to such an extent that it is well-nigh impossible for [the patient] to move. The bed is no longer a bed, it is a nightmare.'[37] Even when a soldier patient 'at last succeeds in loosening the [bed]clothes over him … he is detected [by the nursing sister]' and the bed is 'retucked and patted and the one inside admonished'.[38] Subsequently, 'weeks pass and the patient's spirit is broken; he becomes meek as a lamb and turns the corners of the blankets down, just as though it was natural to do so'. Even when transferred to another ward, to the care of another sister, the scene would be repeated. Again, 'he turns the corners of the blankets', but is caught by the sister. 'How is he to know that in this ward, the bottom of the quilt is tucked along up the edge of the bed, the effects being obtained by pleating each corner twice at an angle of 1314/15 [*sic*] degrees?'[39] Restricted not merely by his bedding but also by the elaborate system dictating its configuration on the bed itself, the soldier patient was at the mercy of the nursing sister who failed to realize that 'a shake-up [of the bed]' caused great discomfort. Such efforts overlooked the fact that 'the poor beggar may have spent all the time since the previous shaking-up in getting them pushed into a comfortable position again'.[40] Enid Bagnold, a VAD nurse during the war, echoed this image in her diary, recalling that she saw a man 'lying high on five or six pillows, slung in his position by tapes and webbing passed under his arms and attached to the bedposts'.[41]

Soldiers' correspondence and individual contributions to nurses' scrapbooks and to articles published in the popular press reinforce a view of the hospital bed as a contested site between soldier patient and medical authority. The bedridden soldier John Middlebrook wrote to his parents of 'the nurses … forever tucking us in and tidying us up'.[42] In the military hospital, he suggested, the official goal of efficiency plainly clashed with his personal goal of being comfortable. A soldier-patient sketch entitled 'Patient's dream of Thornecombe' suggested similar feelings of frustration and hopelessness on the part of the author. Asleep and dreaming in bed, a hospitalized soldier sees signs everywhere around him, on the walls, floor and furniture, that read 'Out of bounds'. Under the sketch is the caption, 'Diagnosis: Thorncombeitis, Treatment – plenty of fresh air and long walks'. The author of this image, which appeared in a nurse's scrapbook, ridicules not only the strict regulation of the hospital bed but also hospital authorities' apparently irrational prescription of the 'fresh-air cure' to soldiers who must remain confined within the hospital (see Figure 5). While some patients associated this predicament with helplessness, others saw it in terms of boredom and even death. 'Here in this coffin of a bed,' wrote Wilfred Owen, 'I've thought/I'd like to kneel and sweep [the] floors for ever', like the orderly.[43] Similarly, as one soldier explained in a poem published in the *Socialist*:

Dost thou know the fate of soldiers?
They're but ambitions' tools, to cut a way
To her unlawful ends; and when they're worn,
Hack'd, hewn with constant service, thrown aside
To rust in peace and rot in hospitals.[44]

The soldier patient's sense of physical constriction, which could be understood as little different from the experience of any bedridden civilian, reinforced his perception of the passage of time. For Maurice Gower, time passed quickly while in bed 'due to the uneventful regularity, or more often than likely [*sic*] to the fact that one can go off into a doze when one pleases'.[45] G. Norman Adams found himself in the same circumstance while receiving treatment for his injuries at the Second Western General Hospital, Manchester. 'The days go fairly quickly here,' he wrote home, 'there is something going on all the time, hardly time to keep one's correspondence up to date, if it isn't dressing it's washing and if it is not washing it's meals. The morning is gone before you know your [*sic*] awake …'[46]

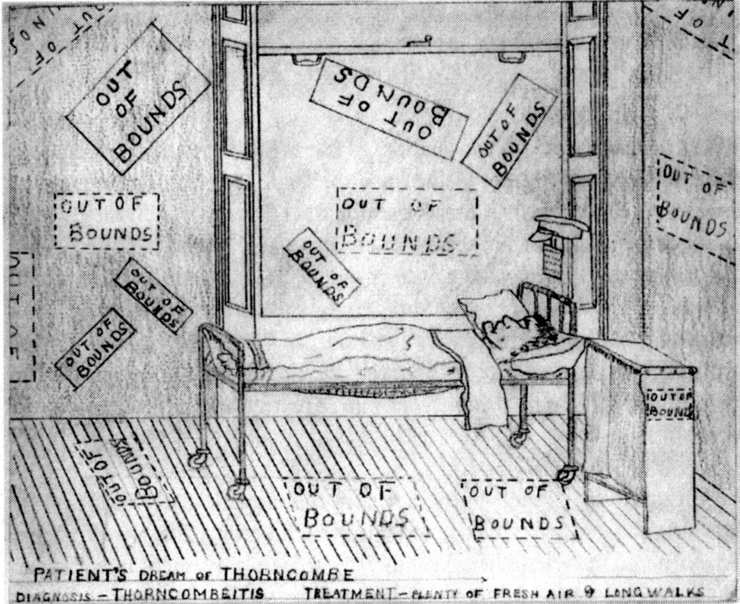

Figure 5 Soldier patient sketch contained in a nurse's scrapbook from Thornecombe Military Hospital, *c.* 1914–18

For other men, however, being bedridden caused 'nothing but sighs'[47] and a sense of the suspension of time. A hospital magazine poem entitled 'The base hospital' described such experiences of one soldier who has a heightened sense of his immediate surroundings. 'The dim half-light of dawn' and the 'alluring warmth' of the bed itself, which 'lately lulled my every sense/And soothed me to a poppied dream'.[48] He 'listens to the wand'rings of his mate's delirium; the frogs; the million strange sounds that make a day; and waits and waits the setting of the sun'.[49] An unnamed subaltern in the story *Contemptible* had a similar experience in a field hospital while he received treatment for head, spine and extremity wounds.

> Somehow, when he awoke from his horrible dreams it was always dark. And the remarkable thing was that the same nightmares seemed to haunt him with persistent regularity. Always he lay down upon a hillside – nebulous, black and furry. Always too, he had been left 'left' and the enemy was swooping quickly down upon him. He would wake up to find himself once more inert upon the bed, would curse himself for a fool and vow that never again would he allow his mind to drift towards that terrible thought again

> … When he awoke from his fever, he would always make frantic efforts to hang on to consciousness. To this end he would always call the Orderly, ask the time, demand water or Bovril – anything to keep him a little longer in touch with the world.[50]

Being bedridden therefore heightened the soldier patient's awareness of the physical environment of the hospital itself. As an untitled poem by a soldier patient suggested, many spent a great deal of time in the hospital observing the 'clean wide room', where there are 'quilted beds arow/each tidy locker, gay with nodding flow'rs' and 'white-capped sisters, hast'ning to and fro/Thro' all the silent hours'. Here, too, were 'weary white-gowned surgeons, skilfully/With probe and forcep, search[ing] each gaping wound'.[51] In the sterile atmosphere of the ward, this soldier felt the 'the morning's cold air' through which 'drearily/The stifled groanings sound'.[52]

Historians have argued that for many men, particularly those of the working classes, 'army life offered a more wholesome diet than they had encountered in civilian life'.[53] While true, this improvement is not apparent in the food-related content of hospital magazines. Echoing traditional working-class responses to institutional food, these expressions convey a view among men that their hospital diet, like their beds and their wards, did not make the hospital the hero's haven that authorities intended it to be.

The kinds of meals provided to men recovering in military hospitals varied widely and generally depended on three factors: individual health, supplies and rationing. Convalescent patients consumed 'ordinary' meals consisting of different combinations of the classic institutional diet, including mushy foods like puddings, soups and cooked vegetables. When available small servings of fish, eggs or bacon and large amounts of bread complemented these dishes. Authorities could also offer small amounts of pickled or tinned beef, called 'bully beef', like that provided to soldiers on the front lines. They restricted newly admitted patients to the 'milk diet', which was part of the classic 'rest cure' that hospital authorities regularly prescribed for recovering soldiers.[54]

Soldier patients associated dependence and degradation with nearly everything they ate, but above all with mushy foods, which they saw as inappropriate for men who had served King and Country. As one soldier observed wryly in a prose commentary on hospital food: 'Unless you are on a starvation diet, your food, consisting mainly of fish, soup and eggs, is fit for the gods – the gods being ethereal creatures and not standing much in the need of solid sustenance.'[55] Soldiers also saw such food as insubstantial owing to lack of flavour, quality, quantity and consistency. 'P is the Pudding to use up stale bread/Q is the Quantity at which we revile,' declared one patient in a hospital magazine ABC rhyme.[56] Dinner, which was, according to one soldier patient, 'oh my, quite the event of the day', would likely have included a 'small heap of beans that curdle your blood'.[57] And when it included chicken, soldier patients called this meal 'names of such manner/That wouldn't look nice on a Sunday School banner'. The author of another poem, entitled ''Ungry 'Enry', saw the Tommy ''Enry' choosing not to eat the meat on his plate but rather to 'see it off'. After the meal, ''Enry' is still hungry and asks for 'more grub' until he is 'heartily tired'. In the end, his effort is futile and he declares: 'Roll on the day when our punishment expires.' The author of ''Ungry 'Enry' continued his criticism of the hospital dinners, pointing out that they included 'cocoa … , quite essential and light,/But I can't see how cocoa's going to win a fight'.[58]

The poem 'A skit on Cambridge Hospital' also revealed a close association between deprivation and diets of both red and white meats. At the First Eastern, the author claimed, the 'dinners are served out in classes three – /One chicken, two fish and three ordinary'. The chicken, the author declares, is 'Oh, my, but … really … foul,/And the ordinary, well, we hear many a growl'. And the fish, he adds, 'it is fish, without any doubt', but it is 'very fishy indeed' and 'when sometimes … we find sticking wishbones,/That is really enough to produce many groans'. Every day during dinner, this patient explained further, the hospital's food inspector 'comes around/To see if complaints with the dinners is [*sic*] found'. The disenchantment felt while eating the meal was reinforced as patients greeted the man with 'Hi, guv'nor, this sparrow has only one leg', only to receive the response: 'Oh, poor little thing.'[59]

As mentioned, military hospitals occasionally included red meat in the soldier-patient diet to help improve morale. This was particularly the case in some hospitals on Saturdays, following meatless Fridays. But this policy likely produced little change in soldiers' responses to hospital food. They saw 'bully beef' and its cheaper white-meat substitutes merely as representative of the austere and repressive wartime food economy.[60] As one patient put it, 'F for the fish that you have with light diet;/It won't buck you up, but it do keep you quiet.'[61] A veteran recalled biscuits and bully beef 'were to appease the appetites of those who found the provided meal insufficient'.[62] Soldiers' songs of the day underscored these views. The arrival of stew at the table prompted the chant:

Oh, hell! What bloody big lumps of beef!
Bloody big lumps, bloody big lumps,
Blo-o-o-dy big lumps!

or sometimes its variant:

Over the swedes and mangolds
Bloody big lumps of duff.
Pick up the duff! Pick up the duff![63]

Convalescent patients' views of their milk diet mirrored such negative perceptions of stew and other solid food. Throughout the war in many hospitals these patients became 'ferocious with hunger' and often resorted to stealing food from patients who had more substantial diets.[64]

Restless with throbbing hopes, with thwarted aims,
Impulsive as a colt,
How do you lie here month by weary month
Helpless and not revolt?
What joy can these monotonous days afford
Here in a ward?[65]

The soldier patient saw his surrounding ward environment, like his bed, as a site of substantial discipline where nurses and doctors upheld a range of rules and regulations to ensure institutional efficiency, economy and social order. But, as the chief communal environment of the hospital, the ward was also an arena in which the individual soldier patient became a member of a larger community. It housed a group of men whose common endurance of institutional discipline and routines reinforced their shared front-line experiences.

A sense of solidarity among soldier patients is particularly evident in hospital magazine poems, prose and illustrations that address specific illnesses, injuries and treatments. 'Back from the land of the almighty franc', wrote one soldier, identifying his own predicament as well as that of his comrades. 'Through drinking foul water and other things dank,/ We've got typhoid with an extra Para. B.' Common suffering is the result of the illness, he suggests.[66] Similarly, two sing-along 'nursery rhymes' reveal medical crises being endured by a community of sufferers. Together, soldier patients:

Sing a song of sickness,
Jaundice in the eye,
Four and twenty gallstones,
Chloledocotomy.

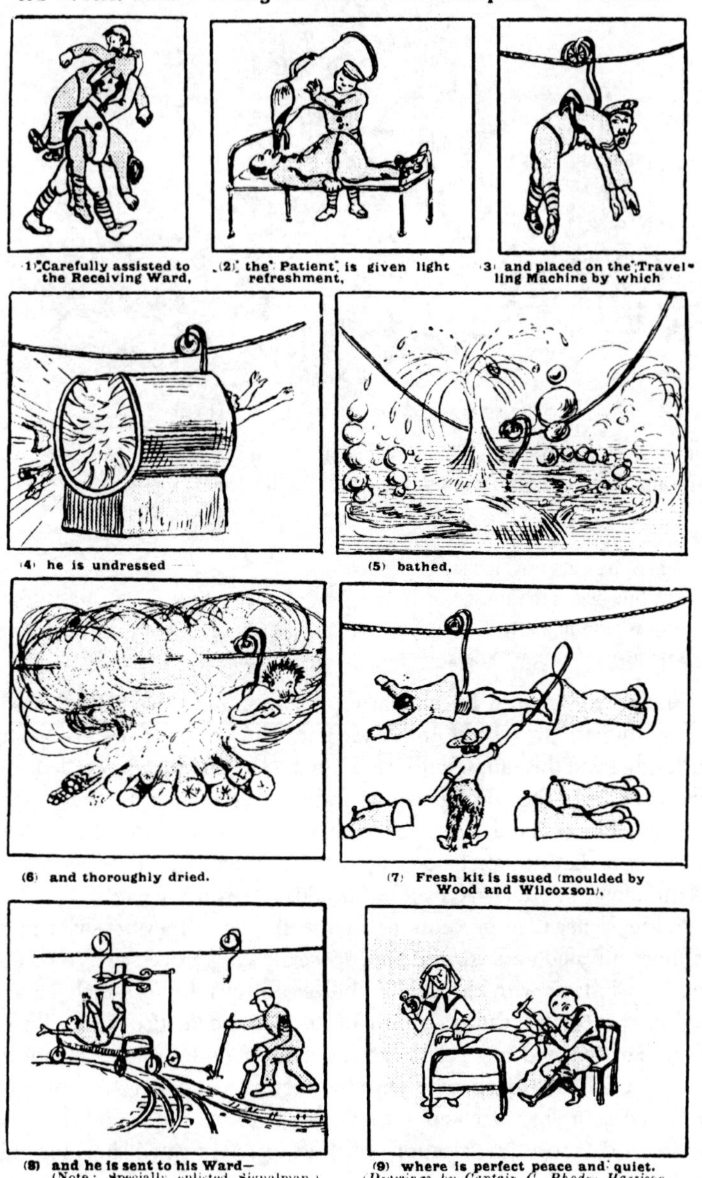

Figure 6 C. Rhodes Harrison, '3rd L.G.H. Labour-saving Devices for the Reception of Wounded', *Gazette of the Third London General Hospital* (February 1916): 131

"THE TANK" GIANT VACUUM CLEANER.

Figure 7 D. Newhouse, '"The Tank" Giant Vacuum Cleaner', *Magazine of the Fourth London General Hospital* (December 1916): 159

When the duct was opened
The bile began to flow,
And when the deuce it's going to stop
The surgeon doesn't know.[67]

The poem 'Spanish flu' similarly conveys a bond that united hospitalized soldiers during the influenza pandemic of 1918–19. Associating suffering from this illness with traditional sport, the author recalled when the flu came to Monyhull Hospital and infected many staff and patients. The flu, he observed, was 'played' like a 'game', endured through the realization that 'it won't be long' until everyone would be well again. Eventually it was defeated by all who said, 'We won't give in.'[68]

Soldiers' negative perceptions of the therapies they received in the military hospital underscored their sense of being processed by a medical machine in tune with a society mobilized for war. In his sketch 'Labour-saving devices for the reception of the wounded' Private C. Rhodes Harrison depicted an orderly at the Third London General Hospital issuing a 'fresh kit' as a newly arrived soldier patient dangles by pulley and rope along a line stretching from the bathing rooms to the ward. Suspended above a selection of stiff, prefabricated hospital blue uniforms, the orderly fits the patient with a rod and wire. This image suggests authorities' efforts to maximize hygienic conditions as well as their desire to establish and maintain a regimented and efficient healing environment (see Figure 6). Another sketch, entitled '"The Tank" giant vacuum cleaner', similarly conveys the idea of the recovering soldier as a cog in a medical machine which processes human wreckage of war. This image also suggests that soldier patients saw the hospital itself and the routine therein as a continuation of the experience of being rotated from trench to trench and accounted for as 'wastage' (see Figure 7).

Soldier patients held similar views when they were 'dosed up' with the frequently prescribed 'No. 9' laxative remedy.[69] As one man wrote in verse:

> If you've blisters on your feet,
> Or you're feeling, well, dead beat,
> Or contracting prickly heat –
> Cerebro-spinal meningitis, measles, mumps, mulekick, delirium tremens, dyspepsia, toothache, heart disease, flatfoot, brain fever, housemaid's knee, appendicitis, pinkeye, phthisis, enteric and so forth,
> There's a remedy your case to meet,
> And it's safe to bet you get a Number Nine.[70]

Because authorities prescribed the 'No. 9' for such a wide range of ailments and injuries, patients called it the 'The Elixir of Life', suggesting that it was a quack cure left over from the previous century.[71]

Soldier patients also ridiculed the widely prescribed 'fresh-air cure', which they saw as involving impersonal and highly regimented treatments. The sketch entitled 'Sun moustache culture' depicts a group of patients on 'off-duty hours at the Fourth London General Hospital', basking in the sun as it streams through the windows of their ward. The subtitle explains that 'they all want their place in the sun', while a sign in the ward reveals that this is merely because 'command orders' require that 'full moustaches or none will be worn.' While mocking the clearly unreasonable rules, this image suggests that the sunshine rest cure is an over-prescribed treatment. In addition to healing a variety of illnesses and injuries, it can supposedly even help to grow moustaches (see Figure 8).

Similarly, a cartoon entitled 'The rest cure' suggests that rest had little to do with the treatment. The title of the cartoon blares from a wardroom gramophone, the image suggesting that the rest cure is synonymous with a variety of chaotic events. As patients sing popular songs of the day, 'When you come home, dear', 'At the close of a perfect day' and 'Where my caravan is resting,' they do not find peace and quiet, but rather a ward orderly dropping a tray full of hospital instruments and another upsetting a bedridden patient by his sweeping. An officer screams 'Stand to!' and an unidentified individual yells 'Shut that d— door!'. The cartoon

"SUN MOUSTACHE CULTURE."

They all want their place in the sun.

By PRIVATE D. NEWHOUSE.

Command orders—"Full moustaches or none will be worn." Off duty hours at the 4th L.G.H.

Figure 8 D. Newhouse, '"Sun Moustache Culture": They All Want Their Place in the Sun', *Magazine of the Fourth London General Hospital* (November 1917): 146

suggests that these activities, in addition to nurses rushing through wards and patients hunting flies with flyswatters, are what the rest cure really involves (see Figure 9).

A sketch entitled 'Fresh air and exercise by "wireless"' similarly emphasizes the soldier patient's view of the rest cure as impersonal and mechanistic. It depicts a 'suggested apparatus' by which hospital authorities administer essential therapies 'in one-thousandth of a second'. The caption explains that 'the opening of the inlet for fresh air will synchronise with the opening of the main and subsidiary values and the oscillation of the pump man. The man in charge of each operation will take his time from the little finger of the MO [Medical Officer]'. The author of this sketch therefore suggested that in the military hospital authorities administered the rest cure not with any personal touch but rather by subjection to a large, leaky machine. One by one, after waiting in a long line, patients are given ridiculously small doses from a 'fresh-air intake'. The whole procedure is meant to be quick and easy, the caption explains,

THE REST CURE.

Figure 9 A.F.W.G., 'The Rest Cure', *Searchlight: Monthly Publication of the Royal Army Medical Corps* (November 1916): 8

involving 'no red tape'. Ridiculing the application of factory-like efficiency systems to the hospital, the author of this sketch concluded that this 'apparatus has already proved its worth in General Hospitals as a Fire Extinguisher'[72] (see Figure 10).

Soldier patients saw other medical treatments in the same light. For example, although the standard bandage was meant to comfort and heal, men disliked it for the way it constrained their movements. As one soldier observed, 'B is the Bandage that Binds you, of course.'[73] Another Tommy abhorred the way in which nurses fitted bandages, arguing that they 'should first realise that there is a right and a wrong way of doing things. Experimenting [with bandages] must be rigorously eschewed. No matter [if] a University training course in aesthetics condemns a bandage as 'inartistic', [a] patient ought not to be joggled about [during the application of the bandage] until the effect is pleasing to the eye'.[74] While some soldier patients saw the bandage as promoting a sense of helplessness and confinement, others, particularly those who were blinded, saw it as representing death and loss. As Wilfred Owen suggested, 'This bandage feels like pennies on my eyes.'[75] Soldier patients who underwent hydro- and physical therapies for bone and muscle injuries experienced a comparable sense of physical restriction and helplessness. 'Water cure for wounded soldiers' depicts a bath-ridden soldier pleading, 'Please, doctor, may I come out? I've been in the bath twenty-one days already.' His plea is met only by a sign on the wall indicating that 'No one to leave bath without doctor's orders'.[76]

Figure 10 A.W. Mawer, 'Fresh Air and Exercise by "Wireless"', *Searchlight: Monthly Publication of the Royal Army Medical Corps* (August 1917): 6–7

Although not drawn by soldier patients, a series of contemporary postcards by the popular artist A.G. Bliss underscores the negative view of physical therapy held by hospitalized men. Chronicling the work of the Almeric Paget Massage Corps (APMC), the series includes a final card, entitled 'It never rains but it pours!' which depicts a patient confined to his bed by a Schnee bath treatment. His right leg and his right arm receive electrical therapy. His left leg is submerged in water for hydrotherapy and his left arm is tied to the bedpost to keep it from interfering in the treatment. A contemporary photograph of this treatment suggests the reality of the Bliss image (see Figures 11 and 12).

These criticisms of military hospital life challenge the official vision of the hospital as an environment of peace and balance and its inmates as idle patients. Moreover, they reveal disillusionment with the tyranny of modern technology and with the efficiency systems with which the wartime healing environment was connected. Hospital magazines therefore demonstrate how in the eyes of the recovering soldier the environment of the military hospital worked in conjunction with the trenches not only to discipline body and mind but also to underscore comradeship among men.

Recreation in the form of musical activities formed one cornerstone of the standard wartime convalescent regime. For authorities concerned about efficiency and economy, provision of these activities was easy and inexpensive since they fitted in with the YMCA's ongoing efforts to provide hospitalized and convalescent soldiers with musical instruments and entertainments. Association leaders initiated their programme in 1916 to help create a 'region of joy and brightness' in the lives of soldiers. They considered this aid so essential that their official publicity campaigns once featured a modified version of the sacred YMCA logo, the red triangle, to show the dedication of the Association to providing music to men at home and overseas.[77]

Musical programmes gradually became popular among authorities. Within a few months after the establishment of the convalescent depot at Trouville, physical education parades, under the direction of the divisional commander, began with marches to the beach 'headed by some tin whistles, which constituted a Band'.[78] While some officers initially criticized this arrangement for being somewhat chaotic, they nonetheless 'organized' and 'gradually developed' such work until the '[whole] well conducted' affair involved '120 Bandsmen, Full Brass Band, Pipe Band, Drum & Fife'. Subsequent months saw the band trained to play music that regulated the

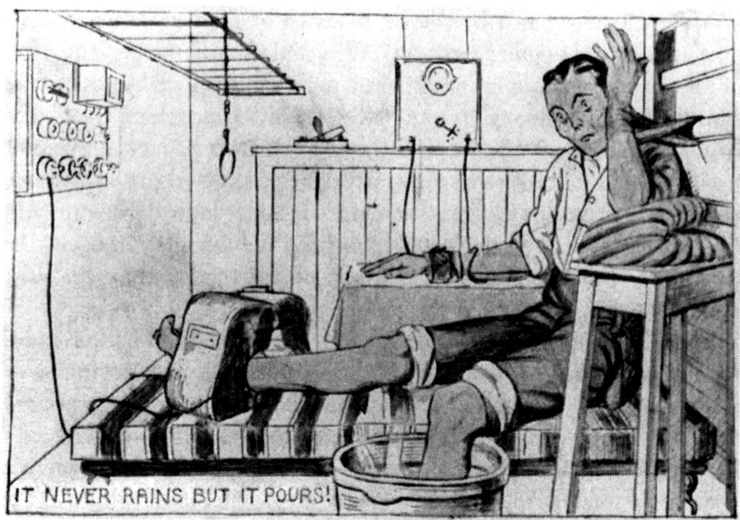
IT NEVER RAINS BUT IT POURS!

Figure 11 'It Never Rains But It Pours!' Bliss postcard, *c.* 1916

pace of exercise as needed. By winter 1917 the YMCA brass band had started to accompany marches on a regular basis, the depot commander observing 'considerable improvement in march discipline' as a result.[79] The YMCA itself recognized the value of this music, one volunteer noting that commanding officers nearly always encouraged 'singing, humming or whistling' to 'keep up [their] spirits and to lessen the fatigue resulting from a long march'.[80] Such observations and practices connected with music and convalescence likely pleased HM Inspector of Music of the Board of Education, Dr Arthur Somervell, who remarked during the war years that 'nothing trained men to work together better than the sound created by music and rhythm'.[81]

Indoor and outdoor concerts were also a key feature and a popular component of the convalescent programme at Trouville and its counterpart sites. As Trouville's commanding officer observed, these activities went far to help maintain discipline among the men, keeping them 'out of the town and getting into mischief'.[82] Concert audiences, the CO also recalled, were 'magnificent, especially in winter, [when] some 3,000 odd men packed in the Dining Hall heaving with merriment, joining in the choruses being a great revelation'. He continued, again suggesting the value of these events in terms of discipline as well as morale, 'They were quite the most critical and best behaved audiences I have ever seen. There

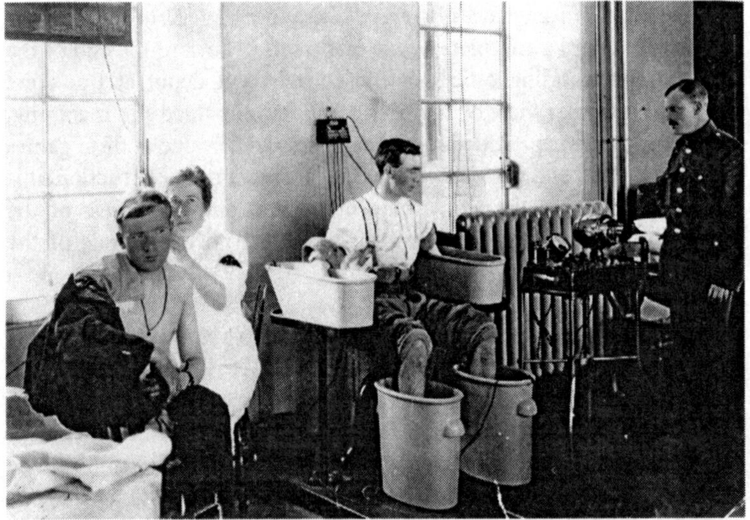

Figure 12 Photograph of a Schnee bath for poor circulation, *c.* 1914–18

was no doubt about their appreciation.'[83] Concerts also served effectively to connect men with their familiar lives at home. As Lieutenant-Colonel Brown explained, 'As a rule such a company of artists exerted a tremendous influence upon its audiences and, as regards the convalescent patient, served to take his mind altogether off the war and to bring him in touch with softer influences and memories of his home life in England or other country whence he came.'[84]

This range of musical activities was unique neither to Trouville nor to one period of the war. From 1915, authorities at the convalescent depot in Wimereux gave convalescent soldiers permission to 'organize and carry out' a variety of 'social amusements', including musical concerts. The commanding officer at Wimeraux observed that his men 'derived much pleasure … from the various concerts which are provided. The men are brighter in spirit for them and I look upon them as being of distinct assistance towards … ultimate fitness.'[85] Subsequently he observed that these activities demonstrated 'a distinct tendency towards assisting the early convalescence of the men and the nature of the functions make for a brighter and healthier disposition becoming apparent among the men'.[86] Down to 1916, the authorities at Wimereux were still doing 'everything possible for the comfort and entertainment on the Convalescents'.[87] The advantages to sponsoring these activities were plainly evident to the commanding officer, who observed: 'Everything very successful. It is pleasing to record a complete absence of crime.'[88] Toward the end of the war, the commanding officer of the convalescent depot at Boulogne expressed a similar view of the music that accompanied the marching, games and dancing provided to his men. 'Beside the value of these games in giving mental and physical exercise to the men under instruction, it is quite apparent that the wholesome merriment and brightness of the music and rhythm will have a very good effect on the morale of the camp.'

In July 1915 the popular actress, singer and YMCA volunteer Lena Ashwell offered an intriguing description of YMCA-sponsored musical concerts and their effect on British soldiers in convalescent facilities overseas. '[T]he Tommies out in France look upon [these events] as "a gift from home" that [is,] "Better than Physic",' Ashwell wrote in the *Newcastle Illustrated Chronicle.* As for the value of entertainers themselves, she added, 'the doctors tell us that we do more than physic in putting heart into war-torn convalescents'.[89] Hospital magazines reveal a very different view of music on the part of soldiers, challenging Ashwell's perception, that of authorities and even that of some historians who have noted the widespread appreciation of music among soldiers and munitions workers.[90] Like medical treatments and institutional diet, music became a substantial target of soldier-patient criticism. Gramophone music 'upsets many men in our ward', wrote one Tommy,

> and I'm never alone
> When it's playing, in saying, 'Oh Gawd.'
> For it starts the first thing in the morning,
> And it plays with few rests in between,
> But I'm forced to refrain,
> It's just starting again,
> Hence I'll sign, Yours, in pain.[91]

Patients also found annoying the competition between gramophone music and piano playing.[92] And they expressed negative reactions toward ward concerts, whether these events were performed by the YMCA-directed Music in War-time Committee or by independent local musicians. Often men disliked these events for being obligatory for those who were not able to leave the ward owing to illness or injury. As Maurice Gower explained in a letter to his sister written from the VAD hospital at Kingsbury, Shortlands, Kent:

> We had a concert in this house on Saturday. I had to attend. The audience was made up of the men who could not get out and some WAACs [Women's Army Auxiliary Corps members] and nurses and relations. The programme for a thing of this sort was not too bad and I should say quite up to the standard of those inflicted on the men round Walthamstow. There were some really good instrumentalists who played classical music, which was not appreciated by the men who talked and played with the WAACs during the performance and applauded violently when it was finished. I hope next time to go for a walk when we are next given a similar treat ...[93]

Men also disliked such gatherings because they often involved performers who were, in the opinion of some soldier patients, not 'doing their bit' for King and Country. As an editorial in the *First Eastern General Hospital Gazette* revealed about one concert:

> It is much to be regretted that some of the patients were overheard to make remarks as to the advisability of the performers quitting their present jobs and joining his Majesty's Forces abroad. To show how wrong it is to express hasty opinions and what injustice may thereby be done to loyal persons, we may state on the authority of the Theatre manager, that of the performers at least six have already served their twenty-one years in his Majesty's Forces and all the others who are eligible have attested and are ready to join their groups when called up. We sincerely hope that the artistes who so kindly gave their services to help cheer up our sick and wounded will accept this apology for the unmannerly conduct of a few individuals, who are no doubt heartily ashamed for expressing themselves as they did.[94]

Such 'concert rowdyism' was widespread in military hospitals, especially during the last two years of the war as many men became increasingly frustrated with those who had 'shirked' duty.[95] Despite authorities' intention to use music to make the hospital comfortable, therefore, like food and medical treatment it became a target of the soldier's 'ready wit', viewed at least as an activity that assaulted his senses and too often indirectly insulted his service to King and Country.

Beyond music, soldier patient interactions with upper-class women who visited the hospital also promoted feelings of assault and insult. Hospital magazines portray these women as purveyors of more irritation than consolation, as persons who tended to gawk at the bedridden soldier. The author of 'People Who Ought To Be "Strafed"' suggested reprimands for women who displayed inability or, worse, unwillingness to see the effects of war on the male body and mind[96] (see Figure 13). Other men suggested the same punishment for women who visited limbless soldiers

Figure 13 B. Howells, 'People Who Ought To Be "Strafed"', *Southern Cross: Magazine of the First Southern General Hospital* (August 1916): 188

and asked thoughtless questions. In one hospital magazine sketch a young girl asks a soldier who has lost his leg, 'What will you do when you leave hospital, my poor fellow?' The man responds, 'Oh! I've got a splendid job – in a brewery – making 'ops and my friend here, he's goin' in for short'and!'[97] A similar illustration depicts a young woman asking a legless convalescent, 'Poor fellow! and have you lost your leg?' He responds, 'Oh, no, ma'am. Being wartime, I thought I'd economise and go without it for a bit.'[98] 'Wit from the wards' depicts a bedridden soldier exasperated after witnessing 'a thousand visitors pass[ing] within an hour'. Dismayed with being the object of the public gaze, the soldier proclaims: 'I was in the Expeditionary Force; I seem now to be in the Exhibitionary.'[99] Similarly, in another sketch that depicts an exchange between a middle-aged woman and a bedridden soldier patient, the visitor asks: 'Don't you find it slow and wearisome lying here all day?' Casually puffing on his cigarette, the patient responds, 'Oh no, for we don't have visitors every day.'[100]

Recollections of 'visiting day' in a military hospital by Ward Muir and by two VAD nurses in their respective VAD hospitals confirm these views. For Muir too many visitors were 'comfortable folk' who, even after they have 'drifted in and out of war-hospitals a score of times … have no remotest inkling of the inwardness of what they behold: their eyes are blind …'[101] In a comparable scathing criticism the VAD Enid Bagnold observed that 'It takes all sorts to make a hospital. For instance, the Visitors', among whom:

> There is the lady who comes in to tea and wants to be introduced to everyone as though it was a school treat. She jokes about the cake, its scarcity or its quantity and makes a lot of 'fun' about two lumps of sugar. When she is at her best the table assumes a perfect and listening silence – not the silence of the critic, but the silence of the absorbed child treasuring every item of talk for future use. After she goes the joy of her will last them all the evening.[102]

Bagnold recalls 'another who cried out with emotion when she saw the first officer limp into Mess'. 'And can some of them *walk*, then!' Perhaps she thought they came in to tea on stretchers, with field bandages on. She quivered all over, too, as she looked from one to the other, and I feel sure she went home and broke down, crying, 'What an experience … the actual wounds!'[103] On one occasion in the hospital where E. Chivers Davies worked 'a bevy of gaily dressed damsels entered and spread themselves about the ward, choosing for preference the young and attractive patients'. In one corner 'a lady in an unnecessarily severe bonnet had pinned the unfortunate Fowler to a discussion on the war; … the V.A.D. had to come to the rescue – Fowler's eyes were rolling pathetically in her direction …'[104]

'Of the brutality' in the military hospital 'there can be no doubt', argues Denis Winter in his landmark study of the British soldier's life at war.[105] Hospital magazines confirm this view and demonstrate the implications of this brutality for the *esprit de corps* of sick and wounded men. Like trench journals, which reflect soldiers' anger at the extent of civilian incomprehension and complacency, hospital magazines reflect a continuation of this anger in home-front environments of healing that became stages for display of the hero of war. The uniform of this hero, as we shall see in the next chapter, facilitated such display in remarkable ways, further reinforcing *esprit de corps* and complicating masculine identity.

Notes

1 F.P. Crozier, *A Brass Hat in No Man's Land* (London: Jonathan Cape, 1930), 43–44.

2 Captain J.G.W. Haynes, untitled poem dated 6 August 1917 in sketchbook of nurse Mrs Dorothy McCann, Eighteenth General Hospital, Leeds University Library, Liddle Collection, Papers of Mrs Dorothy McCann.

3 Fussell, *The Great War and Modern Memory*, among many other works.

4 Stephane Audoin-Rouzeau, *Men at War: National Sentiment and Trench Journalism in France during the First World War*, trans. Helen McPhail (Oxford: Berg, 1992).

5 Fuller, *Troop Morale*, 13.

6 On wartime propaganda especially see Messinger, *Propaganda and the State*, Waites, 'The government of the home front' and Winter, 'Propaganda and the mobilization of consent'.

7 Fuller, *Troop Morale*, 10–11.

8 The conclusions that follow are drawn from the author's examination of hospital magazines held by over a dozen London and provincial archives.

9 'Editorial', *First Eastern General Hospital Gazette* (October 1915): 1, which noted that the *Daily Chronicle* had incorrectly stated in an early October 1915 issue that the Third London General Hospital was first to start a gazette. 'We immediately sent the editor a copy of our 13th issue, with a [request] that the matter might be corrected, as the honour of being the pioneer in starting a Hospital gazette certainly belongs to the First Eastern.'

10 Fuller, *Troop Morale*, 10–11.

11 The staff of the *Magazine of the Third Western General Hospital, Cardiff*, for example, printed their work at the local Educational Publishing Co. in Penarth Road. See *Magazine of the Third Western General Hospital* (March 1917): 1. The staff of the *Harefield Park Boomerang*, the official magazine of Harefield Park Hospital for Australian soldiers, printed their work 'with the help of a London firm in White Friars Street' (Mary P. Shephard, *Heart of Harefield: The Story of the Hospital* (London: Quiller Press, 1990), 30).

12 'Editorial', *Gazette of the Third London General Hospital* (31 December 1917): 1. *Huddersfield War Hospital Magazine* was also sold in local bookshops. See *Huddersfield War Hospital Magazine* (1 July 1916): 2.

13 'Editorial', *Gazette of the Third London General Hospital* (13 April 1915): 1. See also *Tommy in Hospital: An Exhibition of Original Black and White Drawings by Patients and Staff of the Third London General Hospital, Wandsworth* (London: Country Life, 1917), which notes that the hospital's gazette could be 'obtained in single copies for 5*d*.' or 'in return for a postal order for half a crown', n.p.

14 See, for example, 'Editorial', *Gazette of the Third London General Hospital* (13 April 1915): 1, which offers a review of the content of the *Gazette of the First Eastern*.

15 The *Magazine of the Fourth London General Hospital*, for example, kept track of its 'continental' circulation. See *Magazine* (September 1916): 99. Both the *Huddersfield War Hospital Magazine* and the *Magazine of the Second Southern General Hospital* kept track of their sales at local bookshops, though their editors did not report statistics in the magazines themselves.

16 Paper imports dropped dramatically as the war dragged on. The government calculated these imports at 1.8 million tons in 1913 and, subsequently, at 0.5 million tons in 1918. See Charles Ernest Fayle, 'Seaborne trade' in Mancur Olson, Jr (ed.), *The Economics of the Wartime Shortage: A History of British Food Supplies in the Napoleonic War and in World Wars I and II* (Durham NC: Duke University Press, 1963), 94.

17 See, for example, 'Editorial', *First Eastern General Hospital Gazette* (6 June 1916): 76, which points out that although 'the enormous increase in the price of paper, and all other materials used in the printing trade [made] it ... impossible to continue to make use of the familiar and popular khaki cover with the Red Cross centre', the magazine continued production with a 'blue cover and no Red Cross'. The first issue of the *Gazette of the Third London General Hospital*, published in the fall of 1915, cost 3*d*. It remained that price for eighteen months, until April 1917, when it was raised to 4*d*. In less than a year the cost rose to 6*d* and remained this price until the magazine's final issue of July 1918, which cost 1*s*. Circumstances were somewhat different in Scotland, however, where paper shortages and rationing seem to have had a more direct effect on the production of hospital magazines. At the Western General Hospital in Craigleith, where the *Craigleith Hospital Chronicle* was published, such conditions caused publication to change from monthly to quarterly, which reduced paper use by two-thirds. See Martin Eastwood and Anne Jenkinson, *A History of the Western General Hospital: Craigleith Poorhouse, Military Hospital, Modern Teaching Hospital* (Edinburgh: John Donald, 1995), 49.

18 See 'Editorial', *First Eastern General Hospital Gazette* (11 May 1915): 57, in which the editor apologizes to his readers for 'any lowering of the high standard of literary merit hitherto preserved in our columns' due to a higher rate of admissions to the hospital, which has brought greater 'calls upon the time of the staff'.

19 Editors of the *Wire*, the official magazine of the 2/3rd East Lancashire Field Ambulance, justified their production on similar grounds: 'A good deal of activity was manifested at Lexden in the production of the *Wire*, a magazine of no particular merit, but a means of furthering any grumbles and literary desires lying dormant in the Field Ambulance. We did make an attempt to keep the pages of the journal light and interesting, and at least we can say that whilst the pages of the magazine of a sister Field Ambulance were used to reprint lectures on scabies and such like horrible topics, we steered clear of such dreadful things ...'. Sergeant Alfred E.F. Francis, *History of the 2/3rd East Lancashire Field Ambulance: The Story of a 3rd Line Territorial Unit* (Salford: W.F. Jackson and Sons, 1930), 37–38.

20 'Editorial notes', *Gazette of the Third London General Hospital* (12 September 1916): 302. See also 'Editorial', *Magazine of the Second Southern General Hospital, Bristol* (April 1916): 1–2.

21 See Medical and Nursing Authorities, *Cassell's Science and Art of Nursing: A Guide to the Various Branches of Nursing, Theoretical and Practical* (4 volumes, London: Waverley Book Co., n.d.), especially 'Mental nursing', IV, 42–43.

22 See Henry C. Burdett, *Hospitals and Asylums of the World* (London: J. and A, Churchill, 1891), which describes 'employment' and 'amusement' as essential features of English asylum life. For evidence of similar 'occupational therapy' in wartime civilian mental hospitals see 'Newspaper reading in mental hospitals', *Hospital* (30 September 1916): 598, and the description of work of the Guild of Help (Birmingham branch), 'Brabazon work party at the Birmingham City Mental Hospital' in 'The After-care Association for Poor Persons Convalescent or Recovering from Institutions for the Insane, Report of the Council, 1916', WLHUM, SA/MAC B1/29.

23 'Editorial', *Magazine of the Third Western General Hospital* (February 1917): 5. This was especially the view of the authorities of Leicester War Hospital, who by 1916 had sanctioned public contributions to their wards of 'ten new gramophones and 264 new double records', in addition to 'another 500 double records for renewals and replacements. Three years later the hospital had received a total of sixty-six gramophones, 5,076 records and 350,000 gramophone needles for use in the wards. 'Second annual report of the Leicester War Hospital (previously Leicester War Hospital Games Committee), a public organisation run through donations from the people of Leicester and purchases made from donations', 30 September 1916; and 'Fifth Annual Report', 30 September 1919, both TD (14D35), Leicester Record Office. For evidence of similar views held by hospital officials behind the lines on the western front see the official war diaries for Convalescent Depots Nos 1, 2, and 3, PRO, WO 95/411. A brief but excellent history of the Fifth Northern General Military Hospital, Leicester, is J.R. Hopkins, 'Leicester's Great War Hospital: The Fifth Northern General Military Hospital, Leicester, 1914–1919', M.A. thesis, University of Leicester, 1995.

24 *First Eastern General Hospital Gazette* (31 August 1915): 208.

25 'Editor's note', *Bath Bun: The Book of the Bath War Hospital* (November 1917): 1.

26 Ibid., 1.

27 Ibid., 1.

28 'Editorial', *Huddersfield War Hospital Magazine* (July 1916): 2.

29 Ibid., 2. At Craigleith Hospital sales of the *Craigleith Hospital Chronicle* raised over £350 for the hospital's library fund, for its tobacco fund, and for extension of the billiard room in its associated Red Cross hut. See also Martin Eastwood and Anne Jenkinson, *A History of the Western General Hospital*, 50.

30 'Editorial', *First Eastern General Hospital Gazette* (13 April 1915): 1.

31 'Every hospital's own gazette: A great success at military hospitals', *Hospital* (18 December 1915): 257–260, at 257.

32 See 'Editorial', *First Eastern General Hospital Gazette* (27 April 1915): 17, and 'The lighter side of the war hospital', *Hospital* (27 May 1916): 186.
33 'Editoral notes: Freedom and discipline', *Gazette of the Third London General Hospital* (October 1915): 3–4.
34 Ibid., 3–4.
35 Editorial, *Rattler: Magazine of the Third Southern General Hospital, Somerville Hospital, Oxford* (November 1917): 1–2
36 IWM, DOD, Papers of Frederick Davison, 3/15/1, September 1917–January 1918.
37 'Ammonite', 'Beds and bed making', *Southern Cross: Magazine of the First Southern General Hospital* (December 1917): 286–287. For another contemporary description of hospital beds, which emphasizes their 'narrowness', see untitled article in *Courage in a Military Hospital: A Book of the Thorncomb [Red Cross Auxiliary] Military Hospital* (n.p., n.d.). British Red Cross Archives and Library, 346/1.
38 'Ammonite', 'Beds and bed making', 286–287. For a similar account of the sense of entrapment in bed see selections of Enid Bagnold's published diary in ibid. 'No. 22 was lying flat on his back, his knees drawn up under him, the sheets up to his chin; his flat chalk-white face tilted at the ceiling …', 171. For a similar account of a nurse's admonishing see Sergeant H.W. Fullerton, 44th Canadians, 'Unedited verses: Life in hospital', *Bath Bun: The Book of The Bath War Hospital*, November 1917): 124.
39 Ibid., 286–287.
40 'Hints on the treatment of invalids (by an experienced patient)', *Craigleith Hospital Chronicle* (July 1915): 78
41 Enid Bagnold, selection from *A Diary without Dates* (London: William Heinemann, 1918) in Jon Glover and Jon Silkin (eds), *The Penguin Book of First World War Prose* (New York: Penguin Books, 1990), 170.
42 IWM, DOD, Papers of John B. Middlebrook, 7822 Con Shelf, Middlebrook to his parents, 25 March 1916.
43 Wilfred Owen, 'Wild with all regret' in Jon Silkin (ed.), *The Penguin Book of First World War Poetry* (New York: Penguin Books, 1981), 193–194.
44 Southerne, 'To members of the working class who have enlisted as soldiers', *Socialist* (July 1916), p. 61.
45 IWM, DOD, Papers of Maurice F. Gower, 255 88/25/2, Gower to his sister, 4 August 1918.
46 IWM, DOD, Papers of Captain G. Norman Adams, 85/4/1, Adams to Elsie, 28 July 1916.
47 C.F. Steane, 'Rambling reflections', *First Eastern General Hospital Gazette* (16 January 1917): 329. See also the untitled poem by RSM Wood, 2/4th Oxford and Bucks. Light Infantry, *Summerdown Camp Journal* (11 October 1916): 3. From the nurse's point of view, the environment described by these poems involved a 'dark and quiet' atmosphere characterized by a 'brooding sense/of waiting – waiting and expectancy' for "Mercy Ships" of "Wounded Arriving"'

See V.A.D., 'A pen picture', *Magazine of the Second General Hospital* (December 1916): 95–96.

48 'Leicestershire', 'Convalescence', *Summerdown Camp Journal* (15 August 1917): 2.

49 Peter Austen, 'The base hospital', *Jackass: First Australian General Hospital Monthly* (June 1918): 20. Compare this with the sense of temporal stasis conveyed by Siegfried Sassoon in his poem 'The death bed'. Here a soldier patient 'drowsed and was aware of silence heaped/Round him, unshaken as the steadfast walls; Aqueous like floating rays of amber light,/Soaring and quivering in the wings of sleep'. The man is comforted by 'silence and safety' as he listens to the rain 'rustling through the dark', Sassoon, 'The death bed' in Silkin, *Penguin Book of First World War Poetry*, 127–128).

50 'Casualty', *Contemptible* (London: William Heinemann, 1916), 206–207.

51 Untitled poem by RSM Wood, 2/4th Oxford and Bucks. Light Infantry, *Summerdown Camp Journal* (11 October 1916): 3.

52 Austen, 'The base hospital', and Captain T.W., 'The casualty clearing station', *Return: Journal of the King's Lancashire Military Convalescent Hospital* (April 1916): 7.

53 DeGroot, *Blighty*, 163. On the working-class diet before the war, especially in terms of its association with masculinity, see Robert Roberts, *The Classic Slum: Salford Life in the First Quarter of the Century* (Manchester: Manchester University Press, 1971), 90ff and Ellen Ross, *Love and Toil: Motherhood in Outcast London, 1870–1918* (New York: Oxford University Press, 1993), 28–32. On institutional diets before the war see especially Valerie J. Johnson, *Diet in Workhouses and Prisons, 1835–1895* (New York: Garland, 1985).

54 Harmke Kamminga and Andrew Cunningham (eds), *The Science and Culture of Nutrition, 1840–1940* (Atlanta GA: Rodopi, 1995).

55 'In hospital', *Magazine of the Fourth Northern General Hospital* (April 1917): 80. Such a grievance emerged at the Royal Berkshire Hospital, for example, where, after soldiers complained about having to buy their own sugar and eggs, the authorities agreed that the diets were 'insufficient in some respects'. They were amended, as best as supplies likely provided, to include more bread, sugar, butter, eggs, porridge and meat. However, by the end of the war, and through 1919, the prices of meat and fish continued to rise, greater shortages occurred, price controls were introduced and meat was rationed. In view of these circumstances, 'the medical staff advised that porridge, peas, lentils and beans should be used to supplement the meat supply'. Margaret Railton and Marshall Barr, *The Royal Berkshire Hospital, 1839–1989* (Berkshire: Royal Berkshire Hospital, 1989), 170, 182.

56 M.C.S.C., 'The hospital alphabet', *Magazine of the Fourth Northern General Hospital* (November 1916): 23.

57 *First Eastern General Hospital Gazette* (9 November 1915): 335. Patients also looked at eggs with suspicion and caution, no matter how they were served. On eggs see the prose piece entitled 'In hospital', where a soldier patient warns,

'As regards eggs, it is a safe rule never to touch one unless it is accompanied by a sworn statement certifying *a.* its length of service; *b.* its previous convictions'. *Magazine of the Fourth Northern General Hospital* (April 1917): 80. See also the pen-and-ink sketch 'Shell shock', *Magazine of the Fourth London General Hospital* (October 1916): 175, which depicts a gloomy-faced patient who has just opened what appears to be either an overcooked or a spoiled hard-boiled egg.

58 *First Eastern General Hospital Gazette* (9 November 1915): 335. In another poem Sergeant John Humphreys defended 'Enry in light of this rebuttal, asserting that ''Enry, like Oliver Twist', rightly 'asked for more' and had 'no fear/to stand where Oliver stood'. John Humphreys, 'In Defence of 'Ungry 'Enry', *First Eastern General Hospital Gazette* (4 January 1916): 428.

59 T. Frankish, 1st Lincoln Regiment, 'A skit on Cambridge Hospital', *First Eastern General Hospital Gazette, Cambridge* (28 September 1915): 256.

60 On the wartime food economy see 'Food in war-time', *Hospital* (17 April 1915): 71, and 'Palatable fare without meat: The importance of flavour', *Hospital* (20 November 1915) (supplement): 1–2.

61 From 'The hospital alphabet', *Wails of the Wounded, or Convalescent Camp Carollings from the Royal Free Military Hospital* (June 1916): n.p.

62 IWM, DOD, Papers of S. Norman, 11948 2/6/1, memoir, undated, pp. 15–16. Norman recalled further that his friend did find value in 'bully beef'. 'The coast being clear [in the dining hall] my friend removed a number of "Bully beef" tins from the tables, went through an end door, and hid them in the space under the floor. Later that day when the Dining Hall area was quiet the tins were recovered. The disposal of the tins for cash was simple, for a contact in the base had not only supplied the idea but had a ready buyer in Rouen. We gained a few francs which kept us going till I received some money from home.'

63 John Brophy and Eric Partridge, *Long Trail: Soldiers' Songs and Slang, 1914–1918* (London: Sphere, 1969), 253.

64 *Hospital* (29 September 1917): 522.

65 Winifred M. Letts, 'To a soldier in hospital' in George Herbert Clarke (ed.), *A Treasury of War Poetry: British and American Poems of the World War, 1914–1919* (New York: Hodder and Stoughton, 1919), 354–355.

66 *First Eastern General Hospital Gazette* (9 November 1915): 335.

67 Anonymous soldier patient, 'Nursery rhymes', *Gazette of the First Eastern General Hospital* (May 1915): 52.

68 The Happy Trio, 'Spanish flu', *Southern Cross: Magazine of the First Southern General Hospital* (January 1918): 90–91. The subject of the flu received similar treatment in a poem by the same title that appeared in *Lead-Swinger: The Bivouac Journal of the 1/3 West Riding Field Ambulance* (12 August 1918): 454.

69 See M.C.S.C., 'The hospital alphabet', *Magazine of the Fourth Northern General Hospital* (November 1916): 23, which points out that 'D is for Drugs of which there are droves ... M for the Mixtures the doctors prescribe ...'. M.C.S.C. also points out that 'A's Anaesthetic, queer merciful stuff ... J is for Jalap no one

likes to take.' For another illustration of drug over-prescription see the sketch by Private F.J. Leigh, 'A patient's feelings under the anaesthetic', *Gazette of the Third London General Hospital* (June 1917): 250.

70 'J.E.P.', 'The elixir of life', *Norfolk War Hospital Magazine* (June 1916): 4.

71 Fuller acknowledges similar mockery in trench journals of the medical officer's reliance on the No. 9 (laxative) pill' in light of 'other medications unavailable to him'. See Fuller, *Troop Morale*, 61.

72 For another cartoon about the rest cure see the six panels of 'Untitled', *Norfolk War Hospital Magazine* (April 1917): 10–11, 'No. 1: Effleurage; No. 2: A Friction; No. 3: Kneading; No. 4: Petrisage; No. 5: Tapotement; No. 6: The Climax'.

73 Charles Thomas and J.G. Russell Harvey, *Tommy's ABC* (Bristol: Bristol Branch Executive Red Cross Committee, 1916), n.p.

74 'An experienced patient', 'Hints on the treatment of invalids', *Craigleith Hospital Chronicle* (July 1915): 78.

75 Wilfred Owen, 'À terre' in Silkin (ed.), *The Penguin Book of First World War Poetry*, 191–192.

76 'Le baionnette, Paris', *Springbok Blue: The Magazine of the South African Military Hospital, Richmond Park, Surrey* (April 1917): 8.

77 The YMCA initiative was similar to that of the instruments programme sponsored by the Red Cross, which also provided gramophones, mouth organs, penny whistles and 'many other things easeful and useful' to 'transform [rest stations and similar environments] into something more habitable'. See British Red Cross Society and Order of St John of Jerusalem in England, 'Our Work: The British Red Cross Society and The Order of St John of Jerusalem in England', 16 (London: *The Times* Publishing Co., 1918), 26. For evidence of the modified YMCA logo see YMCA, 'The Red Triangle and another kind of triangle: How musicians at home can help musicians at the front', a leaflet dated 3 November 1916. LMA, A/FWA/C/D188/1.

78 PRO, WO 95/4121, 'History of Trouville Hospital Centre', No. 13 Convalescent Depot.

79 PRO, WO 95/4122, Official War Diary of No. 14 British Convalescent Depot, 14 December 1917.

80 Arthur Steward Macpherson, 'A hut at the front and its music', *Music Student: A Monthly Paper for All who Study, Teach, or Listen to Music* (1 September 1917), p. 12.

81 Arthur Somervell, 'Singing for soldiers', printed article lodged in Papers of Surgeon General Evatt, WLHUM/CMAC, RAMC o/s 3.

82 PRO, WO 95/4120, Official War Diary of No. 7 British Convalescent Depot, 19 May 1918.

83 Ibid.

84 L. Graham Brown, 'Military convalescent depots in France during the Great War', *Journal of the Royal Army Medical Corps*, 35:3 (September 1920): 187–202 and 284–299, at 285.

85 PRO, WO 95/4120, Official War Diary of No. 5 British Convalescent Depot, 20

August 1915.
86 Ibid., 18 September 1915.
87 Ibid., 25 December 1916.
88 Ibid.
89 Lena Ashwell, 'Cheering up Tommies, concerts are better than physic. Gift from home. Miss Ashwell's experiences in France', *Newcastle Illustrated Chronicle* (1 July 1915), n.p. Article lodged in scrapbooks of Lena Ashwell held in IWM, DOD, uncatalogued.
90 Lawrence Joseph Collins briefly addresses the positive role that music played in wartime medical contexts in *Theatre at War, 1914–18* (New York: St. Martin's Press, 1998), 60–72. On the positive functions of musical entertainment for women munitions workers see Woollacott, *On Her Their Lives Depend*, 141.
91 C.F. Steane, 'Rambling reflections', *First Eastern General Hospital Gazette* (16 January 1917): 329. Such sentiments are also expressed in an auxiliary hospital ABC book, 'G is the Gramaphone [*sic*] – early and late.' Thomas and Harvey, *Tommy's ABC*, n.p. See also depiction of the gramophone as source of noise – not soothing music – in the sketch by A.F.W.G., 'The rest cure'. Vera Brittain's experiences of hospital gramophones uphold the view presented here. She described them as 'oppressive', 'persistent', 'blaring' and 'blatant', adding that 'though the men found them consoling – perhaps because they subdued more sinister noises – they seemed to me to add a strident grotesqueness to the cold, dark evenings of hurry and pain'. Brittain, *Testament of Youth*, 220–221.
92 For a brief account of this phenomenon see 'Queen Alexandra Hospital, Dunkirk: Some impressions', *Fourth Report of the Friends' Ambulance Unit* 21 (September 1917): 8–12.
93 IWM, DOD, Papers of Maurice F. Gower, 255 88/25/2, Gower to his sister, 26 August 1918.
94 'Editorial', *First Eastern General Hospital Gazette* (23 May 1916): 60–61.
95 'Rowdyism at soldiers' concerts', *Hospital* (5 May 1917): 86.
96 For additional evidence of this phenomenon see Anon., 'Obviously', *Southern Cross: Magazine of the First Southern General Hospital* (October 1917): 245, which depicts a young female civilian asking a recovering soldier a stupid question. See also the illustration of an attractive woman accosting a convalescent blue on the street who is on crutches. Top caption: 'The eternal question'; bottom caption: '"Do you want to go back?"' *Magazine of the Fifth London (City of London) General Hospital (St Thomas's)* (May 1917): 158. Similar images appeared in *Punch*. See, for example, 'Disillusioned', *Punch* (13 January 1915), p. 29 and 'People we should like to see interned', *Punch* (28 April 1915), p. 325.
97 *Magazine of the Fourth London General Hospital* (September 1916): 106.
98 Untitled sketch by 'Pullthrough', *Magazine of the Second Southern General Hospital* (June 1916): 30.
99 Anonymous soldier patient, 'Wit from the wards', *Gazette of the First Eastern General Hospital* (8 June 1915): 64.

100 Anonymous soldier patient in the *Royal Army Medical Corps Magazine* (18 May 1917): 1. The preceeding discussion has been shaped partly by the work of Linda Nochlin, including *The Politics of Vision: Essays on Nineteenth-Century Art and Society* (New York: Harper and Row, 1989) and *Women, Art, and Power and other Essays* (New York: Harper and Row, 1988). In *Politics* see especially 44. In *Women* see 32–33.

101 Ward Muir, *The Happy Hospital* (London: Simpkin, Marshall, Hamilton, Kent and Co., 1918), 82.

102 Enid Bagnold, *A Diary without Dates* (London: William Heinemann, 1918), 15.

103 Ibid., 15.

104 E. Chivers Davies, *Ward Tales* (London: John Lane The Bodley Head, 1920), 89.

105 Winter, *Death's Men*, 201–202.

5

Wartime convalescence: the case of the convalescent blues

On 3 November 1917, after entering the Royal Naval Hospital for his 'gaseous adventures', S.J. Wallis wrote to his brother George, informing him that he had 'arrived at the above "house of correction"'. Advising George that he should 'steer clear' of the hospital, no matter how much he would like to visit, Wallis explained that the institution was 'the closest combination of prison and workhouse I know', with 'infamous rules galore, scanty, ill-cooked grub and general treatment rotten'. When patients are well enough, he added, 'half of your time is occupied in washing pots, sweeping etc'. This routine, Wallis suggested, revolved so tightly around official concerns about efficiency and saving money that one would think, 'viewed through this hospital, the nation appears to be bankrupt'. Wallis found some solace in his predicament, however, when he was allowed to 'escape', dressed in 'civilized rig (modern style blue)', to attend recreations in and around the hospital.[1]

The blue clothing described by Wallis was the most distinctive material object that contemporaries associated with the convalescence of soldiers at home, prompting the naming of recovering men 'convalescent blues'. Its connections with the history of institutional garments and with the exigencies of the war make 'the blues' a valuable focus for exploring further connections between the war machine and the contemporary culture of caregiving as well as camaraderie among men, their sense of separation from the public and public articulations of praise for the wounded soldier's service to King and Country.

While some scholars have linked clothing with the expression of politics and gender, with the emergence of modern consumer society and with the health and discipline of the body,[2] historians of the Great War have been relatively slow to explore how clothing worn during wartime helped to represent and shape contemporary forms of patriotism and gender identity. Taking the lead in redressing this historiographical oversight, Angela Woollacott has demonstrated in her study of the British soldier's khaki uniform how wartime debates about 'khaki fever' among young women reflected the gendering of patriotism. While this phenomenon reflected public concern about the social and sexual behaviour of young women, Woollacott argues, it was also a way for the British public to praise its heroes. But, like the patriotic fervour for the war, 'khaki fever' began to fade as 'the public image of the [heroic] soldier had to accommodate the bandaged, the wounded, those on crutches, the limbless, those with disfigured faces, lost eyes and damaged nerves'.[3] Extending Woollacott's work, Nicoletta Gullace has explored the gendered language of patriotism by examining wartime 'white-feather giving'. The provocative practice of women placing white feathers in the lapels and hatbands of men who wore civilian clothes, Gullace argues, represented 'a sort of inversion of "khaki fever" the idea that scorning a coward can be read as the other side of loving a hero'.[4]

The waning of 'khaki fever' raises the question of what replaced this patriotic public response to soldiers. One answer lies in the clothing of men who were recovering from the ravages of the war. Public attachment of the values of duty, honour and country to the convalescent blue outfit helped to make the Tommy who wore it the heroic counterpart to the khaki-clad soldier. Praise of the 'convalescent blue', like 'khaki fever', served as another way of loving a hero.

However, the phenomenon of the blues was not nearly as straightforward as public praise suggests. Contemporary accounts by convalescents suggest that they had mixed feelings about the blues. Some men attached negative connotations to this wear, suggesting that the ill-fitting, bright-coloured and pocketless 'blues' failed to confer a deserved dignity of appearance and sense of independence. Others implied that they found much difficulty with the public praise they received. Some appreciated this attention when its sources were young women or generous individuals who offered cigarettes. Other men suggested that the utter lack of understanding about the war that often if not always accompanied such attention simply underscored their sense of being a class apart from the rest of society. Like the hospital environment, therefore, the phenomenon of the blues was fraught with contradiction. As a mark of difference and a public emblem of heroism, here was *matériel* on the soldier's own body that served in some instances to subvert and in others to reinforce his sense of independence, strength and sexual prowess.

Standard institutional clothing was not at all a new phenomenon in 1914. Since the early nineteenth century, authorities in workhouses, prisons and schools had realized the value of institutional clothing as a means of ensuring personal and communal hygiene as well as institutional discipline and order.[5] And since the Crimean debacle, civilian and military medical officers in hospitals had recognized the similar value of special clothing for patients.[6]

At the outset of the Great War, authorities drew on these established principles of institutional wear as they developed hospital clothing regulations for recovering soldiers. In late August 1914, anticipating the first returns of wounded British soldiers to newly established military hospitals on the home front, the editors of the tailors' professional journal, *Tailor and Cutter*, published an 'urgent call' for 'suitable jackets or blouses for ward-room use of convalescent soldiers'. This clothing, the editors suggested, might be made along the lines of an oversized lounge coat. 'Better still,' they explained, it should be made according to the special 'sealed pattern' of the Army Council, which called for a 'sac-shaped' outfit with a 36-inch chest size, 'loose Prussian collar' and 'easy armholes and one-piece sleeves'

Made of a flannel and flannelette combination this 'Rickett's Blue' outfit and its lounge-jacket counterpart resembled ill-fitting pyjamas.[7] The entire ensemble included a red four-in-hand necktie and was the only item of hospital clothing issued exclusively by the government during the war.[8] Military authorities required that the garment be worn at all times by soldiers of non-officer 'other ranks' who were receiving treatment in military hospitals and convalescent facilities. At the same time, authorities exempted officers from wearing this outfit, providing them a white armband decorated with a red King's Crown,[9] with a personal clothing allowance, or with fancy silk pyjamas donated by the public and voluntary-aid agencies.[10]

The convalescent blue outfit symbolized efficiency and economy during a time of scarce goods and high prices. Regulated by the government, its production was carried out either through military contracts with private provincial factories or directly by the army at the Royal Army Clothing Factory in Pimlico, where 'labour-saving devices' and a 'smooth, efficient and economical' factory system dominated every facet of clothing manufacture.[11] The uniform was also designed so that a handful of sizes would fit all recovering soldiers of 'other ranks'. This standardization made the uniform fit poorly, requiring soldiers to 'flap' or 'cuff' their trouser legs and shirt sleeves.

The blues were above all a means of establishing and maintaining cleanliness in the hospital, where soldiers usually arrived in dirty, worn-out and infested uniforms and 'greatcoats' that required sterilization and thorough disinfection.[12] Ultimately, in serving this purpose, the hospital uniform played an essential role in the system of wartime medical care which sought as rapidly as possible to make men fit either for further military duty or for civilian life.[13]

Authorities also linked the hygienic function of the blue uniform with efforts to establish and maintain 'rigid economy' in individual institutions and the system of wartime care generally.[14] By maintaining a monopoly on its production and distribution, the government guaranteed not only cost control but also fair distribution among military care facilities and efficient cleaning and sorting. Moreover, this monopoly helped to maintain general 'economy in clothing' during a time when the consumption of woollen goods by civilian and military sectors of the population was 'much in excess of normal times'.[15]

However, the most important function of blues was to help improve administrative efficiency within the hospital environment. At convalescent facilities, the administration of soldier patients involved strict division into four 'sections', each distinguished by combinations of the hospital blue uniform and different-coloured armlets. The 'worst cases' wore hospital blue-and-white armlets. Cases well enough for one to six months of retraining wore blue-and-pink armlets. Section three, including ranks who required less than one month of retraining, wore blue-and-light-blue armlets. Finally, section four included men in blue-and-dark-blue armlets who were 'practically well'.[16] This medical organization by sartorial marking expedited the process of convalescent medical exams, helping divisional medical officers to monitor and sort their sections during weekly inspections when men were either 'moved up' or 'put back from Section to Section as [their] condition indicates'.[17]

The soldier patient remained dressed in blue even while he sat periodically before the standing medical board which sought to determine whether he was 'in his proper section, or whether there is no prospect of training him in a reasonable time'.[18] After this assessment, whether he was kept at a convalescent facility or transferred to a military hospital, the soldier patient remained clad in blue, forbidden by authorities from removing it until he passed through all four phases of recovery and was discharged. These strict sartorial regulations suggest that authorities understood the blue uniform to be an effective means of maintaining rigid medical classification.

Use of the blues also reflected authorities' expectations of potential insubordination among recovering ranks. In essential ways, being 'fully clothed' in blue served as a means of maintaining discipline and order both inside and outside institutional confines.[19] This official linkage of soldier patient behaviour with sartorial requirements was evident in all military hospitals. Inside, the outfit helped authorities to distinguish soldier patients from doctors, nurses, orderlies and visitors. Moreover, in facilities set aside specifically for disabled cases, the blue outfit helped to promote good behaviour. At Shepherd's Bush, Britain's flagship orthopaedic hospital, authorities used these sartorial requirements to encourage voluntary unpaid work in the institution's so-called curative shops. If patients participated in these official work programmes, they could receive privileges such as 'permission to wear khaki instead of the hospital blue or grey' or 'more frequent passes out of the hospital, etc'.[20]

When soldiers were granted permission to convalesce beyond the institution's confines, at the seaside or by the riverside or in public parks, authorities insisted that the men 'be correctly dressed in hospital clothing and if the great coat was worn a blue armlet had to be worn'.[21] These regulations, authorities believed, deterred other ranks from getting into trouble by reminding them that they remained military men under watchful eye and subject to punishment for transgressions such as drunkenness or malingering. While the War Office gave authorities permission to 'waive' this sartorial requirement if they felt that 'such [outdoor] relaxation did not delay convalescence or lead to laxity of behaviour or discipline', the rule often, if not always, remained in effect.[22]

The lack of pockets in the convalescent blue uniform was a measure that fitted with disciplinary arrangements, especially the rule that soldiers were not allowed to hold money while in hospital.[23] Significantly, too, this measure reflected a contemporary trend in civilian wear, that 'one of the great differences between garments for gentlemen and ladies is that, in the former, pockets abound, whereas in the latter they are absent'. Women's clothes did not require pockets because women carried their personal belongings in purses. Men's lounge suits on the other hand always included an inner or outer 'ticket pocket' for carrying money and, indeed, tickets to theatre performances.[24] Soldiers' hospital wear overlooked this difference between women's and men's clothing. In hospital soldiers were supposedly provided with both sustenance and leisure, so they did not need pockets for money or tickets. As we shall see, evidence suggests that convalescents themselves were acutely aware of this feature of their mandated outfits.

FREDᴷ SPURGIN
GOD BLESS OUR
RED, WHITE AND BLUE!

Figure 14 Postcard by Frederick Spurgin (original in colour), 'A & H Convalescent Series', No. 325, Art and Humour Publishing Co., *c.* 1914–18

Like rest huts and hospitals, the blues served an important propagandistic function during the war, helping to put the wounded Tommy on public display and facilitate public appreciation of his service to King and Country. A picture postcard created and sold during the war proudly celebrated the blues in the context of the colours of the Union Jack. Here was the convalescent blue praised alongside the beautiful nurse and the revered Chelsea pensioner (see Figure 14). Similar expressions of praise appeared on Flag Days, patriotic events sponsored by voluntary-aid organizations to help raise money for hospitals and general support for the country's wounded heroes. Flag Day posters and other paraphernalia honoured all recovering soldiers, but especially the blue-clad Tommy.[25] Sold by voluntary-aid organizations at Flag Day celebrations, wooden lapel pins shaped like wounded 'blue boys' and small lapel flags that depicted smiling blue-clad Tommies conveyed the public's support.[26] Like the sale of postcards depicting rest huts, a percentage of profits from pin sales was directed toward the provision of comforts for war-weary, sick and wounded soldiers.

Display of the blue-clad Tommy especially served the needs of the upper-class individuals, particularly women, who were concerned to be seen in public helping the wounded. Newspaper accounts of public recreations held for convalescent soldiers testify to this intention associated with the blues. Sketches in the *Illustrated London News* highlighted the pride with which ladies of 'society and stage' entertained blue-clad 'men broken in the Great War'.[27] Material in *Punch* took a more direct aim at upper-class insensitivity toward the wounded. In March 1915 the magazine published 'More people we should like to see interned', a sketch depicting two richly dressed women visiting a hospital in search of Tommies to entertain. 'Well, we'll bring the car to-morrow, and take some of your patients for a drive,' they explain. 'And by-the-by, Nurse, you might look out some with bandages that show – the last party might not have been wounded at all, as far as anybody in the streets could see'.[28] Punch evoked such ludicrous circumstances again in September 1915 when it reported that 'the return of the wounded to England is marked by strange incidents, pathetic and humorous'. Noteworthy was:

> the cheerfulness of the limbless men in blue is something wonderful. They 'jest at scars' but not because they 'never felt a wound'. It is high privilege to entertain these light-hearted heroes, one of whom recently presented his partner in a lawn tennis match with a fragment of shell taken from his 'stummick'. And the recipient rightly treasures it as a love-token ...'[29]

It's just my luck! They will ask me where I was wounded—I tell 'em I can't sit down, never mind going into details!

Figure 15 Postcard (original in colour), 'Witty Series', No. 584. Bamforth and Co., *c.* 1914–18

Interpretations of such women directing thoughtless questions to soldiers, and therefore demonstrating no comprehension of their conditions, appeared throughout the war in *Punch,* in hospital magazines and in popular picture postcards (see Figure 15).

Literary and visual material authored by convalescent soldiers suggests a view of the blues fraught with contradiction. Some men recognized the uniform as a source of embarrassment, failing in large measure to confer a deserved dignity of appearance.[30] Others understood the blues as part and parcel of the orderly, timetabled rhythms of the military hospital that disciplined their minds and bodies and undercut their sense of independence, strength and sexual prowess. Still others suggested appreciation of the blues for marking them as heroes in the eyes of young women or, in the case of S.J. Wallis, enabling them to 'escape' from hospital routines.

In his hospital magazine poem entitled 'Unedited verses: a suit of blues', Private H.S. Bowles described the cheap, mass-produced quality of the convalescent outfit as it played a role in the 'convalescent adventures' of 'Percy', a typical soldier patient. When Percy 'dressed for dinner at Bathampton V.A.D.', Bowles explained, he was 'shaved and neat as usual, but a fearsome sight [was] he'. His coat was 'a vivid blue and fitted p'rhaps here and there in places', but [at] the back it showed 'the end of Percy's braces'. Percy wore a clean white shirt, but one which 'set in fold[s] and

By Rflmn. A. Sutton.

A Bad Fit of the Blues.

Figure 16 A. Sutton, 'A Bad Fit of the Blues', *Gazette of the Third London General Hospital* (November 1916): 36

curls' and complemented his 'screaming scarlet' handkerchief and 'pantaloons [that] would suit a clown performing at a fair'. Completing this ensemble was the silver lapel badge that Percy wore on his chest. As cheap and unflattering as the suit to which it was pinned, this mark was 'no, not a diamond pin, but something shining brave and bright – a button made of tin'.[31] Here, Bowles concluded, was not a hero, but rather a man whose strength, pride and general sense of self were reduced by 'a garb that's so bizarre'.[32] A hospital magazine sketch by Rifleman A. Sutton, entitled 'A Bad Fit of the Blues', offered a visual interpretation of this poor fit, indeed how the blues fell far short of being a distinguished uniform for Tommy (see Figure 16). Sketches by J. Peplow and L. Timpson conveyed a similar message of emasculation. 'It's the clothes that make the man …?', the caption of 'A new arrival/an unknown hero' asks, suggesting that if such a statement is true, the 'convalescent blue' is far from being the proud man he ought to be, thanks to the shoddy quality and fit of his suit.[33] An untitled sketch by Peplow suggests that recovering soldiers were well aware of the absence of pockets in their undistinguished uniforms, a reality that created a music hall-inspired badge of comedy about wartime masculinity and masculine outfits that cloaked effeminacy. Here, two blue-clad convalescents carry purses while strolling in public. 'Owing to the shortage of pockets in the wearing apparel of the convalescents', the caption explains, 'it has been suggested that they should copy the ladies and carry handbags' (see Figure 17). Timpson's diary sketch entitled 'True blue' depicts a blue-clad convalescent declaring to his friend that 'There ain't no ticket pocket in this 'ere suit.' The other Tommy, who is also dressed in blue, responds simply, 'Dinna fret yourself, laddie, yer no likely to be needing one.'[34] An article in the *Courier*, which described the care of wounded men at Edinburgh War Hospital, testified further to the negative view of the blues expressed by Bowles, Sutton, Peplow and Timpson. At Edinburgh:

> few serious cases and a large proportion are able to walk about the grounds. Clad in their hospital suits of blue the soldiers present a smart appearance albeit that the rather large turn up of the trousers, which is found necessary in most cases, does somewhat distract from the real sartorial effect and Tommy is conscious of it too …[35]

Awareness of the ill-fitting blues, and the implication that it was inappropriate attire for heroes, also emerged in a 1916 session of Parliament that addressed care for the wounded. When the outfit was washed, observed one MP, 'the outside shrank at a different rate from the lining'.[36]

Figure 17 J. Peplow, *Return: Journal of the King's Lancashire Military Convalescent Hospital* (17 August 1917): 5

However, alongside such negative views of the blues was a more positive public interpretation of his wear as being the mark of a hero. Frederick Davison wrote in his diary that 'everyone in Wycombe treats exceptionally well the men in the blue & grey'.[37] In subsequent stanzas about Percy's

Figure 18 J.H. Dowd, 'Reminiscences of Donovan I', *Gazette of the Third London General Hospital* (October 1918): 15

adventures we learn that when this figure attended an after-dinner concert at his hospital, he thought the girls would shun him because he was 'such a weird and wond'rous sight'. To Percy's surprise, 'they flocked around, admired and petted him'. In the end, he became the object of sexual desire as the girls discovered 'the man … within' the blues.[38] A poem entitled 'The blue boy's flirtation' similarly conveyed the sexual value associated with the blues. Here, T.W. Strain described an encounter between a strolling convalescent and 'a nice little maiden'. The blue boy 'wink[ed] with his left eye' and 'she responded with her right'. This communication, we learn, 'showed he had practically won the fight'.[39] A nurse's poem entitled 'The blue' echoed these sexual themes. The blues, this woman observed, represented the transformation of 'a callow youngster … into a warrior true'. It had more meaning than khaki ever could, she concluded:

> There's many a one in khaki [who] has shown his valour well
> Yet come unhurt through shrapnel hail and poison fumes of hell
> And other girls may walk with them, but I, I'll dote on you
> My own brave wounded laddie, my soldier in blue.[40]

Hospital-magazine sketches by J.H. Dowd underscore this vision of the blues. In 'The popularity of the boy in blue', a convalescent Tommy approaches an omnibus while policemen hold back the cheering queue. On the bus, passengers offer the Tommy their seats while others ply him with cigarettes. In the street an old man with an umbrella raises his hat and remarks, 'Hail, saviour and protector!' (see Figure 18).

Convalescent blues very likely appreciated their uniforms for another reason not immediately evident. Since the outfit marked him as having served King and Country, no blue boy would receive a white feather for cowardice.[41] Like the disabled ex-serviceman who dressed in civilian clothes and wore a 'King's Silver Badge' to protect himself from white-feather-wielding women, the blue-clad soldier became a symbol of heroic service even as his uniform was a mark of the war machine on his body that complicated his masculine identity and prompted in his own mind mixed feelings at best about his return home.

During the Great War, as women donned uniforms that represented their unprecedented independence, wounded soldiers wore uniforms that simultaneously reinforced and subverted their sense of manliness. The public – particularly young women – saw convalescent blues, like khaki-clad soldiers, as heroes. But, from the convalescent's perspective, the blues fell far short of being an emblem of masculine pride. This uniform – itself representative of wartime efficiency and economy – represented an assault of the war machine on his body, mobilizing, classifying and disciplining and displaying it to the end of serving the state at war. As such themes marked the life of the convalescent, they also informed the rehabilitation of men who had lost limbs in combat. At Shepherd's Bush Military Hospital, Britain's flagship orthopaedic institution, work therapy became a prominent form of healing that served like rest in rest huts and recovery in hospitals to maintain efficiency and economy in mobilized society. Work therapy also served to shape official and public representations of the disabled soldier, as well as appreciation of his service to King and Country. Men disabled in the war are the subject of the penultimate chapter of this book, since they deserve placement in a category by themselves as the war's most conspicuous legacy and as the group most profoundly affected, shaped and reshaped by the conflict.

Notes

1 Leeds University Library, Liddle Collection, S.J. Wallis to his brother George Wallis, 3 and 6 November 1917.

2 See, for example, Paul Fussell and Betty Fussell, *Uniforms: Why We Are What We Wear* (New York: Houghton Mifflin, 2002); Anne Hollander, *Sex and Suits* (New York: Knopf, 1995); Lynn Hunt, *Politics, Culture, and Class in the French Revolution* (Berkeley CA: University of California Press, 1984), 78–79; Victoria de Grazia and Ellen Furlough (eds), *The Sex of Things: Gender and Consumption in Historical Perspective* (Berkeley CA: University of California Press, 1996) and Christopher Harding, Bill Hines, Richard Ireland and Philip Rawlings, *Imprisonment in England and Wales: A Concise History* (Dover NH: Croom Helm, 1985), 227–230.

3 Angela Woollacott, '"Khaki fever" and its control: Gender, class, age and sexual morality on the British home front in the First World War', *Journal of Contemporary History* 29:2 (April 1994): 325–347. See also Cooke and Woollacott (eds), *Gendering War Talk* (Princeton NJ: Princeton University Press, 1993) and Angela Woollacott, 'Dressed to kill: Clothes, cultural meaning and World War I women munitions workers' in *Gender and Material Culture* II, *Representations of Gender from Prehistory to the Present* ed. Moira Donald and Linda Hurcombe (New York: St. Martin's Press, 2000).

4 Gullace, 'White feathers and wounded men', 191.

5 On the use of standard garments in asylums and workhouses see 'The clothing of lunatics: The therapeutic value of a becoming costume', *Hospital* (3 May 1919): 106. On clothing in prisons see Margaret Delacy, *Prison Reform in Lancashire, 1700–1850: A Study in Local Administration* (Stanford CA: Stanford

University Press, 1986), 101; Michael Ignatieff, *Just Measure of Pain*, 93–94 and 190–191; McConville, *English Local Prisons*, 401 and C. Harding *et. al.*, *Imprisonment*, especially 227ff.

6 This development was partly the result of the reform efforts of Florence Nightingale, who argued that clean clothing helped to rid the healing environment of elements that disturbed health and hindered the recuperative process, such as dampness, chills, drafts and smells. See Florence Nightingale, *Notes on Nursing: What It Is, and What It Is Not* (London: Harrison and Sons, 1859), among her other works.

7 This description is compiled from *Hansard Parliamentary Debates*, Commons, vol. 86 (1916), cols 970–971, from the author's first-hand examination of the hospital-blue uniform on display in the First World War exhibit at the Imperial War Museum (case 16) and from 'Convalescent jacket', *Tailor and Cutter* (20 August 1914) (supplement): 688–690, which also contains the Army Council's special 'sealed pattern' (also called a 'specimen garment', for the 'convalescent jacket'. Such patterns were made for all branches of the armed forces.

8 The 'four-in-hand' was one of the four most popular types of necktie worn in Britain between 1900 and 1925. Red was a popular colour of necktie between 1900 and 1914, and this fact could account for why authorities chose it as the colour of the convalescent's necktie. See Alan Mansfield and Phillis Cunnington, *Handbook of English Costume in the Twentieth Century, 1900–1950* (Boston MA: Plays, 1973), 273–274. The only part of the blue ensemble not mandated by authorities was the hat, which, as it signified individual rank, nationality and regiment, could be the soldier patient's own.

9 An example of the armband worn by officers is on display in the First World War Exhibit at the Imperial War Museum (case 16).

10 See B. Abel-Amith, *The Hospitals*, 275. For a vivid account of the fancy pyjamas often worn by officers see Lyn McDonald, *The Roses of No Man's Land* (New York: Penguin Books, 1993), 39. Discharged soldiers who were no longer receiving care in military hospitals did not wear hospital blue but 'their own clothes'. See Charity Organisation Society, 'The Star and Garter Home for Disabled Discharged Soldiers, Commanding Officer's Report (interview with the Matron of the hospital) 27 August 1919'. LMA, A/FWA/C/D.

11 'A visit to the Royal Army Clothing Factory', *Tailor and Cutter* (6 August 1914): 636–639. See the brief official history of the Royal Army Clothing Department (RACD), written by its director at the turn of the century, PRO, WO 33/78, 'The Royal Army Clothing Department, 1897'. According to this history, the RACD was established in 1855, and by the end of the century it 'consistently functioned' as a 'model factory', according to the 'sound principles of economy, combined with efficiency' (7). On the RACD see also 'Military tailoring', *Tailor and Cutter* (4 February 1915) (supplement): 8. For general background on the British textile industry see G.A. Berkstresser, D.A. Buchanan and P.L. Grady (eds), *Automation in the Textile Industry* (Manchester: Textile Institute, 1995).

12 'Clothing, dental treatment, and railway passes', *Hospital* (20 March 1915):

555. See also E.P. Cathcart, *Elementary Physiology in its Relation to Hygiene, Army Medical Department* (London: HMSO, 1919), 13–14.

13 War Office, *General Instructions* (London: HMSO, 1916), 10.

14 'War Office economy', *Tailor and Cutter* (10 May 1917): 368.

15 'Economy in clothing', *Tailor and Cutter* (3 May 1917): 350. See also 'Textile supplies for hospitals', *Hospital* (18 December 1915): 255–256.

16 'Arrangements for the reception and treatment of sick and wounded in hospitals in the United Kingdom during the Great War', appendix VI to 'The King's Lancashire Military Convalescent Hospital in Blackpool: The King's System and Details of Physical Training', TD (1918) (?), n.p., PRO, WO 222/1.

17 Ibid.

18 Ibid.

19 Ibid.

20 *Reports by the Joint War Committee*, 253.

21 'Arrangements', n.p.

22 Ibid.

23 IWM, DOD, Papers of Miss M. Semple, 5821 96/50/1 and Con Shelf, Jock McLeod to Semple, 23 April 1916.

24 'Pockets', *Tailor and Cutter* (25 March 1915): 211.

25 See the poster '"Fag" Day', which was modelled on a typical 'Flag Day' poster, held in the Department of Photographs at the Imperial War Museum (Q80350).

26 Excellent examples of these pins, sold on 'Flag Days' as well as 'Our Days', are on display in the First World War exhibit at the Imperial War Museum (case 33). An example of such a pin is also lodged in the Papers of Howard Cole, WLHUM. Cole recalled that his mother purchased and wore this 'Blue Boy' badge on a Flag Day in Bournemouth in 1917 and 1918 to help collect funds for the welfare of the wounded soldier. See Cole to Royal Army Medical Corps Museum, *c.* 1971.

27 See sketches by Frank Reynolds, 'Entertaining Tommy: A feature of fashionable life in war-time', *Illustrated London News* (12 February 1916): 200 and 'Driving in the park, 1917: an influence of the motor car on the summer habits of society', *Illustrated London News* (1 September 1917): 247.

28 'More people we should like to see interned', *Punch* (24 March 1915): 230. See also P.J.E. and T.C., 'Heroes both', *Stand Easy: Chronicles of Cliveden* (15 June 1918), 4–5.

29 *Mr Punch's History of the Great War* (New York: Cassell and Co., 1920), (54).

30 Some soldiers felt the same way about the uniform issued to Lord Kitchener's army in 1914. This outfit 'was not at all liked, the first men to wear it being mistaken for inmates of an institutional home'. See *Tailor and Cutter* (5 November 1914) (supplement): 877.

31 According to Denis Winter, the War Inquiry Pensions Committee first issued these little silver lapel badges in 1916 to protect convalescents from military police and from patriotic white-feather-wielding women. See Winter, *Death's Men*, 252.

Models of artificial limbs, 1918

Hand and leg made by Clyde shipbuilders.

(ERS 153)

32 *Bath Bun* (November 1917): 125.

33 J. Peplow, 'A new arrival/an unknown hero', *Return: Journal of the King's Lancashire Military Convalescent Hospital* (August 1917): 9.

34 IWM, DOD, Papers of L. Timpson, 1775 92/3/1, diary sketch, 1 June 1918.

35 Untitled and undated article published in the *Courier*, as quoted in W.F. Hendrie and D.A.D. Macleod, *The Bangour Story: A History of Bangour Village and General Hospitals* (Aberdeen: Aberdeen University Press, 1992), 22.

36 *Hansard Parliamentary Debates*, Commons, vol. 86 (1916), cols 970–971.

37 IWM, DOD, Papers of Frederick Davison, 3/15/1, diary, September 1917–January 1918.

38 *Bath Bun* (November 1917): 125.

39 *Summerdown Camp Journal* (15 August 1917): 3.

40 'The Blue', *First Eastern General Hospital Gazette* (31 August 1915): 190. For a similar account of the distinction between khaki and blue see 'Big Boy Blue', *Magazine of the Second Southern General Hospital* (April 1916): 3–4.

41 Gullace, 'White feathers and wounded men'.

6

Reclaiming the maimed at Shepherd's Bush Military Hospital, London

In May 1918, the French and Belgian Ministries of War hosted the second of two annual international conferences on the 'after-care' of soldiers disabled in the Great War. In London, leading medical authorities, voluntary-aid representatives, labour leaders and politicians met to exchange views on two vital questions. How could the war's disabled be healed effectively and, following this, how could they be reintegrated successfully into civilian society? Officials at the previous conference had examined these questions in detail, but with the military campaigns of 1917 efforts to rehabilitate the wounded serviceman became all the more vital for the welfare of the man himself, his family and his nation.

In his introduction to the official conference proceedings, John Galsworthy offered a hopeful description of Britain's rehabilitation scheme for disabled servicemen. 'In special hospitals,' he wrote:

> orthopaedic, paraplegic, neurasthenic, we shall give [the crippled soldier] back functional ability, solidity of nerve or lung. The flesh torn away, the lost sight, the broken ear-drum, the destroyed nerve, it is true we cannot give back; but we shall so re-create and fortify the rest of him that he shall leave hospital ready for a new career. Then we shall teach him how to tread the road of it, so that he fits again into the national life, becomes once more a workman with pride in his work, a stake in the country and the consciousness that, handicapped though he be, he runs the race level with his fellows and is by that so much the better man than they ... [1]

Galsworthy's sketch is revealing for the way in which it suggests how rehabilitating disabled soldiers involved not only conventional rest but also two distinct yet interconnected kinds of work. Through supervised, post-operative manipulation of maimed limbs, using water, weights and electricity, medical authorities sought to repair both the body and the mind. At the same time, administrators of this programme promoted another form of rehabilitative work as a way to prepare disabled soldiers for re-entry into civilian life. Vocational labour, they held, helped to make them workmen once again. As Galsworthy therefore suggested, providing disabled soldiers with these kinds of work thus meant reconstituting them in three respects: as healthy individuals, as able-bodied bread-winners and as productive citizens.

Historians have devoted considerable attention to the ways in which the mental and physical wounds of the Great War helped to shape the identity of the Great War soldier and his perception by government officials, care providers and the public.[2] This chapter extends this literature and furthers our exploration of wartime healing behind the lines by examining the development of Shepherd's Bush Military Hospital, Britain's flagship orthopaedic centre, established in 1916 at London's Hammersmith Workhouse Infirmary.[3] Based on existing therapies for the physically disabled and the mentally ill, as well as on occupational programmes for convict prisoners, unemployed sectors of the working classes and the urban poor, the rehabilitation scheme at this institution reflected the persistence of Victorian modes of medical care and social welfare into the twentieth century. At the same time, wartime concerns among authorities about efficiency, economy and post-war society helped to shape the development of this programme. Analysing Shepherd's Bush demonstrates that this institution was a site where healing time overlapped with productive work time, creating arenas of teaching and industry where medical authorities conceived disabled soldiers as able-bodied workers who could continue to 'do their bit' for their own welfare and for the benefit of wartime efficiency. Like other sites that constituted the wartime culture of caregiving, Shepherd's Bush was an integral component of the war machine that informed nearly every facet of British society during the Great War.[4] Like these sites also, and no less the contemporary work environments of munitions and metalworking factories, programmes at Shepherd's Bush simultaneously undercut and reinforced traditional gender roles. While factory work enabled women to take on men's roles as the producers of weapons it deepened misogyny by highlighting the privileged status of most women as noncombatants and present or future mothers. Similarly, while therapeutic work at Shepherd's Bush was intended to 'reclaim' disabled soldiers, it helped to remind these men of their emasculated condition.[5]

As Roger Cooter has demonstrated, Shepherd's Bush occupies an important place in the history of medicine. It represented the first large-scale mobilization in Britain of orthopaedic and physiotherapeutic specialists. Never before had there been a single hospital set aside uniquely for the care of the adult disabled. And never before had a hospital staff faced such a multiplicity of physical injuries and the impact of total warfare on the human body. But medical authorities at this hospital did not develop their curative scheme *de novo*. They drew extensively upon their experience of caring for crippled children and injured industrial workers.[6] Moreover, this endeavour reflected the broader contemporary shift in conceptions of work and the effect that work had on the human body.

Between the 1880s and the 1920s, as Anson Rabinbach has shown, authorities in scientific and industrial circles were becoming increasingly concerned about the 'wastage' of labour in modern society. Applying metaphors of the machine to the human body to illuminate the extent to which it was becoming plagued, both mentally and physically, by modern 'fatigue', these individuals suggested how the moral value of work, as virtuous and inherently good, was gradually being displaced by more scientific, measured evaluations of work. Although Rabinbach chiefly emphasizes this development on the Continent, a comparable shift in the conception of work simultaneously occurred in Britain, particularly in the fields of medicine and social and penal reform.[7]

During the last quarter of the nineteenth century, British surgeons began to recognize the value of work in surgical after-care schemes for the physically disabled. Based on the long-established 'moral treatment' of the insane and the poor, which sought to reform individual conduct according to ideas of self-discipline and moral self-consciousness,[8] the orthopaedic surgeon and later founder of Shepherd's Bush, Robert Jones, used two kinds of work to help rehabilitate injured industrial workers and crippled children. On one hand, he followed what was essentially an early form of physiotherapy, emphasizing the so-called 'external' movement of a patient's muscles by means of water, machine-mounted and directed weights and electricity. Complementing this scientific evaluation of labour was 'useful' work in the form of craftmaking, which helped the disabled patient to learn how to move his or her own wounded muscles alone, without external aid. This component of the treatment was especially vital, Jones held, because the successful rehabilitation of the disabled depended as much on their relationship to 'social service' as on effective medicine and surgery.[9] It was important, he believed, to make disabled individuals aware of their potential abilities as newly functional and productive members of the community. This twofold view of work, as both morally and scientifically worthwhile, was central to Jones's efforts as medical supervisor of the Manchester Ship Canal project between 1888 and 1891, where he fitted splints on amputation cases that were the result of industrial injuries. It was also crucial to his subsequent work as surgeon at Nelson Street Hospital in Liverpool, where he aided the rehabilitation of shipwrights, ironworkers, boilermakers and dockgatemen of Merseyside who had sustained severe physical disabilities from their work. Beginning in 1909, Jones's view of work also became integral to the healing scheme established at Baschurch Hospital for crippled children. Here, Jones continued his pioneering psychological treatment of physical injury, emphasizing not only the value of 'useful' work but also that of open-air wards in promoting contentment and recovery.[10]

While Jones emphasized the orthopaedic value of work, comparable evaluations of work appeared in sectors of reform-minded individuals. This development reflected both the persistent moral valuations and the emergence of the new 'scientific approach' to poverty and social indiscipline. In Toynbee Hall and Salvation Army classrooms, women organized and taught semi-skilled work as a means of promoting personal edification, physical sturdiness and a sense of civic service among the poor and working classes.[11] From the 1880s, workhouses also reflected this development. In those institutions established by Reginald and Mary Brabazon, women used semi-skilled work to fulfil the principles of the 1847 Poor Law, to 'save the inmates of the workhouse from the terrible monotony of an idle life' by teaching them how to employ their idle hands usefully.[12] These venues later formed the institutional basis of the Soldiers' and Sailors' Workrooms for disabled veterans of the Boer War (established *c.* 1899). This institution, in turn, became the Lord Roberts Memorial Workshops and after-care clinic for disabled veterans (established *c.* 1904). In both the Workrooms and the Workshops, handicraft instructors and medical authorities promoted the idea that semi-skilled work was valuable in social terms as a means to reconstitute disabled persons' sense of individual and communal worth. Moreover, like the original Brabazon shops, the Workrooms and the Workshops were economically productive environments that attracted customers and extended the market for items made by retrained disabled men.[13]

These new attitudes also informed contemporary debates among English prison authorities about the meaning and purpose of institutional punishment and the value of work in convict prisons. These debates stemmed from the application of new scientific measurement to physical and psychological suffering.[14] Having lost faith in the promotion of self-discipline through deterrence, penal reformers claimed that prisons should seek to promote self-realization among inmates through direct therapeutic action, namely various forms of productive work. Such activity, reformers believed, was also useful for the efficient functioning of the institution itself. Despite opposition by some authorities, including Edmund DuCane, chairman of England's Prison Commission, these views took hold among prison officers. By the 1880s, convicts in local and military prisons were being put to work making their own uniforms as well as mailbags for the Post Office and mats, paperclips, packing cases, notice frames and twine and gunny bags for the Admiralty and the Office of Works.[15] Gladstonian penal reform at the turn of the century led to further amelioration of the harsher aspects of penal servitude under the guidance of a more expansive yet less punitive state. Like the orthopaedic centre and the workhouse, therefore, the contemporary convict prison was also becoming a regimented arena of industry where reform-minded observers promoted work not simply as virtuous but also as scientifically worthwhile in terms of advancing personal, institutional and national standing.

Organized and administered by hospital authorities along simultaneously moral, medical and scientific lines, the 'curative workshops' at Shepherd's Bush functioned as productive work environments intended to heal and to retrain disabled soldiers while benefiting the economy of the medical service. Three groups constituted the support base of the Shepherd's Bush scheme: the War Office, the British Red Cross and the public. An examination of how Jones and his colleagues mobilized the aid of each of these institutions reveals key features of the shops themselves and of the multi-faceted official view of disabled soldiers.

From the outset of the Great War, the British government demonstrated little interest in providing comprehensive post-operative treatment for soldiers who sustained severe injuries in battle. Owing to manpower needs and to limited finances, military policy dictated that disabled cases should receive a short period of treatment followed either by quick return to or, if the case warranted, by discharge from, military service. After-care, the government insisted, should be prescribed only after military discharge and under the sponsorship of voluntary-aid organizations like the British Red Cross.[16]

However, in the spring of 1915, when the military began to return increasing numbers of disabled men home for treatment, Robert Jones argued that the government's existing policy on wounded soldiers was inadequate. It provided for the discharge of disabled cases before proper surgical after-care. Moreover, it exempted the state from the essential responsibility of rehabilitating men who could no longer serve their country. As Jones explained in a letter to Alfred Keogh, Director General of Army Medical Services, there was essentially 'a want of cohesion between departments of treatment, such as massage, physical exercises, electricity and manipulative and operative groups of cases, all of which, properly controlled, make for success in orthopaedic surgery'.[17] What was needed in lieu of this situation, Jones argued, was a comprehensive system of state-sponsored after-care, one that could provide an extended period of recovery and continuity of treatment directed toward efficient and complete restoration of locomotor function. Jones concluded that the country required a central hospital where all existing resources could be brought together to bear on the problem of the war disabled.

In late 1915 the government accepted Jones's plan as a viable strategy for dealing with increasing numbers of wounded soldiers. Soon after this acceptance, however, Jones received word that, while the government had approved his plan, it had insisted that finance of such a programme had to remain the preserve of voluntary aid.[18] This policy, a turning point in the development of his scheme, led Jones to refashion the purpose of Shepherd's Bush and the identity of the disabled servicemen who were beginning to receive treatment at the hospital.

From late 1915 both the Joint War Committee and the British public became the foci of intense fund-raising efforts by the chief administrator of the Shepherd's Bush workshops, Manuel II, the deposed King of Portugal.[19] A key element of this campaign involved Manuel himself 'travelling around the country, more or less like a missionary, to explain what it means for the wounded soldiers as well as for the nation to have orthopaedic centres established, with curative workshops attached to them'.[20] On his travels, Manuel emphasized the practical potential of the hospital, essentially redefining the identity of disabled soldiers. Though still crippled in medical terms, he claimed, these men were nonetheless able-bodied individuals who in the workshops could learn new trades and how to regain productive lives after the war. Such appeals were successful in raising voluntary aid for Shepherd's Bush. In October 1916 the Joint War Committee awarded an initial £1,000 grant to Shepherd's Bush based on its agenda to cure and to retrain disabled soldiers. This sum was followed by a £10,000 grant in 1918. Supplementing these funds throughout the war were thousands of pounds donated by the public directly both to Shepherd's Bush and to its associated orthopaedic facilities in the provinces.[21]

Voluntary aid helped to open Shepherd's Bush and keep it operational. However, Jones and his colleagues knew that in order to extend the scope of their work both within the institution and around the country they needed to gain further military authorization and even greater financial support. To achieve these goals, they further manipulated their rehabilitative scheme and the role of disabled soldiers in it. Appealing to the government's concern about the finance of medical services, they constructed an image of the hospital as a factory and identified soldier patients in this environment as able-bodied and efficient workers. As Jones explained in a 1917 speech to the Royal Institute of Public Health, disabled soldiers were 'an essential part of the economic manpower of the nation, independent producers and wage-earners and not helpless dependents'.[22] Playing on the view of women held by the government and the industrial sector of the war economy, Jones thus aligned his conceptualization of retrained disabled soldiers to address concerns about the wartime paucity of labour generally and the economic state of the military medical system in particular.[23]

This approach helped to win Jones the official authorization he needed to expand the Shepherd's Bush programme itself and to establish associated regional orthopaedic centres. In October 1916 he received a £500 grant from the War Office to support the maintenance of new shops at Shepherd's Bush.[24] Subsequently, in November 1918, he received from the War Office 'an unlimited sum for maintenance' of all shops that were part of or associated with the Shepherd's Bush plan, including those established at sixteen regional orthopaedic facilities,[25] which by the end of 1918 were caring for nearly 15,000 disabled servicemen.[26]

From the perspective of government officials, this network of orthopaedic centres was an essential component of post-war reconstruction. As a War Cabinet secretary suggested in a March 1917 memorandum to Prime Minister David Lloyd George, it was an effective way to prepare a soon-to-be-enfranchised population for participation in local and national political life. If the 'whole local machinery for the registration and supervision of the disabled' is not 'carefully thought out', the secretary wrote, the government 'risk[s] opportunities for training being lost and the country being saddled with thousands of untrained idle pensioners, who will ever be available as object lessons to which political wire-pullers can appeal'.[27] Like the People's Budget of 1909, therefore, which sought to rekindle enthusiasm for further liberal social reform in part by providing better pension schemes for veterans,[28] government policy toward disabled soldiers was intended to make these men healthy citizens for the benefit of post-war reconstruction.

An analysis of the curative function of the Shepherd's Bush programme underscores the connections between the rehabilitation of disabled soldiers and official concerns about health, society and economy. In a 1941 speech to the British Association of Occupational Therapists, G.R. Girdlestone, one of Robert Jones's colleagues at Shepherd's Bush, recalled that in the early summer of 1916, when bedside occupations like embroidery, raffia work and basket work were introduced to make daily hospital life more pleasant for the disabled soldier patients, authorities at Shepherd's Bush began to realize the value of such occupations in 'preserving men's mental and physical fitness'.[29] In the summer of 1916 this realization ultimately resulted in the construction on the hospital quadrangle of what authorities called the 'curative workshops'.

The first three of these shops opened in October 1916, becoming the nucleus of the hospital's rehabilitation strategy. They included a direct curative shop, in which disabled soldiers received various forms of mechanical therapy; a central shop, which contained a smithy fitted with an electric forge and anvils; and a site for commercial photographic work. The rapid growth of these sites attests to their great success. Within less than a year, hospital authorities used soldier patient labour to help construct and maintain fifteen additional shops. In engineering shops disabled soldiers repaired motor-car engines, enamelled frames, relacquered fittings and re-upholstered seat cushions. In artistic shops they made decorations for the hospital chapel and wards. In the carpentry shops soldiers made hospital furniture, shelves and cupboards for the institution. And in other shops there were materials for them to learn tailoring, cigarette making, French polishing, signwriting and fretwork.[30]

Three related criteria determined the kind of work done in the shops. Above all, work that was primarily vocational in character had to move muscles and limbs in ways comparable to work intended strictly as medical therapy. Moreover, the trades taught in the shops were those that authorities saw as growing and non-seasonal, that is, work that could provide long-term employment and a decent wage. What was important in this regard was not specialization in any one trade, but work in a number of 'standard trades'. This was the best means of increasing the chances of disabled men at gaining fruitful employment upon discharge. Finally, authorities considered the previous occupations and personal preferences of the men to be vital in what trades were taught in the shops.[31]

Authorities believed that surgery was vital in the uninterrupted system of care offered at Shepherd's Bush, but from late 1916 they consistently held that the curative shops were the centrepiece of the programme for the way in which they gave attention to the physical and psychological conditions of disabled men. The shops were 'a priceless therapeutic boon', Jones claimed, because they established an atmosphere of activity and usefulness, which counterbalanced the monotony of hospital life generally and that of physiotherapeutic activity in particular.[32] The shops, Jones added, effectively rearranged the daily routine and spatial environment of the hospital. From their opening in 1916 until their period of full development in late 1918, they were part of the daily routine of an average of half the patients resident in the hospital.[33] Delineating specific periods of work during each planned five-hour hospital day, Jones explained, this arrangement 'enabl[ed] convalescent patients who were still receiving one or two treatments to work regularly … and cases [who] were receiving three treatments a day to work for shorter hours'.[34] The workshops also became prominent features of the architecture of the hospital. Designed to 'create an atmosphere of contentment among the men', they effectively extended the traditional healing arenas, the ward and operating room.[35]

Jones was proud of the fact that the shops set Shepherd's Bush apart from most hospitals in the country. 'Those of us who have any imagination, cannot fail to realize the difference in atmosphere and *morale* in hospitals where the patients have nothing to do but smoke, play cards, or be entertained, from that found in those where for part of the day they have regular, useful and productive work.'[36] Jones's rationale for the shops was thus straightforward. Work broke up the monotony of hospital life and helped the physical and mental healing process generally. It also gave social value to rehabilitation

The workshops at Shepherd's Bush involved two kinds of active curative treatment in mechanical-therapeutic terms, 'direct and indirect'.[37] Direct mechanical therapy was used 'when we give a man with a stiff shoulder paperhanging or whitewashing, in order to loosen [his shoulder]; or screwing to pronate or supinate his arm, or a plane to mobilise his wrist'. Indirect therapy was used in the case of patients with stiff limbs that they were not likely to use. As Jones put it:

> He may be given a job to do with his hands. In the interest which the work inspires he forgets to nurse his foot, which almost unconsciously and often very rapidly becomes again mobile. A knee joint which could not bear the continued strain of working a treadle will, perhaps, improve in function quickly, which the patient, forgetful of his injury, is working with a saw.[38]

Jones called this indirect therapy 'psychological curative treatment'. It involved disabled soldier patients literally working their own bodies to the end of 're-educating' his own muscles. The right balance of work had to be maintained so that the activity did not 'fatigue [the disabled limb] and so impede recovery'.[39]

Like therapeutic work, vocational work helped to define the disabled soldier as a functional individual. 'He is like a great schoolboy,' Jones observed, 'and with tact and sympathy he can be led by a silken cord'. For all disabled cases, Jones argued further '"From hospital to industry", should become their aim. They should be pulled back from the "blind alleys" of labour. Unless this is done, a great tragedy will occur when the war ends and the wounded soldier is displaced by a more competent worker.'[40] This moralistic configuration of the disabled soldier thus identified him as a member of an undifferentiated working class whose energy could be harnessed to help him build his own 'bridge' from military to civilian life.[41]

By mimicking a classroom environment where disabled soldiers could feel and be productive and useful, the workshops also served to counter the idea among many patients that they would never again be able to work, or would never again be able to earn their living when they were discharged from the army.[42] The shops were intended to be productive centres that sought to help men realize for themselves how wrong they were about their disabled bodies, their usefulness to their communities and their role as productive workers. As Jones explained at the 1918 Inter-allied Conference, these sites helped to 'create a more complete atmosphere of satisfaction amongst them and to give them every possible chance of again becoming useful citizens to their country'.[43]

The fact that authorities actually conceived disabled soldiers as workers for the institution underlines the socio-economic value that authorities attached to the hospital's rehabilitation scheme. In many shops, soldiers produced basic hospital supplies and essential medical equipment, including surgical splints and boots, artificial limbs, operating tables and 'Sinclair' and 'Balkan' surgical frames. Between October 1916 and March 1917 disabled servicemen who were either largely cured of their injuries or already skilled at using their artificial limbs produced over 1,600 splints of two dozen different varieties. During the same period, in workshops for patients who still required treatment by prescribed work therapy, over 2,000 splints were made and over 1,000 were repaired and altered.[44] And by late 1917, nearly all of the new regional orthopaedic centres had installed facilities similar to these 'Orthopaedic Shops'. Together, they constituted a closely associated network of orthopaedic institutions, supported by a complex scheme of fund raising, purchasing, selling and trading for the supply of military hospitals generally and the orthopaedic centres in particular. From the perspective of medical authorities, the disabled soldier's time, energy and first-hand experience of medical equipment were directed toward the construction, repair and improvement of surgical after-care equipment, including artificial limbs. He became a productive member of his own hospital community as well as of communities of men receiving care in regional orthopaedic facilities.[45]

This arrangement, as the commanding officer of Shepherd's Bush observed, enabled disabled men to 'profit' from their own work in the shops, as 'they have in many cases been able to suggest improvements in older patterns of splints'.[46] Here, then, was soldier patient labour that benefited not only the man himself but also his immediate community and the wartime medical service generally. Further emphasizing the economic value of this labour, Manuel pointed out that:

> the gross value of the work done by the patients in the curative shops, including the value of time and materials used, had been £3,209 11*s*. 5*d*., while the actual net saving to the hospital by reason of the work being done in the hospital and not outside was £2,315 1*s*. 6*d*. The last figure was arrived at after deducting the cost of all materials, depreciation of machinery and tools, salaries of paid instructors, sundry expenses, etc.[47]

In light of such statistics Manuel concluded that the shops 'had the enormous advantage of being, not only a more speedy means of obtaining the necessary articles than would have been the case if we had to produce them outside, but also a very considerable economy to the State'.[48] Authorities at Shepherd's Bush underscored this message through hospital publicity postcards, which plainly depicted the workshops as factories and soldier patients as efficient workers.[49] Figure 19 depicts one of the ten cards produced. Significantly all ten of these cards were themselves products of soldier patient industry, being made by disabled men in the hospital's own print shop, and sold by administrators to raise money for the institution.

The similarity between these photographs and those of contemporary factories suggests that authorities intended to represent the hospital to the government and to the public not as a place of rest and healing but rather as an efficient workplace and an arena of retraining. Fitting with the rhetoric of curative and vocational work extolled by Jones and his colleagues, these images demonstrate how officials visually shaped the identity of the disabled soldier as a self-healing machine, a mechanism to be retrained for personal and familial welfare and an efficient human motor for the state at war.

But even as Shepherd's Bush exemplified these factory-like characteristics, it distinguished itself from the wartime workplace in two ways. First, whereas munitions work was directed primarily toward achieving sufficient production of the weapons of war,[50] labour in the Shepherd's Bush was intended to help 'remedy the general discipline problems of the orthopaedic institution', where interesting activity was limited to 'breaking rules', experiencing 'the mild excitement of coming before the commanding officer' and 'having a grievance to grumble about'.[51] Authorities thus intended hospital work to stem these potentially disastrous situations and to deter disabled men from becoming 'foci of seething discontent and ... a menace to successful recruiting'.[52]

Hospital work also distinguished itself from factory work on the grounds of remuneration. While women workers in munitions factories were paid for 'doing their bit', albeit under circumstances of 'dilution',[53] soldiers at Shepherd's Bush received no remuneration for shop work beyond either soldier's pay or pension.[54] In addition, all hospital work was theoretically mandatory.[55] As Jones explained, 'No rigid lines are drawn round the work, but it is constantly enlarged and adapted, giving full play to the initiative and freewill of the patients ... depending largely upon the psychological element to help in the recovery. By this 'psychological component' Jones meant an arrangement that involved specific measures designed to compel participation in workshop work. These included 'gentle methods of persuasion' like 'sympathy and patience' to build a 'spirit of trust' between staff and patient and 'certain privileges, such as permission to wear khaki instead of the hospital blue or grey; [and] more frequent passes out of the hospital'.[56] Promotion of work in this way, Jones believed, helped to create an environment in which authorities could effectively heal and retrain the disabled while stemming disenchantment among them.

Significantly, British authorities looked to 'mandatory' Continental rehabilitation schemes as a means of differentiating the 'voluntary' work

Figure 19 Postcard showing the stock splint shop at Shepherd's Bush, *c.* 1916–18

schemes at Shepherd's Bush and its associated regional hospitals. I.G. Gibbon, a War Cabinet secretary, observed that in France and Germany 'special measures have to be adopted to induce the disabled generally to take advantage of the opportunities of restoration and training which may be available for them. So great is the difficulty that compulsion has been suggested in some quarters.'[57] Similarly, in his speech to the first Inter-allied Conference on the After-care of Disabled Men, Arthur Boscawen, MP and Parliamentary Secretary to the Ministry of Pensions, criticized Continental schemes by way of praising the British efforts. In French and Belgian hospitals, Boscawen explained, 'the man himself appears to have little voice in deciding his future, while a battle royal between the doctor and the technical expert often rages over his mutilated body'.[58] Considering the fact that British authorities were themselves torn between using a carrot- or a stick-type approach to making their patients work suggests that both Gibbon and Boscawen could well have been describing the approach taken by Jones and his colleagues. These reports testify to the battle that was indeed being fought in Britain over the disabled soldier's body, one that was intimately connected with official concerns about health, society, economy and politics.

Evidence suggests that soldier patients viewed hospital work with resentment at best. Despite assurances by government and military-medical authorities to the contrary, soldiers feared that their well deserved, albeit meagre, pensions would be reduced or, worse, taken away completely because they were making efforts to compensate for their disabilities.[59] Thus soldier patients often refused work altogether, rebelling when work time in the hospital impinged on what they saw as well deserved recreational time. As an instructor at the Roehampton shops suggested in a report to the executive committee of the hospital, patients consistently refused to attend his classes, preferring to take advantage of fresh-air cures, which included river-boat outings on the Thames.[60]

Many disabled soldiers also saw hospital work as a 'kind of charitable action', comparable to being sent to the workhouse.[61] This view had been articulated by medical authorities and newspaper columnists since early 1915. It became more pronounced after early 1917, when many local pension committees were still sending disabled cases to the workhouse, despite the existence of regional orthopaedic facilities.[62] Even when this was not the case, disabled men and their families 'loathed' Government Relieving Officers who visited orthopaedic hospitals, regarding them as 'the front doorstep to the Workhouse'.[63]

This animosity became more pronounced toward the end of the war even as the British Legion lobbied the government for a law that would oblige employers to hire retrained disabled soldiers.[64] As it had done throughout the war, the government insisted that employment schemes for the disabled should remain the preserve of the voluntary sector.[65] The outcome of the Legion's efforts, the King's National Roll scheme, only encouraged employers to take on disabled ex-servicemen to a minimum of 5 per cent of their work force.[66] By 1926, 28,000 firms were participating in this scheme, employing 365,000 disabled ex-servicemen.[67] But the National Roll was not as successful as these numbers suggest. For the most part, it provided temporary work schemes that became vulnerable to elimination as the economy became more depressed and unemployment rates soared. Moreover, the National Roll failed to stave off the tendency of government and private employers to prefer to hire able-bodied men in the post-war work force. Disabled veterans thus found it difficult to compete with the able-bodied for an ever shrinking pool of jobs.

The publications of veterans' groups clearly registered these concerns. From 1916 the Association of Ex-service Civil Servants, which represented the interests of many disabled veterans, fiercely supported 'the principle of the right of ex-servicemen to priority and consideration for permanent posts in Government offices and to something more than a mere struggle for existence'.[68] And from 1917 the Association of Disabled Sailors and Soldiers levelled harsh criticism at women workers who took jobs from deserving veterans.[69] Veterans' groups also accused trade unions of ruining any chances of the retrained disabled veteran gaining decent employment.[70]

Like the King's Roll, Shepherd's Bush ultimately failed to achieve its goal of successfully rehabilitating the men who 'did their bit'. The hospital provided comprehensive after-care for disabled soldiers until 1922, when government authorities transferred the facility from the possession of the War Office to the Ministry of Pensions (MOP). This transfer did not go smoothly. Since the establishment of the MOP, government officials had been increasingly 'uncertain where the duties and obligations' of this department and the War Office 'began and ended'.[71] At the same time, the Council of the Royal College of Surgeons raised concerns about orthopaedic specialists continuing to claim an area of surgical after-care that had traditionally been the territory of the general surgeon.[72] Between 1922 and 1924 Jones made numerous appeals in the *Times* for public support of the hospital. His efforts ultimately failed and in April 1925 Shepherd's Bush ceased to exist when the government returned the building to the control of the Hammersmith Board of Guardians.

In light of the promising rhetoric of work extolled at Shepherd's Bush and its counterpart institutions across the country, disabled men, like many working women, ultimately found themselves being swept out of the labour market. But whereas women could reclaim their roles as mothers, sisters, daughters and wives in homes fit for heroes, disabled ex-servicemen faced substantial difficulty in reclaiming their role as breadwinners. Instead, they became the most conspicuous legacy of the war in Britain, a constant reminder of a generation lost, former heroes who, as one disabled ex-serviceman explained, now found themselves in a 'waste land' where they 'searched for work' with 'sickening heartbeats while being driven to prison or to beg for [their] bread in the streets'.[73]

Notes

1 John Galsworthy, foreword to *The Inter-allied Conference on the After-care of Disabled Men (Second Annual Meeting, Held in London, May 20 to 25): Reports Presented to the Conference (by various authors)* (London: HMSO, 1918), 14–15.

2 Koven, 'Remembering and dismemberment'; see Bourke, *Dismembering the Male* and Cohen, *The War Come Home*.

3 I am indebted to Roger Cooter's pathbreaking study of Shepherd's Bush in *Surgery and Society*, 113ff. Whereas Cooter is chiefly concerned with the implications of Shepherd's Bush for orthopaedics, I focus here on how this

institution and its work-oriented rehabilitation programme helped to shape the wartime and post-war identities of disabled soldiers.

4 Pick, *The War Machine.*

5 On the implications of wartime factory work for gender see especially Downs, *Manufacturing Inequality* and Woollacott, *On Her Their Lives Depend.*

6 Cooter, *Surgery and Society*, 105ff. On these points of continuity see also Koven, 'Remembering and dismemberment', 1186–1188 and Bourke, *Dismembering the Male*, 31–75.

7 Anson Rabinbach, *The Human Motor: Energy, Fatigue, and the Origin of Modernity* (Berkeley CA: University of California Press, 1990), 38.

8 Andrew Scull, Charlotte McKenzie and Nicholas Hervey, *Masters of Bedlam: The Transformation of the Mad-doctoring Trade* (Princeton: Princeton University Press, 1996).

9 Frederick Watson, *The Life of Sir Robert Jones* (London: Hodder and Stoughton, 1934), 50.

10 Ibid., 114ff. See also Cooter, *Surgery and Society*, 53–78.

11 Himmelfarb, *Poverty and Compassion*, 226–243.

12 'The Brabazon Employment Society', *The Times* (26 January 1899), p. 7.

13 'Employment for disabled soldiers and sailors', *The Times* (26 July 1905), p. 8.

14 Wiener, *Reconstructing the Criminal.* This development was certainly not uniform across the English prison system. Late-century penal reform measures, for example, did not improve conditions of imprisonment for debt. Victor Bailey has recently questioned the trend toward therapeutic work in English prisons. See Bailey, 'English prisons, penal culture, and the abatement of imprisonment, 1895–1922', *Journal of British Studies* 36:3 (1997): 285–324.

15 PRO, WO 33/47, Paper A.88, 'Report of Committee on the Employment of Military Prisoners' (1887). Acknowledging the economic benefits of productive work programmes in civilian prisons, this report emphasized the value of implementing these programmes in military prisons. Sean McConville has suggested that this trend in convict-prison work began earlier in the century. See McConville, *A History of English Prison Administration* I, *1750–1877* (New York: Routledge and Kegan Paul, 1981), 350–351 and *English Local Prisons*, 254–255.

16 *Reports by the Joint War Committee*, 248–253 and 732–744.

17 Jones to Keogh, as quoted in Watson, *Robert Jones*, 164–165. This correspondence also implied criticism of the general surgeon, who, as Jones saw it, could not effectively treat severe physical injuries. This criticism later prompted the Royal College of Surgeons to oppose Jones's naming of Shepherd's Bush a 'Special Military Orthopaedic Hospital'. From the perspective of the college, Shepherd's Bush represented a 'hoarding of disabled cases' and an attempt to 'break up surgery into sections'. See 'Report of Orthopaedic Committee', 16 July 1918, in Royal College of Surgeons, *Minutes of the Council of the Royal College of Surgeons, 1917–1919* (London: Taylor and Francis, 1919), 159–160.

map / plan the workshops

18 *Reports*, 732.

19 The Joint War Committee consisted of the British Red Cross and Order of St John. These organizations combined in 1914 for the duration of the war in an effort to provide the best possible aid to the country. Manuel had been a long-time supporter of the International Red Cross. After being deposed by republican forces during the Portuguese civil war, he emigrated to England, where British Red Cross officials placed him in charge of the organization's effort to establish curative programmes for soldiers.

20 *Reports*, 734.

21 Ibid., 733.

22 Robert Jones, 'The Problem of the Disabled' (lecture delivered at the Royal Institute of Public Health, 14 November), as reprinted in *American Journal of Orthopaedic Surgery* 16:5 (May 1918): 273–290.

23 Of the first 1,300 men who entered the hospital and passed through its workshops, no fewer than 1,000 were sufficiently rehabilitated to return to military action. See Cooter, *Surgery and Society*, 118.

24 *Reports*, 733.

25 Ibid., 733.

26 Robert Jones, 'Orthopaedic outlook in military surgery', *British Medical Journal* (12 January 1918): 41–45, at 42.

27 Thomas Jones, 'Notes on the Arrangements for the Treatment and Training of Disabled Soldiers', a War Cabinet memorandum dated 5 March 1917. House of Lords Record Office, Lloyd George Papers, F/79/15.

28 See Powell, *The Edwardian Crisis*, 44–48.

29 G.R. Girdlestone, *Occupational Therapy for the Wounded* (lecture given at the annual general meeting of the Association of Occupational Therapists, March 1941) (London: Association of Occupational Therapists, 1941), 7.

30 A plan of the 'curative workshops' at Shepherd's Bush is contained in D.H. Eade (ed.), *Organisation and Methods of the Military Orthopaedic Hospital, Shepherd's Bush, London W.* (London: n.p., *c.* 1918 (?)), 48.

31 Jones, 'The Problem of the Disabled'. See also Douglas C. McMurtrie, 'The rehabilitation of war cripples', *Medical Review of Reviews* (1918): 409–485.

32 Jones, address to the Inter-allied Conference on the After-care of Disabled Men, second annual meeting, as quoted in *Reports*, 253. James Mennell, Medical Officer in charge of the massage department at Shepherd's Bush, similarly observed the positive psychological effect that shop work had on patients. See Mennell, 'Massage in orthopaedic surgery', in Jones, *Orthopaedic Surgery of Injuries* (London: Oxford Medical Publications, 1921), 511–512.

33 'Meeting the problem of the war cripple: Fighting in the front-line trenches of the army of reconstruction is the American Red Cross', *American Red Cross Bulletin* 12 (London: American Red Cross, 1918), 6–7. At its opening in 1916, Shepherd's Bush contained 800 beds and roughly as many patients. By the following year, approximately half of this number was working in the curative workshops. See *Hammersmith Hospital and the Postgraduate Medical School of*

London: A Short History, 1905–1955 (London: Hammersmith Hospital, 1955), 9. Evidence suggests that when the number of patients at the hospital increased to nearly 1,200 in 1918, participation in the shops also increased to half this number. See 'Meeting the problem of the war cripple'.

34 Jones, *Notes on Military Orthopaedics* (New York: British Red Cross Society and Cassell and Co., Ltd., 1917), preface.

35 Manuel II, 'Scheme and organisation of curative workshops', in Jones, *Orthopaedic Surgery*, 629–644.

36 Jones, *Notes*, preface.

37 Watson, *Robert Jones*, 164–168.

38 Jones, 'The Problem of the Disabled'.

39 Jones, 'The Orthopaedic Outlook in Military Surgery', lecture delivered at the Hunterian Society on 2 June 1918, as reprinted in *British Medical Journal* (12 June 1918): 41–54.

40 Jones, 'The Problem of the Disabled'.

41 Jones, address to the Inter-allied Conference on the After-care of Disabled Men, second annual meeting, as quoted in *Reports*, 253.

42 Jones, 'The Problem of the Disabled'.

43 Jones, *Notes*, preface.

44 *Reports*, 253.

45 Reproduction of a magic-lantern slide depicting the 'Surgical Splint Shop' at the Queen Mary Hospital. A sign in the background announces, 'Bring your repairs'. Image held by Archives of Queen Mary University Hospital Library and Postgraduate Medical Centre, Roehampton.

46 Major Walter Hill, 'The training of the disabled: The Military Orthopaedic Hospital, Shepherd's Bush', *War Pensions Gazette*, 41 (August 1917), 40–41. The Red Cross similarly noted that hospital workshops 'had the enormous advantage of being, not only a more speedy means of obtaining the necessary articles than would have been the case if we had to produce them outside, but also a very considerable economy to the State'. *Reports by the Joint War Committee*, 1921, 248–253. See also 'Report by Sir John Tweedy and Mr Eccles of Royal National Orthopaedic Hospital's application to King's Fund for Hospital Extension', 7 January 1920. LMA (A/KE/255/7). According to this report, disabled soldiers who worked in the shops at the Royal National Orthopaedic Hospital, which were modelled on those at Shepherd's Bush, also helped to 'turn out efficient instruments at a much lower cost than is charged by the trade, and in less time'.

47 *Reports*, 252.

48 Ibid., 734.

49 The American Red Cross used similar images in it publicity pamphlets. See, for example, Douglas C. McMurtrie, *Reconstructing the Disabled Soldier* (New York: Red Cross Institute for Crippled and Disabled Men, 1918), especially 26.

50 Woollacott, *On Her Their Lives Depend*, 72.

51 Jones, 'The Orthopaedic Outlook', 42.

52 Letter from Jones to Sir George Makins, as quoted in Watson, *Robert Jones*, 147–148.
53 See Downs, *Manufacturing Inequality*, 33–43 and 82–85 and Woollacott, *On Her Their Lives Depend*, 27–30.
54 *Reports*, 150.
55 See clauses 16 and 17 of Ministry of Pensions, *Instructions and Notes on the Treatment and Training of Disabled Men* (London: HMSO, 1917), 8. Authorities certainly realized that this policy might well court disciplinary problems. Jones himself believed that it wasn't proper to link hospital work with the soldier's receipt of a pension. See official memorandum on the care of disabled soldiers written in November 1916 by Knowsley Derby, Undersecretary of State for War, to Lloyd George, which reveals Jones's position on this matter early in the development of Shepherd's Bush. Lloyd George Papers, House of Lords E/1/1/9.
56 Jones, *Notes*, preface. Jones echoed this statement in his address to the Inter-allied Conference on the After-care of Disabled Men, second annual meeting. Manuel similarly observed that although the work in the shops was 'ordered by the surgeon directly, and can therefore be considered as theoretically compulsory, it is still voluntary'. On the privileges used to promote work see *Reports*, 250.
57 I. G. Gibbon, 'Confidential Report to the War Cabinet from Intelligence Department, Local Government Board: Care of Disabled Soldiers in France and Germany', Lloyd George Papers, House of Lords F/79/15.
58 Arthur Boscawen, in *Report on the Inter-allied Conference for the Study of Professional Re-education and other Questions of Interest to Soldiers and Sailors Disabled by the War* (Paris, 8 to 12 May 1917) (London: HMSO, 1917), 3–10.
59 DeGroot, *Blighty*, 257–258. The meagre pension offered to disabled soldiers itself promoted grievances among disabled veterans. See 'The plight of the disabled soldier', *Labour Leader* (10 August 1916), p. 2; 'Disabled men's inadequate pension', *Call* (5 September 1918), p. 1; A.A. Watts, 'Disabled heroes: Pensions or pittances', *Call* (27 July 1916), p. 1, and 'The pensions and allowances scandal', *Call* (20 December 1917), p. 4.
60 J.M. Andrew, 'Employment Bureau and Instruction Classes, Queen Mary's Auxiliary Convalescent Hospital, Roehampton, Reports for May and June 1917', LMA (H02/QM/A).
61 This was the observation of T.J. Passmore, a member of the Birmingham Citizens' Committee, who spoke at the Inter-allied Conference on the After-care of Disabled Men, second annual meeting. See *The Inter-allied Conference on the After-care of Disabled Men (Second Annual Meeting, Held in London, May 20 to 25): Supplement to the Reports Presented to the Conference (by various authors)* (London: HMSO, 1918), 57. Passmore also pointed out that this view was widespread among the families of disabled soldiers.
62 *Hospital* (9 July 1917): 267 and Sidney Lee, 'Soldiers in workhouse infirmaries: sad cases after discharge', letter to the editor, *The Times* 9 April 1917, p. 8. The

Hospital also reported that the 'discharged soldier, technically capable of work, but really incapacitated and thrown aside [was] once more knocking at the infirmary door'. See *Hospital* (9 June 1917): 180. Public complaints about this phenomenon had been occurring since early in the war. See *Poor Law Officers' Journal* (22 October 1915): 1229.

63 Captain W.G. Wilcox, Organizing Secretary of the British Legion, Appeal Department, in a draft speech on 'raising funds for the relief of distress among ex-servicemen and their dependents', accompanying letter to General Haig, dated 16 January 1926, Papers of Field Marshal Haig (236/H/C) held in the National Library of Scotland.

64 DeGroot, *Blighty*, 260ff.

65 The Ministry of Labour, for example, provided retraining centres for ex-servicemen in its 'Government Instructional Factories', but it left the subsequent hiring of these men to the initiative of civilian employers. For an excellent description of how these government-run factories sought not to 'produce component or finished goods, but [rather] skilled men' see 'Ministry of Labour', *Memories: The Magazine of the 19th London Old Comrades' Association* 1:1 (June 1920): 23. Why the MOL took such a position is made clear in the minutes of the Cabinet Committee on Unemployment, which explained that it would be 'unwise' to do more than 'train' ex-servicemen, since 'owing to Trade Union objections and trade depression, there was a likelihood that the men trained would be unable to find employment'. PRO, CAB 27/114, Minutes of 14 September 1920 Meeting.

66 For an excellent description of the debate surrounding the King's Roll, whether it should be voluntary or compulsory, see the King's Roll National Council, 'Memorandum on Compulsory Employment of Disabled Ex-servicemen', item 3 on the council's agenda for 20 May 1924. Papers of Field Marshal Haig (Acc. 3155/236s) held in the National Library of Scotland.

67 DeGroot, *Blighty*, 260.

68 'The President's Message', *Live Wire: Official Organ of the National Ex-Service Men's Union of Temporary Civil Servants* 1:1 (1 June 1920): 2.

69 For criticisms of women see especially the series of poems entitled 'Fit for heroes', in the first volume of *Live Wire*. See also National Association of Discharged Sailors and Soldiers, *Proceedings of the First Annual Conference, held in Blackburn, 6 October 1917*, held in the IWM, Department of Printed Books.

70 See, for example, J. Paterson Bryant, 'Are we trade unionists?' *Live Wire* 1:12 (May 1921): 2.

71 Watson, *Robert Jones*, 210–212.

72 See note 18 above and J. Trueta, *Gathorne Robert Girdlestone* (Oxford: Oxford University Press, 1971), 27. For further details on this debate see 'Report of Orthopaedic Committee', 16 July 1918, in Royal College of Surgeons, *Minutes of the Council of the Royal College of Surgeons, 1917–1919* (London: Taylor and Francis, 1919), 159–160.

73 'How you were fooled', in J. Snooks, *To Hell with War* (London: National

Committee for the Declaration of Ex-servicemen against War/Holborn Labour Party Rooms, 1927), 3–4. On this phenomenon see especially Arthur Marwick, *The Deluge*, 284.

7

Conclusion: memories, legacies and landmarks

The Great War in Britain saw military authorities work independently and with voluntary-aid associations to prepare and repair men for battle. The culture of caregiving they developed from precedential knowledge and experience and from the exigencies of the conflict was not simply an essential part of the war machine. It was integral to shaping wartime experiences of soldiers and civilians alike. For soldiers, this culture helped to foster a comradeship of healing that combined with comradeship of the trenches to underscore sentiments of being a class apart from the rest of society. For the public, it served as a means to express appreciation of Tommy despite the existence of a true gulf in experience.

In rest huts located along the lines of communication, voluntary-aid workers emphasized traditional forms of religion and domesticity alongside established ideas of manhood to help men sustain their efforts as fighters and retain their traditional role as breadwinners. In so doing hut culture helped to satisfy official concerns about manpower, discipline and morale, particularly the expectations of military authorities that men should be well rested soldiers prepared for battle. Hut culture also met the expectations of the men themselves, who felt deserving of familiar comforts, the company of women and the right to manage and spend what money they had as they chose. The emergence of huts as practical places of business, aligned with concerns about wartime profiteering, underscored the identity of the soldier as a consumer of the comforts available to him in the wartime public sphere. Voluntary-aid efforts to raise funds and attract named sponsorships for homes away from home also served wartime propaganda needs. These aid efforts gave the public an opportunity to express support of the war effort and of the soldier's service.

Wartime reflections on rest huts, especially huts established by the YMCA, conveyed the sense of masculine comradeship that the culture of these sites helped to foster among their soldier patrons. Post-war recollections of rest huts seem to underscore the wartime *espirit de corps* that centred on hut culture. In his memoir published one year after the Armistice Captain Jeffrey Ramsay recalled YMCA huts and their women workers being 'a *vital factor* in the carrying-on of the struggle'. He encouraged his readers to:

> Imagine a crowd of soldiers arriving in a vast camp officers and men alike hungry and tired after their long journey on sea or land. They may, or may not, have finished their Army ration, but there is nothing on earth which cheers them so thoroughly as a cup of hot tea of coffee at a Y.M.C.A. canteen. And no praise is too great for the devoted band of women who work without ceasing for the welfare of the troops ... And their work – to it there is no end. We tell them that they represent a kind of magic carpet: one has only to ask for anything and, *presto*, it is there. From chocolate biscuits to 'footer togs', from boiled eggs in the early hours of a bitter morning to a last soothing cup of cocoa at night – if it is humanly possible one gets what one desires...[1]

Private Allan Jobson echoed Ramsay's view over ten years later in his own published memoir as he recalled the YMCA hut at Eastbourne's Summerdown Convalescent Camp in similar terms. Here, Jobson explained, 'day followed day across those Sussex hills, crammed with the incidentals of Army routine'.

> 'Form fours' was followed by 'Quick March' and such intricacies as fatigues, lectures on the hillside by youthful officers, inspection by this man and that and the incidental calls of 'Cook House', complemented the round. To say nothing of the hut labeled [*sic*] YMCA, where we drank tea, wrote letters and sang lustily, 'Keep the Home Fires Burning' and 'There's a Silver Lining'. Those hearty melodies to some were fraught with a catch in the throat ...[2]

Jobson found respite with YMCA once more near Le Havre harbour during the winter of 1916. There, he recalled, 'everyone discovered, under the snow, one of the most comfortable night's rest they had ever had. As snug as any hibernating creature ...'[3]

Like rest huts, general military hospitals registered concerns about wartime efficiency and economy as well as enduring ideas about and approaches to institutional caregiving. Conceived by many authorities as havens for heroes where comfort was supposedly a priority, hospitals became foci of official efforts to maintain discipline and morale among men and to win and sustain public support for the war effort. However, the positive rhetoric of military hospital culture stood in stark contrast to the experience of soldiers, who, even as they could appreciate hospitalization for offering respite from trench life, saw military hospitals as extensions of the larger, negative disciplining war machine. These institutions, with their harsh medical treatments, inadequate food, mandated clothing and gawking visitors, framed a continuation of the combined rationalization-anarchy-madness that soldiers experienced at the front. The front-line identity of soldiers as 'cog wheels' remained intact within military hospitals and became more defined through the kinship that emerged from common experiences of hospitalization and convalescence.

How this kinship manifested itself across ranks according to specific illness and injuries and how it played out between men and officers are questions that deserve attention in future research. We also need to consider how the wartime 'cog-wheel' mentality of weary, sick and wounded men, as well as their memories of hospital and convalescent life in general, changed over time after the war. Several post-war recollections suggest the role that the subject of caregiving played in memories of kinship among men who were quick to forget the worst aspects of the period. In a recollection of his journey to a civilian hospital commandeered for military use in connection with Manchester's Second General Hospital, Leonard Ounsworth emphazised the chaos of the process and the apparent insensitivity of the civilians around him:

> When we came out of Manchester station I'd never seen anything like it. The crowd was such that they had mounted police to hold it back...But you can imagine the hysteria when I tell you they were giving us such things as balaclava helmets in the middle of July. They gave us cigarettes, sweets, all sorts of things – enough to stock a shop – but balaclava helmets, I ask you! Of all the stupid things ...[4]

S.T. Kemp recalled his care and recovery in a more positive light. 'I spent three happy months at Brighton [where] the people...were so kind and understanding and they had many soldiers in blue at the hospitals. We were given free rides on the buses, free seats in cinemas and theatres, free approaches to the piers and often, yes often, these kind generous people of Brighton would buy cigarettes or sweets and give them to chaps who were seated or walking along the sea front ...'[5] Kemp's time in Brighton was especially memorable for the camaraderie it helped to foster: 'the very first time that I went out ... I left the tram at the Aquarium and walked across to the Promenade, there was Gus Ball (one member of my old Battalion) leaning against the railings with a pair of crutches and just one leg. How pleased we were to meet ...'

Victor Shawyer remembered his convalescence at Launceston's VAD hospital in a similar spirit. Launceston itself 'was a gem of a place and I loved every hour I had to stay there'. Shawyer recalled further:

> It appealed tremendously to my small town upbringing...Wonderful scenery, lovely country lanes along which we were encouraged, nay, almost compelled to stroll as part of our treatment and which, with the early spring around these parts, were already bursting with buds and leaves, primroses and violets. But, oh! Those hills! But we became accustomed to them. To see soldiers returning from walks, carrying bunches of flowers – primroses and anemones, etc. – which they had gathered on their walks, was a sight for sore eyes, especially when one remembers that only a few weeks earlier, these same men had been living a life of such awful vileness and exposure that it could and very frequently did kill horses and made beasts of men.[6]

Allan Jobson shared Shawyer's sense of serenity that led to feelings of camaraderie. At Eastbourne's convalescent depot, he recalled, 'the line of white tents, the whitewashed stones, the martial sounds and atmosphere welcomed the embryo soldier to the service of his country and to a fellowship, unique and abiding'. Jobson explained that:

> From South, North, West and East came these men with whom we were to live, eat and sleep. Whom we were destined to love or tolerate and be amused with or annoyed by the peculiarities that went to the making of the individual, our brother in the ranks. Soon sun and rain, the splash of the sea and the eternal parade ground, bronzed these pale faces of shops, officers and factories into premature veterans. In three brief years we were to experience all phases of war and crowd into service the lifetime of old campaigners.[7]

While the subject of caregiving served in personal recollections as a means to remember and to forget, it functioned in a similar fashion at the level of mass memorialization of the war. This process began long before the Armistice as battles yielded ever greater numbers of missing and dead and returned home unprecedented numbers of maimed men. Wartime memorialization involved healing the nation writ large, society as a whole coming to terms with life, death and suffering. As we have seen, sites of rest, recovery and rehabilitation played their own roles in this process, becoming foci of public interest in aiding and honouring the manhood of the nation. In many ways, these roles did not change after the guns fell silent and the need arose more than ever before to remember the

Figure 20 Front cover of *Remember! Work made by some of Britain's Crippled Heroes: Church Army work for Ex-Service Men* (London: Church Army Disabled Ex-service Men's Industries, *c.* 1918–19) (original in colour)

'glorious dead', the generation that survived the war in shattered form and those who lost lovers, husbands, fathers and brothers. Post-war memorialization therefore involved many wartime sites of healing taking centre stage to assist the nation in coming to terms with loss. Voluntary-aid authorities augmented wartime resources that complemented rest huts as these sites were gradually dismantled during demobilization. Missing Soldiers' Bureaus and Troubled Relatives' Bureaus of the Salvation Army served to comfort the bereaved, as did YMCA and Young Women's Christian Association (YWCA) hostels for soldiers' relatives and wives and Church Army hostels for 'graves pilgrims', relatives who needed assistance in locating and visiting the graves of loved ones.[8] By encouraging the public to 'Remember!', Church Army retraining schemes and hostels for disabled pensioners helped to heal the men they served as well as the nation coming to terms with loss (see Figure 20). Hundreds of similar memorial campaigns developed across the country as means to help survivors of the era, ex-servicemen and civilians alike, cope with loss. Only a fraction of these efforts have received our attention, and much work remains to be done before we can claim to have comprehensive study of the work of healing the nation both during and after the war.

Hospitals also became memorials. Statistics from the United Kingdom National Inventory of War Memorials reveal the extent of this phenomenon, which historians have only begun to explore.[9] Of the 33,000+ memorials connected with the Great War, nearly 650, or 1.9 per cent, involve hospitals in one respect or another. Nearly 275, or 0.82 per cent, are hospital buildings themselves.[10] How do these statistics compare with the numbers and types of other utilitarian memorials? What circumstances led contemporaries to establish war memorial hospitals, or to overlook these institutions in favour of more monumental sites of remembrance? How did objects function in tandem with memorial environments to help individuals and communities cope with loss? Consider the painting in the entrance hall of Cardiff Royal Infirmary, formerly King Edward VII Hospital War Memorial, that depicts the institution's commanding officer, matron and staff tending the head wounds of a bedridden soldier. How did this artefact serve as a war memorial in place of the hospital itself that effectively 'lost its memorial element' in 1923 when the institution gained its charter?[11] Down to the present day artefacts such as candlesticks, crosses, paintings and illustrations remain intact and prominently on display at Talbot House in Poperinghe. A 'home away from home' for soldiers during the war, this 'Every Man's Club' became afterwards and remains today a popular memorial site for visitors to France and Flanders.[12] What roles have objects played here and elsewhere as means to evoke memories of a generation lost? Ubiquitous every Armistice Day, paper poppies worn on our lapels help us remember not only the fallen but also the lives of those men broken by the war. How has the meaning of this artefact changed over time as subsequent wars have taken away lives, limbs and senses? As Great War Internet sites abound, trench art and other contemporary artefacts are readily available for purchase on the online market place eBay. How have such efforts and the commodification of wartime artefacts shaped our memory, and what will be their implications as we approach the centennial anniversary of the war? Answering such questions of memory and materiality and of meaning embedded in physical and virtual landscapes will open new avenues of research and enrich our understanding of the war and its legacy.[13] Our work can begin with any of these examples, or we can turn to the memorial banner hanging in the Consistory Court of Chester Cathedral, which commemorates the work of local auxiliary hospitals and their staffs during the war.[14] What is most striking about this artefact is the role that disabled soldiers played in its creation. Their assistance in its embroidery suggests the vital role they played in healing the nation shaping *matériel* for memorialization. But if the culture of caregiving helped to give them this opportunity, we cannot forget the role that it played with the war itself in what Miss Irene Rathbone, the wartime YMCA volunteer, described so aptly as the 'extinguishing and degrading of an entire generation'.

Notes

1 Jeffrey Ramsay, Captain, RAMC (TF), *The Outside Edge of Battle: Some Recollections of a Casualty Clearing Station* (Blackburn: Standard Press, 1919), 4–5.

2 Allan Jobson, Private, RAMC, *Via Ypres: Story of the 39th Divisional Field Ambulance* (London: Westminster Publishing Co., 1934), 3.

3 Ibid., 14.

4 Leonard Ounsworth, as quoted in an interview in Max Arthur, *Forgotten Voices of the Great War* (London: Random House, 2002), 168.

5 IWM, DOD, Papers of S.T. Kemp. 3644 85/28/1, 1973 memoir entitled 'Remembrance: The 6th Royal West Kent Regiment, 1914–1918'.

6 Papers of Bandsman Victor Shawyer held at the National Army Museum.

7 Jobson, *Via Ypres*, 1.

8 'The Salvation Army and National Service', *Salvation Army Year Book* (1919) (London: Salvationist Publishing and Supplies, 1919), 1 and Evelyn W. Moore, *Four Studies* (n.a.: Young Women's Christian Association, 1955), 27–33.

9 See Mark Connelly, *The Great War, Memory, and Ritual: Commemoration in the City and East London, 1916–1939* (London: Boydell Press, 2002); Angela Gaffney, *Aftermath: Remembering the Great War in Wales* (Cardiff: University of Wales Press, 1998); Alex King, *Memorials of the Great War in Britain: The Symbolism and Politics of Remembrance* (Oxford: Berg, 1998) and Jay Winter, *Sites of Memory, Sites of Mourning*. See also Watson, *Fighting Different Wars*.

10 The author collected these statistics in late September 2003.

11 See Gaffney, *Aftermath*, 93. A reproduction of this painting appears in Arnold S. Aldis, *Cardiff Royal Infirmary* (Cardiff: University of Wales Press, 1984), 25.

12 See Chapman, *A Haven in Hell*.

13 Work in these important directions has already begun, thanks to scholars who are willing to think across disciplines in order to assess the value of historical artefacts alongside written, printed and photographic sources. See especially Nicholas J. Saunders (ed.), *Matters of Conflict: Material Culture, Memory and the First World War* (London: Routledge, 2004).

14 A reproduction of this banner appears in Arthur R. Smith, *From Battlefield to Blighty: Frodsham Auxiliary Military Hospital, 1915–1919* (Wirral: Avid, 2001), 69–71.

15 IWM, DOD, Papers of Miss Irene Rathbone, 557 90/30/1, diary entry, 27 July 1918.

Select bibliography

Archival Sources

Bodleian Library

John Johnson Collection of Printed Ephemera

British Red Cross Archives, National Headquarters, London and Barnett Hill, Guildford, Surrey

Department files and other records relating to the work of the British Red Cross Society

Official reports, minutes and other records of the Joint War Finance Committee of the British Red Cross and Order of St John

Papers of Lord Wantage

Records of the Star and Garter Home for Disabled Sailors and Soldiers

Cambridge University Library

Church Army Archives held in the archives of the Bible Society

Cambridgeshire Collection and Local Studies Archive

Ramsey and Muspratt collection of photographs

Printed and photographic materials relating to the First Eastern General Hospital

Cambridgeshire Record Office, Shire Hall, Castle Hill

Printed and photographic material relating to the First Eastern General Hospital, Cambridge

Church Army Archives, Church Army Headquarters, Blackheath

Records and periodicals of the Church Army

Select bibliography

Cordwainers College Archive

Records of the College

Dorset House School of Occupational Therapy, Library and Archive, Oxford Brookes University, Oxford

Printed and photographic material relating to the First World War

East Sussex Record Office

Records of Chailey Heritage Hospital

Records of Steyning Workhouse

Printed and Photographic material relating to the Royal Pavilion Hospital for Indian Soldiers

Guildhall Library, London

Records of the City of London Asylum

Hammersmith and Fulham Archives and Local History Centre

Printed and photographic material relating to Shepherd's Bush Military Hospital

Hampshire Record Office

Correspondence, printed papers and architectural plans relating to Enham Village Centre, Hampshire

House of Lords Record Office

The papers of David Lloyd George

Imperial War Museum

Department of Documents: Papers of the following individuals: John B. Middlebrook, Miss M. Semple, Frederick William Sutcliffe, Reverend H.D.F. Pollock, Maurice F. Gower, G. Norman Adams, Frederick Davison, S. Norman, Captain Arthur Guy Osborn, L. Timpson, S. T. Kemp, Miss Irene Rathbone, Alfred Thomas, Lena Ashwell, H.J. Chappell, Rev. P.B. Clayton, Miss M. Denys-Burton, Captain L. Gameson, Miss L.J.D. Griffith, Miss Haigh, Miss D.E. Higgins, Miss R.B. Manning, Rev. M.W. Murray, Miss M.B. Peterkin, R.G. Prew, F. Orchard, R. Read, W. Robb, Miss D.C. Seymour, Osmund Smith, E.H. Stack, A. Thomas, L. Timpson, W. Tyrrell, Miss O. Whiffen, Howard Williams and H.B. Woods.

Department of Printed Books: Red Cross Collection; Women at War (Microfilm) Collection

Photograph Archive

Film and Video Archive

Department of Art

Select bibliography

Lambeth Palace Archives and Library

Correspondence and papers of Archbishop Randall Thomas Davidson

Leeds University Library

Liddle Collection of First World War Material, including papers of Signaller J. Cockcroft, Reverend H.B. Fawkes, Mrs Dorothy McCann, T.H. Newsome, S.J. Wallis, Private Harold Wilson, C.J. Woosnam and the YMCA

Leicestershire Record Office

Records of Evington War Hospital

Records of Leicester War Hospitals Committee (previously Leicester War Hospitals Games Committee)

Correspondence, photographs and printed material relating to Fifth Northern General Hospital, Leicester

London Metropolitan Archives

Records of the Charity Organisation Society

Records of King Edward's Hospital Fund for London

Records of Nightingale School

Nightingale Collection

Hospital records, including those of: School of Physiotherapists, St Thomas's; Guy's Hospital School of Physiotherapy; Queen Mary's Hospital, Roehampton

Lord Roberts Workshops archives held by the Forces Help Society and Lord Roberts Workshops, London

Records of the Soldiers' and Sailors' Help Society

Museum of London, Docklands

Records of the Port of London Authority

National Army Museum

Photograph Collection

Correspondence and papers of Field Marshal Lord Roberts

First World War Papers of Mary Francis Maxwell, Victor Shawyer and M. Harrison Purfleet

Papers of Bandsman Victor Shawyer

National Library of Scotland, Edinburgh

Papers of Field Marshal Haig

National Register of Archives (Scotland) and Scottish Record Office, Edinburgh

Records of the Scottish National Council of YMCAs

New York Public Library

Collection of First World War material

Norwich Record Office

First World War Papers of Canon W. Hewetson

Order of St John, Archives and Library, St John's Gate, London

Official reports, minutes and other records of the Joint War Finance Committee of the British Red Cross and Order of St John

Papers of Lord Wantage

Diary of Miss Daisy Dawson

Records of the Brigade Hospital

Records and reports of various individual hospitals and convalescent homes in the UK

Public Record Office, Kew

Document classes consulted include: CAB 4, 5, 24, 23, 27–29, 35–37, 42, 103; INF 4; LAB 6, 26; MH 47, 48, 79, 101, 106, 120; MN 2, 164, 156, 258; MUN 4, 7; NATS 1; PIN 9, 15, 28, 38, 56, 59, 67; WO 7, 23, 30, 32, 33, 60, 61, 68, 71, 73, 95, 106–108, 115, 123, 158, 161–163, 208, 222, 237, 241, 277, 293; WORK 69–76

Queen Mary's University Hospital Library and Archive, Roehampton

Printed material, manuscripts and photographs relating to the history of Queen Mary's Hospital

Royal College of Music

Correspondence and papers of Marion Scott (relating to Ivor Gurney)

Royal College of Surgeons of England

Printed material relating to the life and work of Sir Frederick Treves

Royal London Hospital, Archives and Medical College Library

Records and photographs of the Hospital, including its School of Physiotherapy

Salvation Army, International Heritage Centre, London

Collection of First World War material

Sheffield City Archives

Correspondence and papers of Henry Coward

Records of Painted Fabrics Ltd

Theatre Museum, Covent Garden

Correspondence and papers of Lena Ashwell

Thoresby Society, Leeds Local Historical Society
Correspondence and papers of Leeds Music in War-time Committee

University of Westminster Archives
Printed material relating to Regent Street Polytechnic

Wandsworth Local Studies Archive
Periodicals and other printed matter relating to the Third London General Hospital

Wellcome Library for the History and Understanding of Medicine, London
General Collection
Manuscript and printed material relating to the Mental After-care Association
Royal Army Medical Corps Muniments Collection
Western Manuscripts Collection

West Sussex County Record Office
Records of Royal West Sussex Hospital, Chichester
Material relating to officers hospital established at Slindon House
War diaries of Ralph Ellis

YMCA archives held by Geoffrey Palmer, Honorary Historian, London Central YMCA
Periodicals, diaries, correspondence, photographs and miscellaneous material relating to the history of the YMCA

Newspapers and periodicals

All the World
American Journal of Occupational Therapy
American Journal of Orthopaedic Surgery
American Journal of Psychiatry
American Physical Education Review
American Red Cross Bulletin, London
Annual of Physical Medicine
Architect's and Builder's Journal
Architectural Review
Archives of Occupational Therapy
Bath Bun: Book of the Bath War Hospital
British Journal of Physical Medicine
British Medical Journal
Brunswick Monthly: Official Organ of the Church Army Head Quarters
Builder

Building News and Engineering Journal
Bulletin of War Medicine
Call
Christian
Craigleith Hospital Chronicle
First Aid
First Eastern General Hospital Gazette
Gazette of the Third London General Hospital
Hospital
Hospital Gazette
Huddersfield War Hospital Magazine
Illustrated London News
Jackass: First Australian General Hospital Monthly
John Bull
Journal of Mental Science
Journal of the American Medical Association
Journal of the American Medical Women's Association
Journal of the Royal Army Medical Corps
Labour Leader
Lancet
Live Wire: Official Organ of the National Ex-Service Men's Union of Temporary Civil Servants
Liverpool Medical-Chirurgical Journal
Magazine of the Fifth London General Hospital
Magazine of the Fourth Northern General Hospital
Magazine of the Second Southern General Hospital
Magazine of the Third Western General Hospital
Medical Press
Medical Press and Circular
Medical Record
Medical Review of Reviews
Medico-Chirurgical Review
Memories: Magazine of the Nineteenth London Old Comrades
Military Chest
Music Student
Musical Quarterly
Nineteenth Century
Norfolk War Hospital Magazine
Poor Law Officers' Journal
Punch
Rattler: Magazine of the Third Southern General Hospital Somerville Hospital, Oxford
Red Cross Supplement
Red Triangle
Red Triangle Bulletin (A Weekly Supplement to the Red Triangle)

Return: Journal of the King's Lancashire Military Convalescent Hospital
Reveille
Salvation Army Year Book
Searchlight: Monthly Publication of the Royal Army Medical Corps
Social Hygiene
Socialist
Springbok Blue: Magazine of the South African Military Hospital, Richmond
Summerdown Camp Journal
Tailor and Cutter
Times
Transactions of the Medical Society of London
Treatment: Monthly Journal of Practical Medicine and Surgery
War Cry
War Pensions Gazette
World
Y.M.: The British Empire YMCA Weekly

Contemporary works: books, articles, and official publications

Bagnold, Enid. *A Diary without Dates.* London: William Heinemann, 1918

Benson, S.H. *A Few Specimen Advertisements Used in Recent Press Campaigns in Great Britain for the YMCA.* Designed, Written and Placed on Behalf of the YMCA by S.H. Benson, Ltd. London: S.H. Benson, Ltd, 1918.

Booth, Eleanor Florence Bramwell. *The Army Uniform.* London: Salvationist Publications and Supplies, 1920

Booth, Evangeline and Grace Livingston Hill. *The War Romance of the Salvation Army.* Toronto: William Brigges, 1919

Brabazon, Lord (ed.). *The Diaries of Mary, Countess of Meath.* London: Hutchinson and Co., 1928

Brabazon, Reginald. *The Soldier's Pocket Companion.* London: Charles Lockwood and Sons, 1915

Brereton, F.S. *The Great War and the R.A.M.C.* London: Constable and Co., 1919

Bryant, John. *Convalescence: Historical and Practical.* New York: Sturgis Fund of the Birke Foundation, 1927

Buckton, Catherine M. *Our Dwellings, Healthy and Unhealthy.* London: Longmans, Green, 1885

Burdett, Henry C. *Helps to Health.* London: Paul Trench, 1885

——. *Hospitals and Asylums of the World.* London: J. and A, Churchill, 1891

Burns, Mary (ed.). *The Pearl Divers: Picture of the Life and Work of Prebendary Carlile and the Church Army.* New York: n.a., 1920

Cairns, David Smith (ed.). *The Army and Religion: An Enquiry and its bearing opon the Religious Life of the Nation.* London: Macmillan, 1919

Camus, Jean. *Re-education of the Maimed.* Translated by W.F. Castle. London: Bailliere, Tindall and Cox, 1918

Cathcart, E.P. *Elementary Physiology in its Relation to Hygiene.* London: HMSO, 1919

Chapman, John. *The Medical Institutions of the United Kingdom: A History Exemplifying the Evils of Over-legislation.* London: Churchill, 1870

Cecil, Rupert William E. Gascoyne. *The Church Army: What it is and What it Does.* Oxford: Church Army Press, 1908

Church Army, *Holidays at Home.* n.p. [1914–18]

Clarke, George Herbert (ed.). *A Treasury of War Poetry: British and American Poems of the World War, 1914–1919.* New York: Hodder and Stoughton, 1919

Clayton, P.B. *Tales of Talbot House: Everyman's Club in Poperinghe and Ypres, 1915–1918.* London: Chatto and Windus, 1920

Clifford-Smith, J.L. *Hospital Management: Being the Authorised Report of a Conference on the Administration of Hospitals. Held under the Auspices and Management of the Social Science Association, 3 and 4 July 1883.* London: Kegan Paul, Trench and Co., 1883

Combe, R.G. Nicholson. *A Treatise upon the Law of Light: Including an Exposition of the Law relating to the Nature, Acquisition, Preservation and Extinguishment of the Easement, or Right to Light and the Remedies Afforded for the Protection of Window Lights.* London: Butterworth and Co., 1911

Copping, Arthur E. *Tommy's Triangle.* New York: Hodder and Stoughton, 1917

Crossett, Lewis Abbott. *The Real Truth about the YMCA.* London: n.a., 1918

Cunningham, Bertram. *This also happened On the Western Front.* London: Hazell, Watson and Viney, 1932

Dearle, Norman Burrell. *Industrial Training, with Special Reference to the Conditions Prevailing in London.* London: P.S. King and Son, 1914

Devine, Edward T. *Disabled Soldiers and Sailors: Pensions and Training. Carnegie Endowment for International Peace, Preliminary Economic Studies of the War.* Oxford: Oxford University Press, 1919

Disabled Society. *Handbook for the Limbless.* London: Disabled Society, 1920

Dunton, William Rush. *Occupational Therapy: A Manual for Nurses.* Philadelphia: W.B. Saunders Co., 1915

Eade, D.H. (ed.). *Organisation and Methods of the Military Orthopaedic Hospital, Shepherd's Bush, London W.* London: n.p., n.d., ca. 1918

Fraser, Helen. *Women and War Work.* New York: G. Arnold Shaw, 1918

Gadd, Arthur John. *Under the Red Triangle.* Gateshead: R. Kelly, 1918

Galton, Douglas. *Healthy Hospitals: Observations on Some Points Connected with Hospital Construction.* Oxford: Clarendon Press, 1863

Gordon, Hampden Charles. *Rhymes of the Red Triangle.* London: John Lane, 1917

Hansard. *House of Commons Debates*

Harris, Garrard. *The Redemption of the Disabled: A Study of Programmes of Rehabilitation for the Disabled of War and of Industry.* New York: D. Appleton and Co., 1919

Henderson, George. *The Experiences of a (YMCA) Hut Leader at the Front.* London: Simpkin, Marshall, Hamilton, Kent and Co., 1918

Inter-allied Conference on the After-care of Disabled Men. Second Annual Meeting, Held in London, May 20 to 25, 1918. Reports Presented to the Conference. London: HMSO, 1918

Jones, Robert. *Notes on Military Orthopaedics.* New York: BRCS and Cassell and Co., 1917

—— (ed.). *Orthopaedic Surgery of Injuries* (2 volumes). London: Oxford Medical Publications, 1921

Keith, Arthur. *Menders of the Maimed: The Anatomical and Physiological Principles Underlying the Treatment of Injuries to Muscles, Nerves, Bones and Joints.* London: Hodder and Stoughton, 1919

Koch, Theodore Wesley. *Books in Camp, Trench and Hospital.* New York: Rider Press, 1917

McKenzie, F.A. *Serving the King's Men: How the Salvation Army is Helping the Nation.* London: Hodder and Stoughton, 1918

Mackenzie, R. Tait. *Reclaiming the Maimed.* New York: Macmillan Company, 1918

Macpherson, W.G. *History of the Great War Based on Official Documents: Medical Services, General History.* London: HMSO, 1921

McMurtrie, Douglas C. *The Evolution of National Systems of Vocational Re-education for Disabled Soldiers and Sailors.* Washington DC: US Government Printing Office, 1918

——. *The Evolution of Systems of Vocational Re-education for Disabled Soldiers and Sailors.* Washington DC: US Government Printing Office, 1918

——. *Reconstructing the Crippled Soldier.* New York: Red Cross Institute for Crippled and Disabled Men, 1918

Ministry of Pensions. *Instructions and Notes on the Treatment and Training of Disabled Men.* London: HMSO, 1917

——. *Places of Worship.* London: J. Truscott and Son, 1918

Mitchell, P. *Memoranda on Army General Hospital Administration.* London: Bailliere, Tindall and Cox, 1917

Mott, John Raleigh. *Criticisms about YMCA War Work and Answers.* New York: n.p., 1919

Mouat, F.J. and H.S. Snell. *Hospital Management and Construction.* London: Churchill, 1883

Muir, Ward. *Happy, Though Wounded!* London: Country Life, *c.* 1917

——. *Observations of an Orderly; Some Glimpses of Life and Work in an English War Hospital.* London: Simpkin, Marshall, Hamilton, Kent and Co., Ltd., 1917

Murray, Mary. *The Salvation Army at Work in the Boer War.* London: Salvation Army International Headquarters, 1900

Nightingale, Florence. *Hospital Statistics and Hospital Plans.* London: Faithful and Co., 1862

——. *Notes on Hospitals: Being Two Papers Read before the National Association for the Promotion of Social Science, 1858.* London: John W. Parker and Son, 1859

——. *Notes on Matters Affecting the Health, Efficiency and Hospital Administration of the British Army.* London: Harrison and Sons, 1858

——. *Notes on Nursing: What It Is and What It Is Not.* London, Harrison and Sons, 1859

One of the Church Army Hut Superintendents on the Western Front. *Over the Top.* London: n.a., 1917

Prince of Wales' Hospital for Limbless Sailors and Soldiers, Wales and Monmouthshire, Cardiff: The Story of the Hospital. n.a.: n.a., 1918

Ramsey, J. and R.E. Rawson. *Rest-pauses and Refreshments in Industry.* London: National Institute of Industrial Psychology, 1939

Report of the Commissioners Appointed to Inquire into the Regulations Affecting Sanitary Conditions of the Army, the Organisation of Military Hospitals and the Treatment of the Sick and Wounded, with Evidence and Appendix. London: HMSO, 1858

Report of a Committee Appointed by the Secretary of State for War to Inquire into and Report on the Present State and on the Improvement of Libraries, Reading Rooms and Day Rooms. London: HMSO, 1861

Report on the Inter-allied Conference for the Study of Professional Re-education and other Questions of Interest to Soldiers and Sailors Disabled by the War, Held at Paris, 8 to 12 May, 1917. London: HMSO, 1917

Report Presented to the Army Council on the National Scheme for Co-ordination of Voluntary Effort Resulting from the Formation of the Department of the Director-General of Voluntary Organisations, Covering the Period September 1915 to April 1919. HMSO: London: 1919

Reports by Joint War Committee and the Joint War Finance Committee of the British Red Cross Society and the Order of St John of Jerusalem in England on Voluntary Aid Rendered to the Sick and Wounded at Home and Abroad and to British Prisoners of War, 1914-1919, with Appendices. London: HMSO, 1921

Richardson, Ethel. *Remembrance Wakes.* London: Heath Cranton, 1934

Roberts, Henry D. (ed.). *The Inter-allied Exhibition on the After Care of Disabled Men, Central Hall, Westminster, 20 to 25 May 1918, Catalogue.* London: Avenue Press, 1918.

Robinson, Gertrude. 'Musical therapeutics', *Medical Review of Reviews* 24 (February 1918): 92–4

Roscoe, Edward Stanley. *A Digest of the Law of Light.* London: Reeves and Turner, 1881.

Royal College of Surgeons. *Minutes of the Council of the Royal College of Surgeons, 1917–1919.* London: Taylor and Francis, 1919

Shipley, A.E. *The Open-air Treatment of the Wounded at the First Eastern General Hospital, Cambridge.* London: Hudson and Kearns, 1915

Snooks, J. *To Hell With War.* London: National Committee for the Declaration of Ex-servicemen against War/Holborn Labour Party Rooms, 1927

Tatham, Meaburn and James E. Miles (eds). *The Friends' Ambulance Unit, 1914–1919: A Record.* London: Swarthmore Press, 1920

Thomas, Charles and J.G. Russell Harvey. *Tommy's ABC.* Bristol: Bristol Branch Executive Red Cross Committee, 1916

Tommy in Hospital. *An Exhibition of Original Black and White Drawings by Patients and Staff of the Third London General Hospital, Wandsworth.* London:

Country Life, 1917

Treves, Frederick. *The King George Hospital: A Short Pamphlet History.* London: Abbey Press, 1915

Vredenburg, Edric Walcott. *West and East with the E.F.C. (Expeditionary Force Canteen).* London: Raphael Tuck, 1919

War Office. *General instructions.* London: HMSO, 1916

——. *Rules for the Management of Garrison and Regimental Institute.* London: HMSO, 1916

Watt, H.J. *The Psychology of Sound.* Cambridge: Cambridge University Press, 1917

Whitehair, Charles W. *Out There.* New York: D. Appleton and Co., 1918

Wilder, Robert Parmelee. *The Red Triangle in the Changing Nations.* New York: Association Press, 1918

Williams, J.E. Hodder. *The Father of the Red Triangle: The Life of Sir George Williams, Founder of the YMCA.* New York: Hodder and Stoughton, 1918

Yapp, Arthur. *The Romance of the Red Triangle: The Story of the Red Triangle and Service Rendered by the YMCA to the Sailors and Soldiers of the British Empire.* New York: Association Press, 1918

Young Men's Christian Association. *Red Triangle Handbook: Issued for the Personal Information of Workers in the Huts and other Institutes of the Association.* London: Red Triangle Press, 1917

Secondary works: books and articles

Abel-Smith, Brian. *Changes in the Use of Institutions in England and Wales between 1911–1951.* Manchester: Lockwood, 1960

——. *A History of the Nursing Profession.* New York: Springer, 1960

——. *The Hospitals, 1800–1948: A Study in Social Administration in England and Wales.* London: Heinemann, 1964

Adams, Ann Marie. *Architecture in the Family Way: Doctors, Houses and Women, 1870–1900.* Buffalo NY: McGill-Queen's University Press, 1996

Alderson, Frederick. *The Comic Postcard in English Life.* Newton Abbot: David and Charles, 1970

Alper, Helen (ed.). *A History of Queen Mary's University Hospital, Roehampton.* London: Richmond and Twickenham and Roehampton Healthcare NHS Trust, 1996

Anthony, P.D. *The Ideology of Work.* New York: Tavistock, 1978

Armstrong, David. *The Political Anatomy of the Body: Medical Knowledge in Britain in the Twentieth Century.* Cambridge: Cambridge University Press, 1983

Ashelford, Jane. *The Art of Dress, Clothes and Society, 1500–1914.* London: National Trust, 1996

Ashworth, Tony. *Trench Warfare, 1914–1918: The Live and Let Live system.* New York: Holmes and Meier, 1980

Audoin-Rouzeau, Stephane. *Men at War: National Sentiment and Trench Journalism in France during the First World War.* Translated by Helen McPhail. Oxford: Berg, 1992

Audoin-Rouzeau, Stephane and Annette Becker. *1914–1918: Understanding the Great War*. London: Profile Books, 2002

Bailey, Peter. *Leisure and Class in Victorian England.* Toronto: University of Toronto Press, 1978

Bailey, Victor. 'English prisons, penal culture and the abatement of imprisonment, 1895–1922', *Journal of British Studies* 36:3 (July 1997): 285–324

——. 'In darkest England and the way out: The Salvation Army, social reform and the labour movement', *International Review of Social History*, 29 (1984): 133–171

—— (ed.). *Policing and Punishment in Nineteenth-century Britain.* London: Croom Helm, 1981

Barnes, R. and J.B. Eicher (eds). *Dress and Gender: Making and Meaning in Cultural Contexts* Oxford: Berg, 1995

Barry, Jonathan and Colin Jones (eds). *Medicine and Charity before the Welfare State.* New York: Routledge, 1991

Benyon, H. *Perceptions of Work: Variations within a Factory.* Cambridge: Cambridge University Press, 1972

Biernacki, Richard. *The Fabrication of Labour: Germany and Britain, 1640–1914.* Berkeley CA: University of California Press, 1995

Binfield, Clyde. *George Williams in Context: A Portrait of the Founder of the YMCA.* Sheffield: Sheffield Academic Press, 1994

Bogacz, Ted. '"Tyranny of words": Language, poetry and anti-modernism in England in the First World War', *Journal of Modern History* 58 (1986): 643–668

Bonadeo, Alfredo. *Mark of the Beast: Death and Degradation in the Literature of the Great War* Lexington, KY: University of Kentucky Press, 1989

Bond, Brian. *War and Society, 1870–1970.* Oxford: Oxford University Press, 1986

Bourke, Joanna. *Dismembering the Male: Men's Bodies, Britain and the Great War.* London: Reaktion,1996

——. 'The experience of medicine in wartime', in John Pickstone and Roger Cooter (eds), *Medicine in the Twentieth Century* (New York: Harwood Academic Publishers, 1998

Bracco, Rosa. *Merchants of Hope: Middlebrow Writers of the First World War.* Providence RI: Berg, 1993

Braybon, Gail and Penny Summerfield. *Out of the Cage: Women's Experiences in Two World Wars.* New York: Pandora Press, 1987

Brittain, Vera. *Testament of Youth.* New York: Penguin Books, 1989

Butlin, Robin A. *Historical Geography: Through the Gates of Space and Time.* Oxford: Oxford University Press, 1993

Calder, John. *The Vanishing Willows: The Story of the Erskine Hospital.* Guildford: Biddles, 1982

Cantile, Neil. *A History of the Royal Army Medical Department.* London: Churchill Livingstone, 1974

Cecil, Hugh and Peter H. Liddle (eds). *Facing Armageddon: The First World War Experienced.* Barnsley: Pen and Sword, 1996

Checkland, Olive. *Philanthropy in Victorian Scotland: Social Welfare and the Voluntary Principle.* Edinburgh: John Donald, 1980

Chomeley, J.A. *History of the Royal National Orthopaedic Hospital.* London: Chapman and Hall, 1985

Cohen, Deborah A. *The War Come Home: Disabled Veterans in Britain and Germany, 1914–1939.* London: University of California Press, 2001

Collins, Lawrence Joseph. *Theatre at War, 1914–18.* New York: St. Martin's Press, 1998.

Connor, Jennifer J. 'Book culture and medicine', *Canadian Journal of Medical History* 12:2 (1995): 203–214

Cooke, Miriam and Angela Woollacott (eds). *Gendering War Talk.* Princeton NJ: Princeton University Press, 1993

Cooter, Roger. 'Medicine and the goodness of war', *Canadian Bulletin of Medical History* 7 (1990): 147–159

——. *Surgery and Society in Peace and War: Orthopaedics and the Origin of Modern Medicine, 1880–1940.* London: Macmillan, 1993

Cooter, Roger, Mark Harrison and Steve Sturdy (eds). *War, Medicine and Modernity.* Stroud: Sutton Books, 1998

——. *Medicine and Modernity.* Amsterdam: Rodopi, 1999

Creek, J. (ed.). *Occupational Therapy and Mental Health.* London: Churchill Livingstone, 1990

Cunningham, Hugh. *Leisure in the Industrial Revolution.* London: Croom Helm, 1980

de Grazia, Victoria and Ellen Furlough (eds). *The Sex of Things: Gender and Consumption in Historical Perspective.* Berkeley CA: University of California Press, 1996.

DeGroot, Gerald. *Blighty: British Society in the Era of the Great War.* New York: Longman, 1996

Delacy, Margaret. *Prison Reform in Lancashire, 1700–1850: A Study in Local Administration.* Stanford CA: Stanford University Press, 1986

Delaporte, Sophie. *Les Gueules Cassées: Les blessés de la face de la Grande Guerre.* Paris: Editions Noêsis, 1996

Denning, Michael. *Mechanic Accents: Dime Novels and Working-class Culture in America.* New York: Verso, 1987

Dickson, Gilbert. *The YMCA in Scotland, 1844–1994.* Edinburgh: YMCA Scotland, 1994.

Diehl, James M. (ed.). *The War Generation: Veterans of the First World War.* Port Washington, NY: Kennikat Press National University Publications, 1975

Digby, Anne. *Madness, Morality and Medicine: A Study of the York Retreat, 1796–1914.* Cambridge: Cambridge University Press, 1985

Donnelly, M. *Managing the Mind: A Study of Medical Psychology in Early Nineteenth-century Britain.* London: Tavistock, 1983

Downs, Laura Lee. *Manufacturing Inequality: Gender Division in the French and British Metalworking Industries, 1914–1939.* Ithaca NY: Cornell University Press, 1995

Driver, Felix. 'Discipline without frontiers?', *Journal of Historical Sociology* 3 (1990): 272–293.

——. *Power and Pauperism: The Workhouse System, 1834–1884.* Cambridge: Cambridge University Press, 1993

Duncum, B. 'The development of hospital design and planning' in F.N.L. Poynter (ed.), *The Evolution of Hospitals in Britain.* London: Pitman, 1964

Dunton, William Rush and Sidney Licht. *Occupational Therapy.* Springfield IL: Charles C. Thomas, 1950

Edwards, Tim. *Men in the Mirror: Men's Fashion, Masculinity and Consumer Society.* London: Cassell, 1997

Eksteins, Modris. *Rites of Spring: The Great War and the Birth of the Modern Age.* Boston MA: Houghton, Mifflin, 1989

Evans, Martin and Kenneth Lunn (eds). *War and Memory in the Twentieth Century.* Oxford: Berg, 1997

Evans, Robin. *The Fabrication of Virtue: English Prison Architecture, 1750–1840.* Cambridge: Cambridge University Press, 1982

Eyler, John M. *Sir Arthur Newsholme and State Medicine 1885–1935.* New York: Cambridge University Press, 1997

Fairbank, Jenty. *Booth's Boots: The Beginnings of the Salvation Army Social Work.* London: Salvation Army, 1985

Fiddes, Nick. *Meat: A Natural Symbol.* London: Routledge, 1992

Figg, Laurann and Jane Farrell-Beck. 'Amputation in the Civil War: Physical and social dimensions', *Journal of the History of Medicine and Allied Sciences* 48 (1993): 454–475

Foucault, Michel. *The Birth of the Clinic: An Archeology of Medical Perception.* Translated by Alan Sheridan. New York: Vintage Books, 1995

——. *Discipline and Punish: The Birth of the Prison.* Translated by Alan Sheridan. New York: Vintage Books, 1995

——. *Power/knowledge.* New York: Pantheon Books, 1980

Friedson, Eliot. *The Hospital in Modern Society.* New York: Free Press, 1963

Fuller, John. *Troop Morale and Popular Culture in the British and Dominion Armies, 1914–1918.* Oxford: Clarendon Press, 1990

Fussell, Paul. *The Great War and Modern Memory.* London: Oxford University Press, 1975

Gaffney, Angela. *Aftermath: Remembering the Great War in Wales.* Cardiff: University of Wales Press, 1999

Garland, David. *Punishment and Welfare: A History of Penal Strategies.* Brookfield VT: Gower, 1985

Gilbert, Sandra M. and Susan Gubar. 'Soldier's heart: Literary men, literary women and the Great War' in Sandra M. Gilbert and Susan Gubar (eds). *No Man's Land: The Place of the Woman Writer in the Twentieth Century* II, 258–323. New Haven CT: Yale University Press, 1989

Gillis, Leon. *Fifty Years of Rehabilitation at Queen Mary's Hospital, Roehampton.* London: British Council for Rehabilitation of the Disabled, 1989

Girdlestone, G.R. *Occupational Therapy for the Wounded: Lecture Given at the Annual General Meeting of the Association of Occupational Therapists, March, 1941.* London: Association of Occupational Therapists, 1941
Glover, Jon and Jon Silkin (eds). *The Penguin Book of First World War Prose.* New York: Penguin Books, 1990
——. *Foucault and the Writing of History.* Cambridge MA: Blackwell, 1994
Gosling, F.G. *Before Freud: Neurasthenia and the American Medical Community, 1870–1910.* Bloomington IN: University of Indiana Press, 1987
Gower, E.S. (ed.). *Queen Mary's Hospital, Roehampton: General Hospital and Limb Fitting Centre.* n.p.: *c.* 1960
Granshaw, Lindsey and Roy Porter (eds). *The Hospital in History.* New York: Routledge, 1989
Grayzel, Susan R. *Women and the First World War.* New York: Longman, 2002
——. *Women's Identities at War: Gender, Motherhood and Politics in Britain and France during the First World War.* Chapel Hill NC: University of North Carolina Press, 1999
Gregory, Adrian and Senia Paseta. *Ireland and the Great War: 'A War to Unite Us All'?* Manchester: Manchester University Press, 2002
Gregory, Adrian and Jay Winter (eds). *The Silence of Memory: Armistice Day, 1919–1946 (The Legacy of the Great War).* Oxford: Berg, 1994
Gritzer, Glenn and Arnold Arluke. *The Making of Rehabilitation: A Political Economy of Medical Specialization, 1890–1980.* Berkeley CA: University of California Press, 1985
Gullace, Nicoletta. *The Blood of our Sons.* New York: Palgrave Macmillan, 2002
——. 'White feathers and wounded men: Female patriotism and the memory of the Great War', *Journal of British Studies* 36 (April 1997): 178–206
Haley, Bruce. *The Healthy Body and Victorian Culture.* Boston MA: Harvard University Press, 1978
Hamlin, Christopher. *Public Health and Social Justice in the Age of Chadwick: Britain, 1800–1854.* Cambridge: Cambridge University Press, 1998
Hammersmith Hospital, *Hammersmith Hospital and the Postgraduate Medical School: A Short History, 1905–1955.* London: Hammersmith Hospital, 1956
Harding, Christopher, Bill Hines, Richard Ireland and Philip Rawlings. *Imprisonment in England and Wales: A Concise History.* Dover NH: Croom Helm, 1985
Hareven, T. *Family Time and Industrial Time.* Cambridge: Cambridge University Press, 1982
Harris, Charles. *Lord Haldane.* London: Oxford University Press, 1928
Harris, Jose. *Private Lives, Public Spirit: A Social History of Britain, 1870–1914.* Oxford: Oxford University Press, 1993
Harrison, Mark. 'The medicalization of war – The militarization of medicine', *Social History of Medicine* (September 1996): 267–276
——. 'Medicine and the management of modern warfare', *History of Science* 34:4 (1996): 379–410
Harvey, John. *Men in Black.* Chicago: University of Chicago Press, 1995

Haste, Cate. *Keep the Home Fires Burning: Propaganda in the First World War.* London: Allen Lane, 1977

Higonnet, Margaret (ed.). *Behind the Lines: Gender and the Two World Wars.* New Haven CT: Yale University Press, 1987

—— (ed.). *Nurses at the Front: Writing the Wounds of the Great War.* Boston MA: Northeastern University Press, 2001

Himmelfarb, Gertrude. *The Idea of Poverty: England in the Industrial Age.* New York: Knopf, 1984

——. *Poverty and Compassion: The Moral Imagination of the Late Victorians.* New York: Vintage Books, 1992

Hobsbawm, E.J. and T.O. Ranger (eds): *The Invention of Tradition.* Cambridge, Cambridge University Press, 1983

Hopkins, C. Howard. *History of the YMCA in North America.* New York: Association Press, 1951

Hutchinson, John F. *Champions of Charity: War and the Rise of the Red Cross.* Oxford: Westview Press, 1996

Hynes, Samuel. *The Soldiers' Tale: Bearing Witness to Modern War.* New York: Penguin Books, 1998

——. *A War Imagined: The Great War and English Culture.* New York: Collier Books, 1990

Ignatieff, Michael. *A Just Measure of Pain: The Penitentiary in the Industrial Revolution, 1750– 1850.* New York: Pantheon Books, 1978

James, W. Paul. *Hospitals: Design and Development.* London: Architectural Press

Jeffery, Keith. *Ireland and the Great War.* Cambridge: Cambridge University Press, 2000

Johnson, Valerie J. *Diet in Workhouses and Prisons, 1835–1895.* New York: Garland Publishing, 1985

Jones, Ann Hudson (ed.). *Images of Nurses: Perspectives from History, Art and Literature.* Philadelphia: University of Pennsylvania Press, 1988

Joyce, Patrick. *Visions of the People: Industrial England and the Question of Class, 1848–1914.* Cambridge: Cambridge University Press, 1991

——. *Work, Society and Politics: The Culture of the Factory in Later Victorian England.* New Brunswick NJ: Rutgers University Press, 1980

—— (ed.). *The Historical Meanings of Work.* Cambridge: Cambridge University Press, 1987

Kamminga, Harmke and Andrew Cunningham (eds). *The Science and Culture of Nutrition, 1840–1940.* Atlanta GA: Rodopi, 1995

Kent, Susan Kingsley. *Making Peace: The Reconstruction of Gender in Interwar Britain.* Princeton NJ: Princeton University Press, 1993

Kern, Stephen. *The Culture of Time and Space, 1880–1918.* Cambridge MA: Harvard University Press, 1983

King, A.D. (ed.). *Buildings and Society: Essays on the Social Development of the Built Environment.* London: Routledge and Kegan Paul, 1980

King, Alex. *Memorials of the Great War in Britain: The Symbolism and Politics of*

Remembrance. Oxford: Berg, 1998
Knight, Francis. *The Nineteenth-century Church and English Society*. Cambridge: Cambridge University Press, 1995
Koss, Stephen. *Lord Haldane: Scapegoat for Liberalism*. New York: Columbia University Press, 1969
Koven, Seth. 'Remembering and dismemberment: Crippled children, wounded Soldiers and the Great War in Great Britain', *American Historical Review* 99:4 (October 1994): 1167–1202
Laffin, John. *World War I in Postcards*. Stroud: Sutton Publishing, 1989
Leed, Eric J. *No Man's Land: Combat and Identity in World War One*. Cambridge: Cambridge University Press, 1979
Liddle, Peter H., Ian Whitehead and John Bourne. *The Great World War, 1914–1945: Who Won, Who Lost*. New York: HarperCollins Publishers, 2003
Lipovetsky, Gilles. *The Empire of Fashion: Dressing Modern Democracy*. Translated by Catherine Porter. Princeton NJ: Princeton University Press, 1994.
Louden, Stephen H. *Chaplains in Conflict: The Role of Army Chaplains since 1914*. London: Avon Books, 1996
Lucic, Karen. *Charles Sheeler and the Cult of the Machine*. Cambridge MA: Harvard University Press, 1991
Lynch, Donald. *Chariots of the Gospel: The Centenary History of the Church Army*. Worthing: H.E. Walter, 1982
MacDonald, Catriona M. M. *Scotland and the Great War*. East Linton: Tuckwell Press, 1998
Macleod, David I. *Building Character in the American Boy: The Boy Scouts, YMCA and their Forerunners, 1870–1920*. Madison WI: University of Wisconsin Press, 1983
Mandler, Peter (ed.). *The Uses of Charity: The Poor on Relief in the Nineteenth Century Metropolis*. Philadelphia: University of Pennsylvania Press, 1990
Mangan, J.A. *Athleticism in the Victorian and Edwardian Public School*. Cambridge: Cambridge University Press, 1981
Mansfield, Alan and Phillis Cunnington. *Handbook of English Costume in the Twentieth Century, 1900–1950*. Boston MA: Plays, 1973
Marwick, Arthur. *The Deluge: British Society and the First World War*. New York: Norton, 1965
Mason, Tony (ed.). *Sport in Britain: A Social History*. Cambridge: Cambridge University Press, 1989
Maurice, Frederick. *Haldane*. Westport CT: Greenwood Press, 1970
Mayer, Arno. *The Persistence of the Old Regime: Europe to the Great War*. New York: Pantheon Books, 1981
McConville, Sean. *English Local Prisons, 1860–1900: Next Only to Death*. New York: Routledge, 1995
——. *A History of English Prison Administration* I, *1750–1877*. New York: Routledge and Kegan Paul, 1981
McDonald, Lyn. *The Roses of No Man's Land*. New York: Penguin Books, 1993

Melman, Billie. *Women and the Popular Imagination in the Twenties: Flappers and Nymphs*. Baskingstoke: Macmillan Press, 1988

Messinger, Gary S. *Propaganda and the State in the First World War*. Manchester: Manchester University Press, 1992

Metcalf, Thomas R. *An Imperial Vision: Indian Architecture and Britain's Raj*. Boston MA: Faber and Faber, 1989

More, C. *Skill and the English Working Class, 1870–1914*. New York: St. Martin's Press, 1980.

Mosse, George L. *Fallen Soldiers: Reshaping the Memory of the World Wars*. New York: Oxford University Press, 1990

——. *The Image of Man: The Creation of Modern Masculinity*. New York: Oxford University Press, 1996

Murdoch, Norman H. *The Origins of the Salvation Army*. Knoxville TN: University of Tennessee Press, 1994

Murphy, Lamar. *Enter the Physician: The Transformation of Domestic Medicine, 1760–1860*. Tuscaloosa AL: University of Alabama Press, 1991

Myerly, Scott Hughes. *British Military Spectacle: From the Napoleonic Wars through the Crimea*. Cambridge MA: Harvard University Press, 1996

Nochlin, Linda. *The Politics of Vision: Essays on Nineteenth-century Art and Society*. New York: Harper and Row, 1989

——. *Women, Art and Power and other Essays*. New York: Harper and Row, 1988

Olson Jr, Mancur. *The Economics of the Wartime Shortage: A History of British Food Supplies in the Napoleonic War and in World Wars I and II*. Durham NC: Duke University Press, 1963

Ouditt, Sharon. *Fighting Forces, Writing Women: Identity and Ideology in the First World War*. New York: Routledge, 1994

Pahl, R.E. *On Work: Historical, Comparative and Theoretical Approaches*. New York: Blackwell, 1988

Panchasi, Roxanne. 'Reconstructions: Prosthetics and the rehabilitation of the male body in World War I France', *Differences* 7:3 (1995): 109–140

Peacock, John. *Men's Fashion: The Complete Sourcebook*. London: Thames and Hudson, 1996

Pedersen, Susan. *Family, Dependence and the Origins of the Welfare State*. Cambridge: Cambridge University Press, 1993

Peiss, Kathy. *Cheap Amusements: Working Women and Leisure in Turn-of-the-Century New York*. Philadelphia: Temple University Press, 1986

Pick, Daniel. *War Machine: The Rationalisation of Slaughter in the Modern Age*. New Haven CT: Yale University Press, 1993

Pickstone, John V. *Medicine and Industrial Society: A History of Hospital Development in Manchester and its Region, 1752–1946*. Manchester: Manchester University Press, 1986

—— (ed.). *Medical Innovations in Historical Perspective*. London: Macmillan, 1992

Poovey, Mary. *Making a Social Body: British Cultural Formation, 1830–1864*. Chicago: University of Chicago Press, 1995

Porter, Roy and Colin Jones (eds). *Reassessing Foucault: Power, Medicine and the Body*. New York: Routledge, 1994
Powell, David. *The Edwardian Crisis: Britain, 1901–1914*. New York: St. Martin's Press, 1996.
Poynter, F.N.L. *Medicine and Culture*. London: Wellcome Institute for the History of Medicine, 1969
Prior, L. 'The architecture of the hospital: A study of spatial organisation and Medical Knowledge', *British Journal of Sociology* 39:1 (March 1988): 86–113
Prost, Antoine. *In the Wake of War:* Les Anciens Combattants *and French Society*. Translated by Helen McPhail. Providence RI: Berg, 1992
Purcell, William. *Woodbine Willie*. London: Hodder and Stoughton, 1962
Rabinbach, Anson. *The Human Motor: Energy, Fatigue and the Origin of Modernity*. Berkeley CA: University of California Press, 1990
Rabinow, P. *French Modern: Norms and Forms of the Built Environment*. Boston MA: MIT Press, 1989
Radley, Alan (ed.). *Worlds of Illness: Biographical and Cultural Perspectives in Health and Disease*. New York: Routledge, 1993
Raven, James, Helen Small and Naomi Tadmor (eds). *The Practice and Representation of Reading in England*. Cambridge: Cambridge University Press, 1996
Reid, D. 'The decline of St Monday, 1766–1876', *Past and Present* 71 (1976): 76–101
Reznick, Jeffrey S., 'Work-therapy and the disabled British soldier in Great Britain in the First World War: The case of Shepherd's Bush Military Hospital, London' in David A. Gerber (ed.), *Disabled Veterans in History*. Ann Arbor MI: University of Michigan Press, 2000.
Riberio, Eileen. *The Art of Dress: Fashion in England*. Chicago: University of Chicago Press, 1997
Richardson, Harriet (ed.). *English Hospitals, 1660–1948: A Survey of their Architecture and Design*. Swindon: Royal Commission on Historical Monuments of England, 1998
Richardson, Ruth and Robert Thorne (eds): *The* Builder *Illustrations Index, 1843–1883*. London: Builder Group and Institute of Historical Research, 1994
Roach-Higgins, Mary Ellen (ed.). *Dress and Identity*. New York: Fairchild Publications, 1995
Robb, George. *British Culture and the First World War*. New York: Palgrave Macmillan, 2002
Robbins, Keith. *The First World War*. Oxford: Oxford University Press, 1984
Roberts, Robert. *The Classic Slum: Salford Life in the First Quarter of the Century*. Manchester: Manchester University Press, 1971
Roche, Daniel. *The Culture of Clothing: Dress and Fashion in the Ancien Regime*. Cambridge: Cambridge University Press, 1994
Roper, Michael and John Tosh (eds). *Manful Assertions: Masculinities in Britain since 1800*. New York: Routledge, 1991
Rose, Nikolas. *Governing the Soul: The Shaping of the Private Self*. New York: Routledge, 1990

Rosen, G. *From Medical Police to Social Medicine: Essays on the History of Health Care.* New York: Science History Publications, 1974

Rosenberg, Charles. 'Inward vision and outward glance: The shaping of the American hospital, 1880–1914', *Bulletin of the History of Medicine* 53 (1979): 346–391

—— (ed.). *Healing and History.* New York and Folkestone: Dawson, 1979

Rosenberg, Charles E. and Janet L. Goldin (eds). *Framing Disease: Studies in Cultural History.* New Brunswick NJ: Rutgers University Press, 1992

Ross, Ellen. *Love and Toil: Motherhood in Outcast London, 1870–1918.* New York: Oxford University Press, 1993

Rothman, David. *Conscience and Convenience: The Asylum and its Alternatives in Progressive America.* Boston MA: Little, Brown, 1980

——. *The Discovery of the Asylum.* Boston MA: Little, Brown, 1971

Russell, David. *Popular Music in England, 1840–1914.* Kingston, Ontario: McGill-Queen's University Press, 1987

Sammons, Jack. 'Hospital Blues', *Military Chest* 2:2 (March/April 1983): 47–48

Sandall, Robert. *The History of the Salvation Army* (4 volumes). London: Thomas Nelson and Sons, 1955.

Scull, Andrew. *Social Order/Mental Disorder: Anglo-American Psychiatry in Historical Perspective.* Berkeley CA: University of California Press, 1989

——. *The Most Solitary of Afflictions: Madness and Society in Britain, 1700–1900.* New Haven CT: Yale University Press, 1993

——. *Museums of Madness: The Social Organisation of Insanity in Nineteenth-Century England.* London: Allen Lane, 1979

—— (ed.). *The Asylum as Utopia: W.A.F. Browne and the Mid-nineteenth Century Consolidation of Psychiatry.* New York: Routledge, 1991

Scull, Andrew, Charlotte McKenzie and Nicholas Harvey. *Masters of Bedlam: The Transformation of the Mad-doctoring Trade.* Princeton NJ: Princeton University Press, 1996

Shedd, Clarence Prouty. *History of the World's Alliance of Young Men's Christian Associations.* London: SPCK, 1955

Showalter, Elaine. *The Female Malady.* New York: Pantheon Books, 1985

Silkin, Jon (ed.). *The Penguin Book of First World War Poetry.* New York: Penguin Books, 1981.

Smith, F.B. *The People's Health, 1830–1910.* New York: Holmes and Meier, 1979

——. *The Retreat of Tuberculosis, 1850–1950.* New York: Croom Helm, 1988

Soloway, Richard A. *Demography and Degeneration: Eugenics and the Declining Birthrate in Twentieth-century Britain.* Chapel Hill NC: University of North Carolina Press, 1990

Stedman Jones, Gareth. *Languages of Class: Studies in English Working Class History, 1832–1982.* Cambridge: Cambridge University Press, 1983

——. *Outcast London: A Study in the Relationship between Classes in Victorian Society.* New York: Pantheon Books, 1984

Steward, W.A.C. and W.P. McCann. *The Educational Innovators, 1750–1850* (2 volumes). New York: St. Martin's, Press 1967

Storch, R.D. (ed.). *Popular Culture and Custom in Nineteenth-century England.* New York: St. Martin's Press, 1982

Story, Geoffrey O. *A History of Physical Medicine: The Story of the British Association of Rheumatology and Rehabilitation.* London: Royal Society of Medicine Services, 1992

Strachan, Hew. *The Politics of the British Army.* New York: Oxford University Press, 1997

—— (ed.). *World War I: A History.* Oxford: Oxford University Press, 1999

Summers, Anne. *Angels and Citizens: British Women as Military Nurses.* New York: Routledge and Kegan Paul, 1988

Taylor, Jeremy. 'Circular hospital wards: Professor John Marshall's concept and Its exploration by the architectural profession in the 1880s', *Medical History* 32 (1988): 426–448

——. *Hospital and Asylum Architecture in England, 1840–1914: Building for Health Care.* London: Mansell Publishing, 1991

Thane, Pat. *Foundations of the Welfare State.* New York: Longman, 1996

Thompson, F.M.L. *The Rise of Respectable Society: A Social History of Victorian Britain.* Cambridge: Cambridge University Press, 1988

Thompson, J. and G. Golding. *The Hospital: A Social and Cultural History.* New Haven CT: Yale University Press, 1975

Thompson, Paul. *The Nature of Work.* London: Macmillan, 1983

Tomkins, Sandra M. 'The failure of expertise: Public health policy in Britain during the 1918–19 influenza epidemic', *Social History of Medicine* 5 (December 1992): 435–454

Tosh, John. *A Man's Place: Masculinity and the Middle-class Home in Victorian England.* New Haven CT: Yale University Press, 1999

Trombley, Stephen. *Sir Frederick Treves: The Extra-ordinary Edwardian.* New York: Routledge, 1989

Trueta, J. *Gathorne Robert Girdlestone.* Oxford: Oxford University Press, 1971

Van Emden, Richard and Steve Humphries. *Veterans: The Last Survivors of the Great War.* Barnsley: Leo Cooper, 1999

Vincent, David. *Literacy and Popular Culture.* Cambridge: Cambridge University Press, 1993

Vogel, M. *The Invention of the Modern Hospital.* Chicago: University of Chicago Press, 1980

Waites, Bernard. *A Class Society at War: England, 1914–1918.* New York: Berg, 1987

Walker, Pamela J. *Pulling the Devil's Kingdom Down: The Salvation Army in Victorian Britain.* Berkeley CA: University of California Press, 2001

Wall, Richard and Jay Winter (eds). *The Upheaval of War: Family, Work and Welfare in Europe, 1914–1918.* Cambridge: Cambridge University Press, 1988

Watson, Frederick. *The Life of Sir Robert Jones.* London: Hodder and Stoughton, 1934

Weindling, Paul. *The Social History of Occupational Health.* London: Croom Helm, 1985

Weiner, Deborah E.B. *Architecture and Social Reform in Late Victorian London.* Manchester: Manchester University Press, 1994

Whalen, Robert. *Bitter Wounds: German Victims of the Great War, 1914–1939.* Ithaca NY: Cornell University Press, 1984

Whitehead, Ian. *Doctors in the Great War.* Barnsley: Leo Cooper/Pen and Sword Books, 1999

Wiener, Martin J. *Reconstructing the Criminal: Culture, Law and Policy in England, 1830–1914.* Cambridge: Cambridge University Press, 1990

Wilkinson, Alan. *The Church of England and the First World War.* London: SCM Press, 1996

Winter, Denis. *Death's Men: Soldiers of the Great War.* New York: Penguin Books, 1979

Winter, J.M. *Sites of Memory, Sites of Mourning.* Cambridge: Cambridge University Press, 1995

Winter, Thomas. *Making Men, Making Class: The YMCA and Workingmen, 1877–1920.* Chicago: University of Chicago Press, 2002

Wohl, Robert. *The Generation of 1914.* Cambridge MA: Harvard University Press, 1979

Woodall, Samuel James. *The Manor House Hospital: A Personal Record.* London: Routledge and Kegan Paul, 1966

Woodward, John and David Richards (eds). *Health Care and Popular Medicine in Nineteenth Century England: Essays in the Social History of Medicine.* London: Croom Helm, 1977

Woollacott, Angela. '"Khaki fever" and its control: Gender, class, age and sexual morality on the British home front in the First World War', *Journal of Contemporary History* 29:2 (April 1994): 325–334

——. *On Her Their Lives Depend: Munitions Workers in the Great War.* Berkeley CA: University of California Press, 1994

——. 'Dressed to kill: Clothes, cultural meaning and World War I women munitions workers' in *Gender and Material Culture II: Representations of Gender from Prehistory to the Present*, ed. Moira Donald and Linda Hurcombe, New York: St. Martin's Press, 2000

Woollacott, Angela and Miriam Cooke (eds). *Gendering War Talk.* Princeton NJ: Princeton University Press, 1993

Theses and dissertations

Brehony, Kevin Joseph. 'The Froebel Movement and State Schooling, 1880–1914: A Study in Educational Ideology', Ph.D. dissertation, Open University, 1987

Brown, Alison. 'British Churches in the First World War', Ph.D. dissertation, St Andrews University, 1996

Clifton, Albert Shaw. 'The Salvation Army's Actions and Attitudes in Wartime, 1899–1945'. Ph.D. thesis, King's College, University of London, 1989

Elsey, Ena. 'The Rehabilitation and Employment of Disabled Ex-servicemen after Two World Wars', Ph.D. dissertation, University of Teesside, 1995

Hopkins, J.R. 'Leicester's Great War Hospital: The 5th Northern General Military Hospital, Leicester, 1914–1919', M.A. thesis, University of Leicester, 1995

Latcham, Andrew P. 'Journey's End: Ex-servicemen and the State during and after the Great War', D.Phil. dissertation, Oxford University, 1997

Noonan, David. 'Ships of Mercy: The Hospital Ship in the First World War', BSc. dissertation, Wellcome Institute for the History of Medicine, 1999

Orr, Richard Bryon. 'In Durance Vile: Attitudes Toward Imprisonment in England during the Du Cane Regime, 1877–1895', Ph.D. dissertation, University of Wisconsin, 1968

Schneider, Eric F. 'What Britons were Told about War in the Trenches, 1914–1918'. D.Phil., Oxford University, 1998

Schock, Marya. 'Healing the Patient, Serving the State: Medical Ethics and the British Medical Profession in the Great War'. Ph.D. dissertation, University of California, Berkeley, 2000

Thompson, J. Lee. 'Lord Northcliffe and the Great War: Politicians, the Press and Propaganda, 1914–1918'. Ph.D. dissertation, Texas A&M University, 1996

Index

- Manchester Uni – centre for cult. hist of war
- Palgrave

Lightning Source UK Ltd.
Milton Keynes UK
UKOW05f1031031014

239563UK00001B/39/P